A PACIFIST AT WAR

Ray Jenkins is a film, TV and radio dramatist who lives in London.

A PACIFIST AT WAR

RAY JENKINS

arrow books

Published by Arrow Books 2010
2 4 6 8 10 9 7 5 3 1

First published in Great Britain in 2009 by
Hutchinson
Random House, 20 Vauxhall Bridge Road,
London SW1V 2SA

www.rbooks.co.uk

Addresses for companies within The Random House Group Limited can be found at:
www.randomhouse.co.uk/offices.htm

The Random House Group Limited Reg. No. 954009

A CIP catalogue record for this book is available from the British Library

ISBN 9780099525134

The Random House Group Limited supports The Forest Stewardship Council (FSC), the leading international forest certification organisation. All our titles that are printed on Greenpeace approved FSC certified paper carry the FSC logo. Our paper procurement policy can be found at www.rbooks.co.uk/environment

Typeset by Palimpsest Book Production Limited,
Falkirk, Stirlingshire

Printed and bound in Great Britain by
CPI Bookmarque, Croydon CR0 4TD

For my family.

And

to Joanna and Wole Wey
for their love and support
for Francis and Nan.

Contents

Preface

Why write about Francis Cammaerts ? The answer is simple – he should never disappear. Despite his almost mythical status in SOE legend, his huge active personality led to further momentous achievements in the revolutionary post-war world of education both in the UK and in Africa. Fifty-eight years later he is still remembered warmly in both disciplines. He is a man not to be forgotten.

Happily I met him in the mid-1960s when he was the charismatic Principal of the Teachers Training College at Scraptoft in Leicester. You didn't work under Francis, you worked with him, and like countless others in his long life you soon became aware of what he had done, though never through him. But once you did discover a few gems the more you wanted to know and that became an intriguing quest, seldom abandoned. Above all what he gave was utter trust and what you returned was devotion.

Francis rarely wrote but he did narrate. On one occasion near the end of his life, his friend George Kitson wanted to know why he'd never published 'his stories'. The answer came back – he wrote too slowly. Then get someone to do it for you, George said. And that is where this book was born.

The basic urge was to tell Francis's glittering story in his own words, not to attempt a history of the Second World War or even of SOE – both have been covered by many an excellent book. No, the idea was – give him the mike, go slowly over the whole ninety years and the reward was a personal narrative full of fascinating detail, opinion, humanity, danger and sheer progression; his gimlet mind rarely hesitated. Of course in his eighties he could and did forget, miss the occasional beat, but for Francis France was indelible in his mind, it was his place and it turned a serious loner into a brilliant enabler, a pacifist into a friend for life of hundreds. It was a life to be listened to.

All biography is incomplete, therefore any serious attempt at portraiture inevitably reflects the incompleteness, as it does here. But in this case age plays a critical role. Francis lived a long and very involved life but those who could have helped in any vital double-checking are, regrettably, in most cases no longer with us. Therefore where there is any doubt and the checking of sources almost impossible, then I have deliberately rested with Francis's own words. I trust the man.

Nothing could be told without the help of many people and I would like to express my deepest gratitude to them, whether scholar, family or long friend. But, above all, I must register my total indebtedness to Professor M.R.D. Foot for his books *SOE in France*, both editions, *SOE 1940-46* and *Six Faces of Courage*, to Professor Arthur Layton Funk, Professor of History, University of Florida's *Hidden Ally*, to Duncan Stuart C.M.G., formerly of the Foreign and Commonwealth Office, for great help over Francis's Personal File and to Madeleine Masson for her fine work on Christine Granville.

Many thanks are also due to the following – their books and sources are set out in the Notes. To Hugh Verity, E.H. Cookridge, Jeanne Lindley, N.G. Brett-James, Ronald Blythe, Patricia Cockburn, Emile Cammaerts, Russell Miller, Hugh Dalton, Marcus Binney, Leo Marks, G. Rheams, Peter Churchill, Jerrard Tickell, Frederich Douzet, Xan Fielding, Denise Domenach-Lallich, Henri Rosencher, Max Hastings, George Millar, Pierre Tanant, Joseph La Picirella, Francois Rude, Alberto Torini di Priero, Souvenirs – *Homage à Paul Héraud*, Martha Gellhorn, Roy Close, Sarah Helm, Christopher Burney, Katharine Whitehorn, George Kitson, Sylviane Rey, Maurice Buckmaster, Pearl Witherington, Michael Morpurgo, the Imperial War Museum and the Public Record Office.

Finally I must thank those who gave their time to sustaining the book itself – to the Cammaerts family – Niki, Jay, Elisabeth and Paul, Kia and Wole – and to my own – Ceri, Pascale and Annie. Without their care and patience much might have been lost as would have been the case without the determined backing of Diana Tyler and my editor Tony Whittome.

Thanks to you all.

Note

In the text, Francis's contributions are within inverted commas, whereas the writings of others are set down without inverted commas.

'From the earliest days of his work it was apparent that he was one of the most outstanding organisers in the field. This was borne out on D-Day when his organisation numbered 20,000 men of which at least 15,000 were fully armed'

Part of citation for DSO by Colonel Maurice Buckmaster, Head of F Section, Special Operations Executive, 1945

22–23 March 1943

At last, moonlight.

The slender, half-full-and-half-again 'moon period' each month is vital. Darkness means postponement and precious time and nerve wasted; pilots fly at the gift and mercy of the moon. Moonlight is needed to map-read by, to trace routes to dropping zones for parachuted supplies and to hit the tiny silver fields sedulously chosen as landing grounds for delivery of 'Joes' – agents trained to aid résistants *in combatting the corrosion of German military occupation and the deep French shame.*

Two 'Joes' are ferried in Hugh Verity's 30-foot Lysander across the Channel on this mission. One, a former conscientious objector, Francis Cammaerts, twenty-six, faces the direction of the flight. Georges Dubourdin, the other occupant, will not survive the immediate betrayal to come. Agents are not encouraged to chat; here they are expected to keep their eyes peeled, the pilot being completely blind to attack from the rear. Moonlight also kills.

The chunky 'Lizzie' is camouflaged in dark green and pale grey, which may reduce its silhouette against low cloud and thus allow it to avoid detection from above.

For Francis the flight in the tiny aircraft is a curiously unreal happening: 'As we flew I could see night fighters – friend or foe I couldn't tell – swishing past so fast whereas the Lysander moved very slowly. This strangely was an advantage – fighters move fast but take miles to turn round and return and by then we'd gone elsewhere.'

Hugh Verity agrees: 'Francis remembered that we were chased by a night fighter and shot at with tracer. To escape this I did very violent, steep turns. I made no record of this at the time, merely noting that I had been hopelessly lost for some time on the way to the target.'[1]

They will become lifelong friends.

The landing is on a friendly hop farm at Estrées-St-Denis, near Compiègne, 75 kilometres north-east of Paris and close to where the Germans had built one of their largest concentration camps for captured Résistance fighters, complete with raking searchlights. 'It was a bold choice but a good one; the last place the Germans would expect to be used for the landing and picking up of secret agents . . . and only a few kms west of the N17.'[2]

The field and 'flare path' (consisting of three pocket torches tied to sticks in the shape of an inverted 'L' over a distance of 150 metres), landing and reception, organised by one André Marsac, are flawless, as is the honed procedure for turning about on the field with one agent remaining in the aircraft to haul out luggage and then receive that of the home-bound passengers while the engine is still running. On this occasion there are two returning – Peter Churchill and Henri Frager, a prematurely greying architect and brave, resourceful résistant *– both of them, together with Marsac, members of the CARTE circuit on the Côte d'Azur Francis is to investigate. The fraught condition of CARTE is the reason for the urgent recall of the two men to London, four previous attempts to pick them up having failed.*

Francis cannot remember any communication with Churchill, 'Except that as he climbed on board he said to me – be careful you've always got some paper with you when you go to the toilet, they're very short of rolls.'

The turnabout takes three minutes.

Apart from two car trips across eastern France, Francis stands for the first time in his young life on French soil but his excellent French, together with his height, are legacies of his Belgian father. In the bright darkness he is alert: 'As the plane took off I am led to a waiting car which I'm surprised to see is petrol-driven. Then, to my horror, we make straight for Paris – six young men bottled in a crowded car crossing a Paris under curfew; though one of them did have a doctor's permit to drive at any hour. There appeared to be very little security consciousness in their chatter. My whole reception I felt more and more insecure, dangerous.'

He is told to hand over all compromising material and his revolver is hurled from a bridge into the River Oise, leaving him, he is assured, 'more like a normal French citizen'. The nightmare is momentarily relieved as they reach André Marsac's apartment in the deserted rue Vaugirard. A tall, meagre man of immense energy, Marsac and Francis stay up talking and finishing off a rum flask until five in the morning. Marsac had thought it easier to go direct to Paris than let the arrivals shiver in a haystack. 'Our papers were good for the night, the Paris group is well organised, has the necessary German permits and identity cards as well as an excellent forger of the Kommandantur's various signatures.'[3]

Francis finds his host 'Friendly, intelligent and thoughtful and he proudly told me about things they were doing though I had little chance to talk about the CARTE organisation as such. I was then again shuttled across Paris to No. 1 Quai Voltaire to stay at the flat of Doctor Sperry, a Czech lady, where I slept.

'Marsac and I had arranged a rendezvous at the Pont Neuf just opposite the flat for lunchtime. Paris was grey and gloomy – total black and white photography. Then one of the LeJeaune brothers, who had been part of the reception team at Compiègne, turned up on time and said, "You'd better get out fast – END – [Marsac] has been arrested. The doctor'll help you with necessary passes – but don't hang around!"

Knowing I couldn't leave Paris for twenty-four hours because you had to have a "fiche d'admission" to board a main-line train, I returned to the flat and feverish patience. The doctor got me a pass through the French Red Cross and for the first of many hundreds of times I travelled on the French railway, leaving the Gare de Lyon for Annecy in the Savoie Mountains, immediate trouble . . . and my deep personal silence.'

I

Francis Charles Albert Cammaerts, the names a combination of family and patriotic significance – King Albert had become a hero of his father Emile – was born the third of six children, two years into the First World War, on 19 June 1916 in Kensington.

Here is his light-hearted account of that summer:

> 'A pretty nurse with a white cap, a close-fitting blue dress, black shoes and stockings, pushes a pram with high back wheels and low front ones. In it is a few weeks' old boy baby, his two-year-old sister opposite him and the nurse holds the hand of a trotting five-year-old girl. The little party slopes off left towards Kensington Gardens, the Round Pond and the Peter Pan statue. In the sun on the benches sit soldiers in blue fatigues, some of whom whistle at the nurse. There are many of them for this is the summer of 1916 and the hospital at Hyde Park Corner is full of wounded soldiers. The nurse sits on a bench near the Round Pond next to a soldier who has lost a leg. The nurse and the soldier hold hands while the girls are allowed to romp on the grass.
>
> After half an hour or so the nurse reluctantly gets up and says she has to go. She returns her charges to Launceston Place. There a couple in their thirties greet them. They are both unusual in appearance – the father has a bright red beard and the mother, a heavily built woman, pregnant, wears tweeds in spite of the heat. On the second floor stands her mother, a fairly formidable middle-aged opera singer of renown. The nurse lives in and shares a room with the housemaid.'

Tall, even at eight years of age, Francis had once travelled with his father, on a tram in Brussels, the seats facing each other. Across from them a middle-aged woman kept staring at his father. Finally she leaned forward, tapped him on the knee and said, in French, 'Emile, don't you recognise me? I'm your wife.'

If a son who revered his father to the extent that Francis did ever needed proof of his father's quixotic past this was as good a place as any to start; he had *two* mothers?

Who *were* his parents?

Born into the affluent middle-class of Brussels in 1878, Emile Cammaerts, poet, writer, teacher, distinguished art historian and a gifted explainer of Belgium to the English and the English to Belgium, had grown up in an intellectual melting pot – Brussels at the turn of the twentieth century. Because of his frail health, when his parents divorced he was separated from his two brothers and remained with his mother, Eugénie, a beautiful, demanding early feminist. She had replaced her Catholic faith with wide classical reading, a love of nature, curiosity, music and Jean-Jacques Rousseau. All these she taught her son and such values Emile would in turn pass on to his own children, a heritage to which his father, a rich, abusive lawyer who would ultimately put a bullet into his own head, contributed nothing.

Admitted to the University of Brussels at sixteen, Emile left to join the Université Nouvelle which ran concurrently with the older body but was resolutely modern, democratic and anti-clerical. This was shut down by a Conservative government while he was still there two years later and he left with no degree.

> 'Happily it didn't make any difference because my father's subject was geography in the days when it was a revolutionary discipline, encompassing physical and human geography; but above all because he had met "a great Worshipper of Mankind", Elysée Reclus (1830–1905), together with Prince Kropotkin in the turmoil at the end of the nineteenth century, the undisputed spurs of anarchism.
>
> A drawing of his head was on my bedroom wall as a child. Reclus led to my father joining the anarchists for a number of very mettlesome years. They were men who spurned the extreme methods of Russian terror and preached the gospel of social revolution. In his relative innocence, my father wanted to write to kings and presidents and say "we don't need you" – not quite the route to furious change. Ironically in France, I, a pacifist, blew up manned trains.'

Later Emile wrote: 'Reclus was deeply sincere and his enthusiasm was contagious. I caught the infection myself and embraced the new hard doctrine which denounced God, the State, marriage and property.'[1]

Charles van den Borren, who was to become his greatest friend and himself achieved prominence as President of the Belgian Academy, described the twenty-one-year-old Emile at that time as 'an original, brilliant but a little crazy, not an anarchist with his reason but with his emotions'. As proof, for three years, with friends teaching all subjects between them, Emile ran 'the Little School' over a pub for their friends' children and those of local people who could not afford private education or hated the rigid discipline of the State schools. Ignoring exams and anti-clerical, they sought total individualism and Reclus's 'human interest' in every subject. It closed in 1899.

But as he subsequently became a scruffy teacher commuting daily for nine years to industrial Mons, Emile still attempted to maintain his 'true' way of life in parallel. He had set up a *marriage libre* with an equally committed anarchist, Christine. True to Reclus, they kept an open house but the moment the union was legalised under pressure from Christine's parents, she left him for a fellow anarchist. One presumes Christine's reminder to Emile on the tram was mischievous. Their divorce, at the time, left him devastated.

The second seismic shift in Emile's life at this period would prove even more decisive than Reclus from whom he had gradually moved away.

He and Charles van den Borren, one by now a provincial schoolmaster and the other a not very prosperous lawyer with a passion for music, decided during Easter 1903 to visit Italy. Emile's reasons for going were honest: 'It is characteristic of my romantic state of mind that I escaped to Italy in the hope of finding some salve for my wounds and still more characteristic that I found it there so soon.'[2]

Studying the development of Flemish and Belgian painting they quickly realised the importance of the influence of Italy, so they said, 'we must go and see'. Already great walkers, with little money they slept rough and lived hard. The trip was a superb reconnaissance that would open up the whole world of Italian art to Emile, especially through the Giotto frescoes at Padua and Assisi. It set the pattern for future travelling and thus art became Emile's new religion, a virile constant in his career, writing and future family life. The polymath was born.

For by now Emile was writing seriously, early poetry giving way to a pamphlet on how to teach Geography at school – 'human interest above all'. Enlisting his mother's help, he embarked on translations of

John Ruskin – 'that erratic and impulsive prophet' – who had been his trusted Virgil in Italy, 'and thus began my training as a writer'. Ever industrious, lectures jostled with translations from Flemish into French and occasional freelance reviews on the arts.

On 26 October 1906 Charles van den Borren's diary noted, 'Shakespeare soirée with Tita Brand and Brema'.

Emile used to tell his children that when Charles invited him to go to the Shakespearean soirée he had said, 'I'd like to hear Brema sing, but who is this woman who thinks she can perform Shakespeare on her own? Well, I'll come, it'll make another article for *Le Matin*.'

He also told his children that he left the recital swearing 'I'm going to marry that woman!' which ambition, after a deeply flattering revue of her acting and a fierce courtship of words – at first his in French and hers in English – he duly achieved two years later.

Francis's mother, Tita Brand (her stage name for Helen Braun) was an established actress who played for, among others, George Bernard Shaw, Granville Barker, Johnston Forbes-Robertson and Sir Frank Benson on tour where her 'voice like figured satin' was noted and she kissed nobody. Her mother was her only friend.

A famed English mezzo-soprano and Wagnerian diva, Marie Brema (1856–1925), who was born in Liverpool, in her prime toured widely all over Europe and America and her unhappy marriage to Arthur Braun, a cotton merchant of German origin, having broken down, always took her daughter with her. Tita thus revelled in her corner 'after the performance to hear de Reszke, Cosima Wagner, Richard Strauss, Sir Arthur Sullivan, Stanford, Parry, Hans Richter all talking and laughing with her mother'.[3]

'As a diva, my grandmother was a gifted musician but spoilt by excess of success. She no longer understood the value of money or what it meant in the world. In other senses I never knew her. I did meet her husband who was a cunning bore and she must've had lovers during her life but I never knew about that side of things. Those were skeletons kept hidden in the cupboard with my mother swallowing the key.'

After straining her heart climbing a mountain in an effort to lose weight, Marie concentrated on lavishly refurnishing her house at 17 Launceston Place, Kensington, partly through enthusiasm and partly to help her timid daughter benefit from having a real home in which to study and make friends. But the 'timid daughter' always read voraciously and had minutely studied her mother in action; she had a mind of her own – she was going on the stage.

> 'In her stage career my mother was of her time, in being involved heavily in the evolution of the stage interpretation of Shakespeare and William Poel's revolt against the huge complexities of massive scenery and costume-led productions. I remember her telling me of one over-decorated production of *The Tempest* where the first scene took forty-five minutes – all for a couple of lines! Poel's vision, by contrast, was simple costume and curtains as background to the words – hence the bare white and gold room and potted plant when she so entranced my father. I don't know whether my mother was a good actress or not but she certainly had the respect of a lot of other actors. Her voice reading on our family Sundays was enormously impressive to me.'

But she had also decided she was a Christian Socialist. On tour, away from her mother, Tita saved all she could. Politically she believed she'd found a way of doing her share to help relieve some of the hopeless poverty she saw around her in London and the provinces. Ruskin and William Morris wanted a revival of handicrafts: she would bring it to East London!

She therefore set up Brema Looms. To operate the hand-weaving looms she employed crippled girls from the East End but, more visionary than business manager, her acting had to make good the losses on the looms. Like Emile's Little School, it collapsed though she remained in contact with many of the girls, one of the friendships lasting nearly sixty years. This enterprise and behaviour her daughters found laudable and of her class, but for Francis 'there was my mother in Kensington and the girls, from Shoreditch or wherever, having to trudge over to Brema Looms in Pimlico! She talked about looking after lost women, they were 'lost' she would 'find' them. Very early I found it all so repulsive, patronising.'

Everything was discussed as a couple – Socialism, nature, art, religion and theatre. Where Emile *was* his writing – serious, literary, logical, enthusiastic, fearless and tumultuous in content – Tita, while just as serious, was more innocent in manner while still retaining the iron streak she never lost: 'What leads me to Socialism above everything else is that it is to me essentially Christian – it is because our whole system, our whole society is so blasphemous and un-Christian in every particular that I look to Socialism as a blessed ray of real practical hope.'[4]

George Bernard Shaw was gently exasperated at Tita's behaviour: 'For Heaven's sake do learn to discriminate between yourself and the Almighty! You go about exclaiming, "look at the wickedness of this world of mine. What am I to do?" . . . Monstrous conceit! The only thing you can do for Socialism is to make yourself a first-rate actress and then let everyone know you are a Socialist!

'This bouncing goodness is unbearable. Why can't you enjoy yourself, since you, at least, are not starving? Do you consider it suitable to go on crutches because somebody else's leg is broken? I have no patience with you. A suffering world! Tableau: Tita mourning over Jerusalem. A crucifixion! Tableau: Tita weeping at the foot of the cross. My prophetic eye sees a desperate man hurling himself from Waterloo Bridge into the black, cold, but peaceful river. It is Tita's husband.'[5]

In fact not cold waters but the whole glittering world of the arts opened up for Emile in Marie Brema's court. Because of her mother's power over her daughter, Emile had decided to live in England. If Tita toured he tagged along, reading day and night, devouring English literature with a sheer lust to know, and real friendship led to him translating G. K. Chesterton while keeping up his journalism. But there is no doubt that he became increasingly stifled by Marie's thoughtless generosity and Tita's subservience. They should have their own place – their first child was already three years old. But then came the bombshell of August 1914 and the world was turned upside down.

Belgium was invaded.

Joining the Artists' Rifles at the outbreak of war, Emile was swiftly invalided out during training with a weak heart. He never told his son he regretted that and he never talked about his heart or his health. Yet running with his children they could see he was occasionally breathless, but it was never allowed to become a disturbing factor. Nevertheless, his youngest daughter, Jeanne, probably came nearest to the truth in evaluating Emile's loss to the military: 'My father already had a slight academic stoop and was painfully thin. He would not have been good company in the Officers Mess and one halts before the image of anyone trying to instruct him in the elements of army drill!'

The stream of refugees flooding across to Britain included Belgian government officials and political leaders. With the son of a foreign minister, Henri Davignon, also a writer, Emile combined to set up a bureau to collate and interpret all news on Belgium. Personal stories and military realities were sifted from the dross of propaganda, Emile's quality as a poet being being especially revered. For it was at this point that Emile had set about writing patriotic poems for his country. They were a huge success, appealing to the desperate feelings created by the horrors of invasion.

One poem – 'Sing Belgians, Sing' – was set to music by Edward Elgar and recited by Henry Ainley. Also recited by Tita in her own translation at the Albert Hall, it had been written in October 1914 after the battle of Antwerp and it led to Emile becoming a household name in his absent homeland and being lionised by prominent refugees in England. But the real pain was the thought of his mother, family and friends in constant danger amidst the guilt of his own safety; his anarchism drifted towards patriotism.

2

Zeppelins, immense, lighter-than-air airships, originally developed for surveillance purposes, were quickly adapted by the Germans to launch their bombing attacks against England during the early years of the First World War and the resulting civilian carnage gave birth in turn to the modern concept of 'total war'.

Although the bombing was a factor, it was the need for a decidedly cheaper lifestyle that led, in December 1916, to the family moving to two 'cottages' in Loom Lane, Radlett, then a village of some six to eight hundred souls south of St Albans. Besides the three children – Marie, Elisabeth, plus Francis – there were two servants, Jeanie, a Mancunian, and an Irish cook, Florence.

Marie Brema's career was on the wane but she still dominated family and social life with her extravagance and high reputation. Her cottage, Launceston, held her baby grand, a servant and was only 150 yards from her daughter's. A great deal of publicity surrounded the family in those early days, what with Marie Brema's presence and Emile's growing 'heroic' wartime reputation. But fame isolates, too; locally the Cammaerts were regarded as *odd*.

The 'cottages' were badly built, damp, and that meant in cold weather at least six coal fires daily. The coal was delivered by a merchant wearing a cap with a tail to protect his back. For each cottage he needed to haul in half a dozen hundredweight sacks on his annual delivery and he was a fascinating sight for a small boy who'd look forward to the coming of the fierce, coal-dust-spattered man.

As he grew up, the delivery men were Francis's major interest. The milkman, too, was high on the list and his dray, with an open back, a very heavy churn on a shelf with a tap, a bucket with pint and half-pint measures clanking on a bar inside as it was hauled up the path, the deliverer's arm held out to balance the bucket's weight. His white pony mare, Daisy, was one of Francis's first friends. After the milkman came the portly bread man, 'his smell lovely', then the butcher with a bloodstained wooden shelf hollowed out over his shoulder.

Just as vivid in the memory was shopping with his mother and a sister or housemaid in the International Stores, a magical place smelling of biscuits, coffee beans, porridge oats, dried fruit and cheese, with fresh sawdust on the floor and a wire cage with a lady inside who took the money in overhead zinging tubes . . . and a man in a white coat and kind glasses who sliced bacon on a machine with a round hissing knife. Finally the highpoint:

> 'On to Curly Lamb, son of the fishmonger – his smell was divine and I've never lost the excitement of a fish shop – no ice, just running water over a marble slab displaying fish of all sizes and shapes. We got herrings and kippers as they were the cheapest but when we had guests there was sole and occasionally crab. But it was Curly who mattered. He was my hero. Every child has a "Curly".
>
> After the chemist's – to which my mother was addicted – came the small house where Sister Cox lived. She attended the birth of the babies to come – Catherine called "Kippe" (after a Belgian victory), Pieter and Jeanne. We were such a big family that the doctor who helped my mother with the three births after we'd moved there never sent in a bill because he knew a teaching professor with six children couldn't afford to pay – common practice apparently in medicine in the period before the Second World War and such compassion I was only told about much later.
>
> Rather as my father had with his mother, I learnt to read, write and calculate from family lessons with my mother. I didn't go to school until I was eight. Reading was wonderful and stretched early from Beatrix Potter in French and English to Robert Louis Stevenson. The *Fairy Tales* of Grimm, the Norse, the Blue Book and the Red were read aloud to us as a group – especially on the family Sundays when we also had Shakespeare and Dickens to act to. As we grew up we would all read small parts moving on gradually from 2nd Messenger and 3rd Soldier to the occasional Earl or Duke.
>
> Memories of those first ten years are dominated by the colour green – eating out, of the lawn, of lessons outside, games, swimming and gradually realising I was big for my age.'

Francis's elder sister Elisabeth agreed: 'We were very physical. I clearly remember a game of rounders and my father and I colliding – I've still got the scar on my forehead – and my father's eye streaming with blood and Francis being very concerned. He was very caring.'

'He was the centre of attention,' added Jeanne. 'He came out of the womb with leadership qualities that one – but then both our parents had. By the time he was ten he had huge *confidence*. All the veneration we had for him as siblings might not have been good for him but my God it didn't half help set him up. He didn't have to be the best player in any team, sport or whatever, but he was the captain. In our play and plays Francis had all the ideas and Elisabeth made the arrangements – it was amazing, so sharp. They would murder, slaughter each other – total pastiche Shakespeare. He was the *galvaniser* but like my mother he didn't like things to go wrong. In fact the only one who didn't join in the worship to some extent was my mother. But there again there was no hierarchy in her devotion to all of us.'

Nothing was pallid. Intellectually and physically it was a robust, intact world of individuals, immensely self-contained, a hothouse where 'every meal was a seminar'.

'If books and their characters were important,' Francis explained, 'so too was music. Because of my grandmother's and father's interests we heard folk songs, lieder and occasional sonatas on the piano and, through my mother's piety, hymns and carols at Christmas, but no orchestral music. There was no gramophone or radio at Loom Lane, or comics for that matter. But we did have my father's chestful of reproductions of paintings and a magic lantern and slides of Giotto, Fra Angelico, etc; Gerard David's *Christ Nailed to the Cross* affected me most.

'My earliest introduction to History was almost entirely literature/art based – Greece from translations of the great plays of Aeschylus, Sophocles and Euripides while Shakespeare provided Rome, Renaissance Italy and the English Kings, yet the worlds of China, India and Africa would remain blanks to me even up to and including Cambridge.'

Central to all this were the family Sundays; they were sacrosanct. Early worship at eight with Tita, hatless, eager and devout leading, then a slow walk back to breakfast with Emile reading aloud from his friend Garvin in the Sunday *Observer*. Then the family would settle, Emile lighting his pipe – a habit his son later adopted, earning him the nickname 'Shag' in the process – and the reading began. Dickens, Scott, *Alice in Wonderland* side by side with Ibsen, Shaw, Molière, Shakespeare, Chaucer and Cervantes. Such casts were dutifully recorded in Tita's diaries from 1925 to 1930. When Emile's voice grew rough, Tita would take over. Her Fagin, the Aged P, Mrs Gamp, Audrey in *As You Like It* and a host of others none present ever forgot.

This went on uninterrupted till lunch, sweet briar in bowls decorating the table, where every dispute was checked, with Emile usually immensely pleased if one of his children could catch him out with an error. After lunch, music, which most of the children later confessed they hadn't enjoyed as much as they'd pretended to at the time. But Emile would smile: 'I know my dear, "*L'hypocrisie est l'hommage que la vice rend à la vertu.*"' It didn't matter that his children had to be led to love literature, music and pictures; Emile led them by the subtle implication that these were adult joys.

Then a long afternoon walk and the days would end with Racing Demon and rummy or outside games in the summer. Everything mattered in a demanding way and a moral dimension was always present partnering the freedom.

The truth was that both Tita and Emile were, in their differing ways, at the same time individual parents and considerable teachers even if neither could tell one end of a screw from the other. Both had come from broken homes, they had their dream marriage but no role model as guide, yet they worked at its success incessantly.

Comedy, however, could arise from the self-absorption and at the same time feed the reputation for oddity. Alan Bush, the Communist musician, lived in Radlett and his brother and wife came to live next door to the Cammaerts. Alan asked his brother how they got on with them. 'They're nice enough,' came the reply, 'but they *fight* so!' It was a summer evening, with windows wide open. 'Listen – they're at it again!' They listened. It was the family reading *Othello*.

For the children home was a very tight ball. Part of their parents' insecurity was that they felt they had to do everything themselves. Home was, in a sense, an extension of 'the Little School' and there was an air of Emile's former energetic anarchism in a lot of what they did.

But it *was* self-absorbed. Therefore friendships outside the family were few. Like Curly Lamb and the delivery men, the ordinariness outside was exotic and the exotic – the god-parentage of the Chestertons or visits to Sybil Thorndike's dressing room – normal.

At the age of eight Francis was sent to a prep school – Hardenwick – ten miles away by train, where he was joined two years later by his young brother Pieter. Francis could hardly bring himself to talk about this period in his life.

'It was ghastly. Talking about it will make me sound racist. What really mattered in Hardenwick was sport. I wasn't particularly good at games but I was big and as a result I was captain of everything and became wildly conceited and I learnt nothing. Pieter I bullied and he certainly lived under my shadow at that stage. It was only seven or so years later that I became aware of what I was doing. When at last I let him alone at Mill Hill he'd grown six inches and become a very good actor. At twelve years of age I wasn't the kind of boy I would have liked if I'd met myself.'

Ultimately they would all become aware of difference of class and in Francis's case it was the local children mocking him because he wore a cap and tie. His parents were horrified and it became clear to him that his mother and her friends regarded the local children as human beings with whom their own should not associate and the children took it as read. Yet Tita had devoured the Bible avidly while still young ; she was a socialist and a Christian, confusing for a child. For Francis his main consolation at Hardenwick lay in hearing his first pop song – 'Bye Bye Blackbird'.

'One word about French,' explained Elisabeth. 'Father spoke French all the time and I remember Francis, very young, justifying to him why we spoke deliberately "Englished" French – "It's all right, Pa, it's my school French." We were mocked mercilessly at school if we spoke correct French even with our Belgian accent. My God, we were a troupe of actors!'

Marie's death in 1925 left her daughter bereft. Her passionate affection for her mother many found frightening and certainly oppressive yet Francis couldn't recall any sadness at his grandmother's passing.

'I thought she was a very selfish person who considered it duty done if she treated her grandchildren to extravagant outings in London twice a year. I never felt there was much in the way of love or affection, which I did with my father's mother who also died about this time of cancer. With her I knew I was one of the family, even an important one. With Marie every gesture was a duty. She didn't affect me, she was someone remote. My father would go and play on her piano occasionally but she never came to our house, we went to hers. Marie was, I suppose, at the root of my mother's contradictions – social and religious activism tied to living beyond one's means. In the case of my mother, her contradictions repelled me. It was a Victorian morality we encountered with her, brooking no contradiction.

After Hardenwick came Mill Hill and, because of my dislike of the assumptions behind both of these private schools, I had to find a line of my own – which in all truth rejected the schools and accepted and embraced a lot that home had provided; there was no harmony between home and school. I'm already talking about what I will call "the divorce" from my mother but the major influence on me was my father, his mother and maybe her mother; they were the sources of *his* morality and very, very strong. It is perhaps unfortunate that my mother had no one of their calibre in her childhood; all she had were Jesus and Marie Brema.'

The death of Marie meant the need for one house rather than two and the family 'crossed the tracks' to a large ten-bedroom house, 'The Eyrie', atop a steep unmade-up lane, Hillside Road. If the house creaked in every limb and there were splinters all the time from warped floorboards, the gardens were family-perfect – tennis, badminton courts, an exercise bar, a swing and dovecote, acacias, a crab apple and poplar trees. The maintenance costs would prove a drain on Emile's energy, already sapped by crippling lumbago. When he went for spa treatment in Wales, Francis and Elisabeth could sail.

Carrying a basket of Elisabeth's pigeons through the fog, Francis wept at the move:

'I was ten, maybe weeping for the loss of the fun of innocence? The onset of puberty? I don't really know why but I cried helplessly. We lost our neighbours including the farmer Smith, whose gorgeous physiotherapist daughter treated me for flat feet, the curse of my life, and at the bottom of Loom Lane a wealthy family, the Brooks, whose second daughter I was to court years later. But to this day I don't know the name of any of our new neighbours after we'd moved.'

Emile was now commuting daily as a lecturer to Queen's College in Harley Street and would continue to do so until 1931. He lectured on Belgium with eclectic passion. Schools in Leeds, Bradford, Sheffield, Plymouth and Glasgow called for him with the result that he was often absent from the trauma of the new move.

'In any case, my father was not the kind of person to cultivate neighbours; his friends and acquaintances were leading cultural names. So, yes, our crossing the tracks to non-contact was a pretty reversal of the usual social reasons and no doubt increased our isolation. During the Second World War we were even reported to the government as German spies, my father's thick accent perhaps being the unwitting cause!'

Indeed, evidence of this perceived oddness would find its way into Francis's Personal File in SOE Records

On 23.7.40 an informant called at Room 055 to give information concerning Emil [sic], Cammaerts, the Belgian Poet Laureate. It was alleged that he was living with his German wife at The Eyrie, 3 Hillside Road, Radlett, Herts. It was reported that they had a German maid and that all the other German maids in the district are frequently invited to the house for parties. The informant also stated that Emil Cammaerts' wife boasts that they can go where they like and do what they like because they are under the protection of Lord Halifax.[1]

'This was the time when my father began to speak to me in more or less adult terms. He talked about money, the upkeep of the house and about family relations, yet the reality of the dawning General Strike of 1926 received only a single mention. I remember walking with him down to the station, which we as children often did to see him off, and him saying, "You'd better tell your mother to get some coal in because I think it might soon be difficult to obtain."'

The movement towards a General Strike should've aroused the political concern of my parents; it didn't and the poverty to be suffered by the strikers was never mentioned. Neither of my parents had any feeling for unionism – and that defined their politics. The turn-of-the-century left-wing movement in Europe was led by a highly educated intellectual minority and the workers only came in marginally and that is why the General Strike was a surprise to the intellectuals who certainly didn't organise it.

I don't think he would have asked one of the girls to pass on the message. He knew a son was different from a daughter, although he had more respect for daughters than many people at that time, but the women in his life were very domineering and overrode him completely. I don't think they were aware they were doing it but they were in fact abusing his foreignness. There was his strong accent; it doesn't explain everything but his foreignness never disappeared. He never shopped. Seduced into the world of international musicians on getting married, he felt he'd stepped out of one world into another and that new world he worked very hard at understanding and conquering. Yet he was always hoping to go back to Belgium. He realised he couldn't for a variety of reasons – money, his investment in a successful career in this country but above all because of Marie's hold on his wife, or rather her need for her mother, and he wouldn't do anything to upset their applecart. But, wonderfully, because he couldn't go back to Belgium, our yearly holidays in the Ardennes became for all of us so necessary, liberating, alive.

I've talked a lot about my father. He was responsible for seven-tenths of my education.'

By 1928 Emile had moved with increasing sureness into the world of art and art history, partly through his position as a semi-diplomat. He'd always dreamed of a large exhibition of Flemish art which would be held in London. As the idea caught fire he was the go-between, linking the Belgian and English institutions and the scope of the 1927 Royal Academy Exhibition blossomed into covering the whole field of Flemish and Belgian art from 1300 to 1900. It was a huge success and in the New Year's Honours List of 1928 Emile was awarded the CBE for services to the arts.

This would lead directly to an all-consuming interest in Peter Paul Rubens and a great deal of his research dealt with the work of the seventeenth-century Belgian court painters in the reign of Charles I, a perfect melding of the British and the Belgian. Emile travelled from one country house to another, looking at portraits, landscapes and sketches. All this activity flooded back into the conversations at home during the family Sundays; it was education through passion.

'He was a total romantic. He didn't like the literature of the eighteenth century. He couldn't read Pope and Dryden. He could accept Donne and the Elizabethans but otherwise English poetry started with Keats and Shelley. It was in his nature as an anarchist. If I close my eyes the image I see of him is that portrait. That is why it is so important to me.'

'Delights, of course, came with the move to The Eyrie – electricity, a gramophone and radio high among them. Huge names in music could match the great names we were reading and on Sundays I graduated to Horatio and Julius Caesar But already in my head I was drifting away from my mother and home, but in no way from my father.

I was also drifting away from religion. An original flirtation with the Church – I loved the blue cassock and altar serving and being on stage if the truth be known – and the idea that I might become a priest died. Now I was prepared for my divorce from home and religion. I wanted to be away.'

Elisabeth agreed. 'Francis always wanted to be where *other* things were happening.'

'There's a great painting of a stag in a forest with a crucifix caught in his horns.[2] Whether my father had talked about it or no I'm not sure but I *know* every time I saw it it made a fantastic impression on me. At Hardenwick I wrote a four- or five-page essay on it and set it in the Ardennes. And it won me a top scholarship to Mill Hill School.

My mother would have liked to have seen me at Harrow but the conventional public school scared my father and although, I suspect, the faults of Mill Hill were reflected in many other schools in the 1930s, he was suspicious of boarding and so when told that Mill Hill took day boys, he went for that.

Ours was a family where the children were always asked for their opinion when there was a decision to be made; what we felt mattered. But I was never asked if I wanted to go to Mill Hill. Thus at thirteen I was plunged into a society I at first hated; where all forms of recognised quality were sporting, nothing else counted, no matter how good you were. The school had a three-year programme leading to the School Certificate and my scholarship meant I jumped two years. I could keep up in languages but maths defeated me – the first time I'd failed at anything. Socially I was among young men who had already spent two years in adolescence; the result was my first two years were black. Day boys – we were called *day-bugs* – were treated like my mother's "village urchins" – and I begged my parents to let me go as a boarder and they gave way. Those two years formed the most profoundly unhappy period in my life.

Apart from sport the only topic was sex; sex as a dirty thing and that capped my divorce. In my mind it was sinful because that was the kind of morality we had at home – sex was never talked about, it didn't exist, it wasn't something you thought about because it was bad. I was cutting myself off from my family because everything that happened at school was something that would be black and unacceptable at home and I was living at school. Every moment of that life I was ashamed of, there was nothing to be proud of, no self-satisfaction, I couldn't go home and feel comfortable and happy. One night I walked out of the dormitory and took the bus up to London, ate in Lyons Corner House and then went back again. I did it just to feel I *could* do it, be away, be me.

My mother had a hatred of anything that was vulgar and inferior; it was "not to be talked about". Obviously a child's dependence during a motherhood from which you move out very slowly remains important for the first ten years or so of your life. Certainly for that period mine was the love of a child for the mother who treated him well. But basic to what I call the divorce was the *authority* of the mother as imposed on me and my father and this caused a reaction against the imposition of her will on the way we lived. What that divorce from home really meant was a divorce from my mother.'

The early coming together of factors that began to determine Francis's development – his love for his father, alienation from his mother, physicality, natural French, skills in organising, cultural awareness, financial myopia and the cushion of privilege – found further inspiration in summer holidays in Belgium. They mattered to the whole *famille nombreuse*, a designation that granted welcome travel cost reductions. First, pleasure at La Penne, Knokke and the sea, then at Spa where Emile and his brother Francis had bought a house together, Rendoux, which replicated, in a more ordered, blue and white crockery way, the homeliness, complete with deliveries, of lost Loom Lane. Charles van den Borren, '*petit cher*', lived close by.

From the age of nine through to university, the Ardennes meant Francis could walk with his father, be increasingly privy to the older man's raunchy humour and need for male relaxation; both could be away.

'As we walked, I remember listening to silence, the deep silence in the woods and forests and all those holidays are vivid with the experiencing of beautiful things; natural forests with not too much undergrowth and a lot of wild animals . . .

'A very important part of my education via my father was learning the attraction of natural things; it has lasted a lifetime. He talked so much about it, about his and Charles van den Borren's walks in Italy where they weren't simply trekking from one painting to another, they were enjoying the Italian Alps, the beauties of natural environment. I would find the same in France.'

On one holiday Emile wrote back to Tita of a walk towards the village of Francorchamps after a fall of snow:

Suddenly, in a clearing, the boy (Francis) stopped, lifting his hand like a bobby controlling the traffic – you know his way. We nearly stumbled against him, carried along by the rhythmic march. The sun had broken through, a fierce young spring sun, and it lit up the whole wood. It was so dazzling that we had to shut our eyes for a moment. Shall I mention diamonds and silver linings – those miserable poetical expressions – or pillars and palace halls and the tawdry brilliance of gems and pageantry? Rather, imagine the four of us standing there, lost in the vivid flood of the light reflected by every inch of the ground, every twig of the overloaded fir trees – millions and millions of electric bulbs and wires glaring away, white, blue, purple and red. And just at that moment the blackbirds burst into song, a full-throated loud song like that of the angels in Dante's *Paradise*, drunk with God's glory and blinded by his light, unbearable to mortal eyes. It was strange, almost incongruous, that such a sun should beat on such a snow and such a song burst forth in such a place.

I was so happy that I no longer felt your absence. I was sure that at that very moment you were by my side – or at least that essence of you which is free from space and time – or shall I say, space-time?[3]

3

Post-1660, Dissenters were punished by Charles II and the social exclusion of nonconformists for two hundred years drove the cream of them – ejected ministers together with sober and industrious kings of trade – into building their own schools and academies. Of these, Richard Smith's at Mill Hill, was probably the earliest. By the 1930s Mill Hill School, 'austere yet urbane', was a public school, a non-local boarding school in extensive, tree-clad grounds, with imposing buildings, chapel and a growing reputation for sport, slung low against an ancient ridgeway close to the borders of Middlesex and Hertfordshire overlooking Edgware. 'It was the sort of school, which when mentioned, would sometimes make snobbish people confess that they rather thought they had heard of it.'[1]

Although its dissenting tradition had always encouraged religiously tinged social awareness and individuality of thought, it was nevertheless imbued, inevitably, with the public school, upper-class preference for breeding over intellect; it was this strain that had partly produced Francis's blackness. For Mill Hill paraded the usual public school values, including bullying, arrogance of the senior pupils – the Monitors ran the school's discipline – and fagging; it was all there to be marked by. Thirty or so years later a day-bug can remember being slippered with a dead battery in the toe of a plimsoll for failing to recognise the significance of a tie.

However, as, in his final two years, Francis relaxed into its system, a certain laddishness appeared coupled with laziness. He was regarded as being brighter than his achievement though of a Sunday he would often walk home to Radlett, missing his maturing friendship with his father.

Eighteen months before he left school, his need to be challenged intellectually found satisfaction through a classics master, Alan Whitehorn. According to his daughter, Katharine Whitehorn, her father's 'knowledge wasn't world-wide it was world-deep; he reckoned he was teaching two civilizations, two literatures, Greek and Latin. He made his stuff accessible through humour, he was very funny. He thought the linguistic side was very important – "in order to translate you've got to know what you want to say – you can't waffle in Latin!" He made people *think* and yes, Francis is probably right, he was considerably more enlightened than many of his colleagues.'[2]

'Alan Whitehorn gave me something to look up to. He took General Studies and it was during the week after the famous 1933 Oxford Union debate, where the students shocked the Establishment, including Winston Churchill, by voting two to one "that they would under no circumstances fight for King and Country", that Alan, who unknown to us had been a conscientious objector in the First World War, asked us the same question. We were about a dozen and I put my hand up for pacifism and none of the others did. So he said to me, you will write me an essay saying why you would fight for your country and set the others to pen a defence of pacifism. It was the first time in a school I'd encountered good teaching. It was enormously important – a light in what was generally black for me.

The origins of my pacifism are very simple. As little children, my generation, born during the First World War, was brought up under the shadow of poison gas, absent fathers and one-legged lovers in the park. And as we grew up many of us decided that that was never going to happen again. We would never kill. I was sixteen, yes, but it all went back to childhood. I clearly remember seeing a black and white film – *The Angel of Mons* – and being profoundly affected by it and then I could only have been nine. I was a child pacifist and have never ceased to be a pacifist. Yet I would ultimately execute a man.

'Shortly after Alan, I formed a deeply valuable friendship with John Lloyd, who became Captain of the School. It began when he dropped me from the First XV because I couldn't move fast enough. An extremely gifted athlete himself, he knew what it meant to me and so he invited me into his study and played Louis Armstrong and that began a rebirth of my enjoyment of the arts and thinking aright and he gave me jazz; on top of it all he was a socialist, in love and already engaged to be married.

Friend and guru, when I won a prize for French, it was John who suggested a list of choices. He had already looked at the most unusual and eccentric in art, sculpture and music and he introduced me to contemporary writing – W. H. Auden, T. S. Eliot, D. H. Lawrence, ee cummings and critics like F. R. Leavis – all talents whom my father

> ignored. Yet, when he came to Radlett and met my father, he was very excited and enthusiastic about him; he saw what my father had given me years before. In my blackness I thought all that had been lost and then I found that what I had had was precious and valuable and could relate to what I was now feeling; all this and the quick realisation that the pleasure my father got from Jan Van Eyck and what I was getting from Picasso were the same. I was beginning to realise I couldn't do everything, that my abilities were limited. Out of the blackness came more and more light.'

Jeanne agreed. 'In John Philip Lloyd, broodingly beautiful, taller than my brother, lock of hair encouraged to come down over one eye, very thirties, Francis had an *ally*.

> Bringing home John Lloyd was for the first time Francis introducing someone his parents weren't too happy about. John was *raw*, living out D. H. Lawrence. He and Francis went in for string beneath the knees of their corduroys, open necks and cravats – John was a huge influence – both of them just becoming men. John obliterated all other relationships, they mutually blossomed; he was the best friend you never thought you would ever have. I was in awe of him but he scared my mother witless – "*il était farouche*" – wild, fierce, savage – totally untrue, of course, he was as middle-class as we were But for her it was lock up your daughters time – until, that is, Penelope appeared. She was a beautiful girl, a total complement to John. It was a very young affair and when he joined the RAF and had a lung shot away and was very ill for a long time, Penelope was fantastic, always looking as if nothing would break her purple nail varnish for a second, bursting with devotion and love; an amazing relationship.'

For Francis what came out of jazz was a hatred of racism. Jazz came from oppression and it keenly nurtured a desire to experience Africa some day. The nearest he had got to it through his father had been classical Carthage. 'The nature of living in the twenties and early thirties excluded knowledge and understanding of remote parts of the world, partly because travel was so difficult, but not exclusively for that reason, with the result one only had the remotest inkling of what was happening and shouldn't be happening.'

But John Lloyd would continue to feed the dream. Denied a university education by his father, in 1936 he succeeded in buying his way into the publishers Martin Secker & Warburg, long *his* dream.

'John rang up one day and said, "I've just read the most important book on Africa called *Facing Mount Kenya* – come and meet the author." So I ended up having lunch with Jomo Kenyatta and John in a milk bar on the Embankment. Thirty-two years later I would be teaching teachers in his captivating country.'

'There were few Oxbridge Scholarships in which you could offer French and History and as there was little chance of me getting in at Scholarship level I was given an introduction to Tom Henn by a teacher at Mill Hill who had been at St Catharine's College, Cambridge. In addition, my father had taught French conversation to Aldenham School sixth formers at the time Tom had been a teacher there, so Tom knew him and of my existence. He was admissions tutor at St Cats. I had a very impressive tea at his home and was offered a place in the College, an obvious extension of privilege, and there I was up at Cambridge.

'It was agreed I'd do Part I English but Tom knew all about my father's prejudices and said to me as soon as I started my studies, "You've got to stop being a Romantic; there are many other joys in literature." But still in thrall to John's opening up of me, I read contemporary novels and poetry, not bothering about the periods they'd ask questions on. So I got a Third in English and did Part II in History.

I enjoyed those first two years – people were brighter than me – lots of classical music, no jazz really except from records but a lot of laughter and beer. I was very close to the music scholars at Cats and King's and I had friends who were top sportsmen, and although I had a Seniors Trial I didn't go any higher in hockey and the fact that at cricket I had University nets was mainly because Tom had paired me in tutorials with Mark Tindall, the Cambridge captain. I formed a close friendship with Patrick Dickinson whom I regarded as a great poet and still do. Harry Rée, a future brilliant SOE agent, professor of education and long-term friend, I met in our theatre going.

The combination of theatre and St Cats being next to King's led to many friendships with gays. My sister Kippe and her school friends came and performed at King's and I got to know their world. It was all friendly and we didn't talk about gaydom a lot; it was there and illegal but I was never attracted. It was certainly a major factor in life in Cambridge at that time – the political connotations, combinations of poets, the stage – all intermingled. I was three years younger than the Cambridge Communists and, although Guy Burgess was still around, it was all beneath the surface – of necessity as far as recruitment was concerned! I was unaware of a Communist Party in Cambridge. Life was too good.

People say that I have my own way of thinking and acting, that I have an assured but defensive control over my emotions, that I guard myself against intrusion, and ask if Cambridge was responsible for this. In one sense it certainly was – Cambridge was an oasis of total privilege and one was privileged and many of the privileged were ashamed and felt guilty about their privilege *but one didn't show it*. The thirties was still the era in which you couldn't get to university unless your parents paid vast sums of money to see you through private schools. The number of undergraduates who had been to a grammar school was certainly less than a tenth of the whole in any one year. This guilt, I believe, was fundamentally the basis of the Communist route. They were all upper middle-class people who realised that 95 per cent of the population had no chance of experiencing the tremendous advantages they had; they were the haves in an ocean of have-nots and the resulting sense of shame drove them into the arms of Moscow.

There were also different *layers* of self-guarding For instance, I wouldn't have talked any kind of politics or pacifism with my sporting friends – they belonged to one pigeon hole and, say, the gays to another. Patrick Dickinson's time was strictly divided between his life as a golf blue and his poetry. He would never show any of his poems to his golfing friends but he would to me. There was no hostility between the groups. This compartmentalising was quite characteristic of Cambridge because Cambridge was what it was. All my life in France, on the other hand, was sharing.'

Radlett, Mill Hill and then Cambridge had been safe cocoons. But outside the gates, so to speak, lurked emergent fascism, in Britain as well as abroad. Although people didn't become fascists en bloc many believed the solution to the problems of Britain lay outside Parliament. In government there was inertia, the certainties of empire and capitalism seemingly everywhere threatened by revolution, depression and nationalism – all packed into the new Europe which had emerged from the flames of the First World War. Although the radical intelligentsia, through its sentimentalising of Russia, had seemed to have discovered the working class and found them 'beautiful, like the Fulani or Dinka', there was nevertheless ignored paralysis in the shipyard and mining regions of the North of England, Wales and Scotland. The Means Test and its spies persisted and two million unemployed even managed to rouse that most supine of men, Stanley Baldwin, into momentarily recognising that unemployment was 'eating away the energies of the Nation and breeding dangerous thoughts'. A generation of young men had never worked; they stared at their boots on street corners. In 1936, two-thirds of the way through the Jarrow March's month long descent on London, a thousand Mosley blackshirts marched through Bethnal Green, only for such naked anti-Semitism to be defended by the Home Office as the right to free speech . . . and up against the gates there was, too, civil war in Spain, Mussolini and Hitler. To many it was only poets, through their fresh 'unpoetical' words, images, subject matter and detached tone, who first recognised and articulated the violence and sense of impending change the politicians could not see.

Yet for Francis 'the evolution of political thinking wasn't readily discussed in *my* Cambridge.

> Theatre brought people together, talking about change, but in *theatre.* We were fed up with the West End and Noël Coward on tap. We were certainly interested in Auden – *The Dog Beneath the Skin* (subtitled Where Is Francis?) – *The Ascent of F6* and *On the Frontier* – all written for the Group Theatre; yes, for us, the thirties was Auden's decade. Among my closest friends pacifism and conscientious objection, for example, were fields of silence. None of them except Harry Rée thought of opposing the action of the government if it went to war. I did but we weren't going to endanger our friendships by bringing it up. I had one friend – George McAlpine – whose son became Treasurer of the Tory party – who even told me after we'd both left Cambridge that with my views I was a traitor to my class!
>
> No, during this period, right up to the outbreak of war my gospel was *The Week*. What I'd give for a copy now.
>
> When described by its editor, Claud Cockburn, as "unquestionably the nastiest looking bit of work that ever dropped onto a breakfast table", he was referring to its physical appearance and the general effect of dark brown ink rather smudgily transferred to the six sides of three buff-coloured foolscap sheets. He also truthfully boasted that it included among its subscribers the foreign ministers of eleven nations, all diplomatic correspondents of all

the principal newspapers on three continents, a dozen members of the United States Senate, about fifty members of the House of Commons and a hundred or so in the House of Lords, King Edward VIII, the Secretaries of the leading Trade Unions, Charlie Chaplin and the Nizam of Hyderabad.

Blum read it and Goebbels read it, and a mysterious war lord in China read it and Herr von Ribbentrop, Hitler's Ambassador in London, on two separate occasions, demanded its suppression on the grounds that it was "the source of all anti-Nazi evil".[4]

The small cyclostyled sheet made public all the news and rumours of news the official press fought shy of and "exploded effectively in many strange places". With huge malice aforethought, Claud Cockburn used a small team of well-placed international correspondents, mathematically spreading out to countless top contacts and therefore guaranteeing information of prodigious proportions, a team that could fit things together without depending on gossip, to say the unsayable, suggest the unanswerable, destroy the untouchable. He loved adventurer-journalists, civil-servant moles, the indiscreet, foreign angles. All major matters of the decade – Spain, "the Cliveden Set", the rise of the appeasers in England, the Abyssinian War, Munich, the City and the liquid morality of international finance and manufacture – were covered and "the small monstrosity" emerged, possibly through its scabrous concern for truth, largely unscathed from prosecution despite the Official Secrets Acts, libel laws and the police.

Claud Cockburn was the patron saint of the thirties.'[5]

'Cambridge was a genuinely rare society. You came away from school having learnt nothing about life as a whole, you'd never met a woman; as yet sex, if at all, was with another male, then up to University where again women were extremely rare.

Amazingly, through the Organ Scholar at St Cats, I was introduced to Rosalind, the second daughter of the wealthy businessman, Brooks, who lived at the bottom of Loom Lane, Radlett. Emotionally I took her very seriously. What it was really about, of course, was it made my relationship with John and Penelope more balanced. She was a debutante and a beautiful creature. My family thought her marvellous and our engagement was announced in *The Times*.

Through the Brooks I went to Switzerland and skiing and down to Dartmoor and rode horses. They paid for everything and they had a lovely Rover Sports saloon which I drove all over the country for five years. I was plunged into trying to live in a world I didn't belong to. I didn't feel an outsider because they were utterly friendly people. Because of them the mixing was easy, as it was again in France because of the generosity of the people there.

On the other hand she was a Protestant who sniffed at anything a bit smutty. But most of my friends suffered from the same rather absurd Puritanism – which excluded some of the greatest insights in literature, music and painting. The girl who relieved me of my painful virginity was an actress who had been equally helpful to my brother.

In the first month of my teaching in Belfast after University, Rosalind wrote to me and said that our engagement had to be put on hold as she was going to get her nursing qualifications before she got married. I was suicidal. I went down to the docks, all fog, virtually ready to throw myself in. But didn't.

She ultimately married a Czech who in fact worked for a time in the Czech Section of SOE, or SIS – very ironic. Then, four or five years ago, out of the blue, she sent my daughter Jay the engagement ring I'd given her, the most expensive gift I'd ever made – £20 – now worth £600.

'When I left University there were 10,000 unemployed graduates in England. And there were only about five thousand secondary school graduate teachers. That was the situation. There weren't other jobs. Peers at school were selling silk stockings at the back door – women didn't count at all and they weren't even included in the unemployment figures. I felt I had to earn something; I'd cost my parents a hell of a lot of money and I felt guilty. I couldn't lean on them any more, I had to get a job. With the degree I'd got, teaching seemed to be the only thing available. There was no question of training as a teacher but there was a teacher-placing agency in Cambridge which I registered with – "Fox's Martyrs" – I was unaware of the London Institute where Harry Rée went; nobody'd told me about it. That is how I moved towards teaching. I couldn't think of anything else I would possibly enjoy doing more.

I was ready to leave Cambridge. I'd enjoyed it and learnt a great deal from Tom and from friends like Patrick yet my father still held the key . . . still does. I know where my education came from – Peter Paul Rubens and my father's brilliant essay on the British and their sense of humour – "The Poetry of Nonsense." I can still roughly remember passages from it, one in particular:

"On fine days the children prefer playing in the garden, though the nursery is their great refuge in the winter, when they apply themselves conscientiously to wipe away from it every trace of tidiness. Every upturned table becomes a ship, every stick becomes an oar, chairs are harnessed like prancing horses . . . within the child lies the poet."'[6]

4

Perceptibly the pace of panic began to quicken all over Europe during 1937–8. In the three terms up to Munich, Francis taught in Cabin Hill, the preparatory school attached to Campbell College, Belfast, the 'Eton' of Northern Ireland. Despite the slight overtones of Evelyn Waugh's *Decline and Fall* about his appointment, as with Hardenwick and Mill Hill Francis regarded the experience as a disaster even if others recalled his presence with fondness – whether him providing two tins of biscuits for the Debating Society to munch through while dealing with the existence of ghosts or helping protect his local pub, run by a Catholic, from the depredations of the Marching Season. Yet echoing Emile's celebration of the upside-down table as a vividly imagined ship, it is only a production of *Treasure Island* that he remembered with any degree of relish:

'It lasted about four hours and we believed audience participation to be the greatest thing in theatre. For the pirates' attacks on the block-house they had little flasks of red ink and we got some rifles for firing into the audience and they bounced the ink over their mothers' best dresses. It was wonderful and a marvellous lad called Sinclair was on stage for the whole four hours.'

But it was easy to see that Belfast had finally put an end to any religious preoccupation Francis might still have harboured post-John Lloyd's 'you can manage without all that clobber'. He left Belfast an unbeliever. He had seen the processions Sunday after Sunday and they had sickened him. All this was abundantly clear to his youngest sister: 'Francis was a very moral man and when he smelt evil he smelt a devil. He was coming home very tight-lipped. All the same it was not the most sensible thing in those days to leave any teaching job, determined gesture though it was.'

Nevertheless it was *Treasure Island* that convinced him he still wanted to teach.

'I wanted to be in the public sector of education and I managed to get two interviews in south London. One was at Raynes Park Grammar School where I made the mistake of choosing tea rather than a homosexual gin and tonic at four o'clock in the afternoon. The other was at Beckenham and Penge Grammar School, led by Sidney Gammon, a wonderful headmaster, who with his whole family was tragically killed by one of the first bombs to fall on London.

At my interview he showed me a pile of applications and said, "There are 315 there and I've only got time to read about thirty." I was accepted, maybe luck, maybe a nudge from Harry Rée, who was already on the staff together with a number of other enlightened young teachers. In the staff room there was a Berlin Wall between the older and those younger ones who backed Sidney's more flexible form of teaching. At the end of my first term he took me to one side and said, "I've had a look at what you're doing in the classroom and it's awful. You don't know anything about it but everything you do outside is miraculous" – I was running about four or five societies – "You'll be a good teacher when you can introduce a few of your outside skills into the classroom."

I wasn't carefully enough prepared. I didn't know the different pupils and their individual needs to the extent I should have done. He knew I'd had no training and he gave me a lot of guidance.

I don't know what Sidney Gammon saw in me. Whether Harry Rée had said anything or whether Sidney thought it would be a good thing to have two friends teaching together I don't know. Harry and I had met at Cambridge, we were both interested in theatre, we both visited Leavis – though I did so behind Tom Henn's back; he couldn't stand Leavis. Harry was half-gay and together with teaching we talked a lot about our pacifism.'

There is little doubt that the two friends influenced each other – as evidenced, for example, by the almost identical tone in their reasons for ultimately joining the Forces.

Harry: 'I can't say it was simple patriotism that moved most of us – there was very little of that in the last war, it was much closer to simple impatience. You see, after the fall of France most of us in the army in this country had damn all to do. We were pushed off to Exeter or Wales or Scotland, nice safe places where there was very little to do, while wives and families were often in London or Coventry or Plymouth, all places that were being bombed; they were at risk while we weren't. I think a lot of men resented that. And there was another thing. If we were going to get into a risky situation, we wanted to go somewhere where we would be our own masters. We didn't want a stupid colonel ordering us to advance into a screen of machine-gun bullets when we didn't agree with the order – we weren't the Light Brigade! If we were going to advance into a hail of machine-gun fire or do something equally suicidal, we wanted it to be our decision. That was something we shared – and agreed about. But it made us all different. We were all individualists.'[1]

Francis: 'Once you'd accepted the notion of the discipline of an armed force you were bound to accept the probability of stupid and ridiculous orders which you'd have to obey. I might be ordered to kill people in a way that was entirely wrong. I had no intention of getting into any other branch of combat except one where if somebody gave me a silly order I could write back and say "don't be a bloody fool".'

Then, on 19 September, Neville Chamberlain's aircraft touched down at Heston from Munich and he emerged 'transfigured with success' waving his single sheet of paper!

Such a pinnacle of appeasement, garlanded with 'peace with honour' and 'peace in our time', left Czechoslovakia abandoned, Poland ripe for invasion and Jews everywhere hideously vulnerable.

'The news of Munich came while I was in Victoria in the evening after teaching. I had found a flat behind the station in Denbigh Street which made it easy for the trip to school and for contact with Rosalind who was training at King's College Hospital just outside Brixton. But that evening I wandered around alone. My overwhelming feeling was that everyone in the street felt as I did – immense relief and shame forced together, jarring emotions tearing at each other – so thankful we weren't at war yet so bitterly ashamed at the way it had been done. Oh, I trawled from pub to pub – people were all looking as gloomy as I felt, all thinking the same.

John Lloyd had volunteered for the RAF. He was on fighters and then night fighters for some time before he was shot down and imprisoned. He was somewhere else in London.

The emotion! You couldn't talk about it. No one looked elated. You felt, "I can't laugh and I can't cry!" It was extraordinary. As a young person you learnt an enormous lesson – you could feel equally passionate about two totally contradictory things.

It was a very important evening in my life.

'Harry and I talked a lot about the nature of teaching. He was trilingual because he had German family, too. We swopped classes and one thing we were sure about was that teaching a language as if the grammar came first and the spoken word second was not on; five hours a week on five separate days was the worst possible way. You needed to get very fluid, even at the expense of other subjects perhaps, for as much as three months or more, and then make up for the rest at another time.

We got together on popular songs and small dramatic incidents. There was also the conviction we should never attempt to teach pupils anything unless they wanted to learn it, that teaching a bored group meant inevitable failure. Yes, you could of course teach them to like it!

There was no overt hostility towards us – but it was such a short period of time – two years – and quite a lot of what we did was (still!) outside the classroom. We had, for instance, informal Saturday morning groups in Harry's flat where sixth-formers, boys and girls, could meet, hold hands, kiss if they wanted to and listen to good music and poetry. We knew there would be an almighty explosion if the girls' headmistress ever got to know of it but the kids were very adult, discreet and talked to their parents about what was happening. The alternative – be schooled 100 yards from each other and never be allowed to even talk – we found overwhelmingly stupid. I met former pupils recently, after all these years, who said how important those Saturdays had been!'

Both men were admired by many. 'Their English teaching was exciting and informal. Cammaerts introduced us to the new literary world of Penguin paperbacks, Rée encouraged us on one occasion to compose limericks about himself, which he then read aloud with appropriate criticisms. Cammaerts wore strawberry-coloured socks and often sat on his desk with his feet on a chair, both features making him appear very avant-garde. Rée told us that his Southend Road landlady had been Miss United Kingdom – and then after a long pause ". . . in about 1900". Cammaerts was a quiet, no-nonsense man whom we immediately respected; Rée was ebullient and his frequent shout of "Shut up, blast you!" was surprisingly effective because we knew a good teacher when we saw one.'

*

At the end of his first year at Beckenham war broke out and, as compulsory service didn't affect him until twelve months later, Francis didn't have to register as a conscientious objector at that point, but he warned Sidney Gammon that that was his intention. In November 1940 Harry Rée decided he had to accept his call-up. The fall of France earlier in May had forced him to realise his conscientious objection was largely political, never religious and therefore he had no right to refuse to fight the Nazis. He went into the Intelligence Corps and subsequently the Field Security Police before becoming an agent.

'We were very close friends, both respecting the integrity and intelligence of the other yet the very freedom of our thinking was bound to create areas of difference and we both accepted that.'

Even so, it is remarkable how closely the trajectories of the two friends' experiences mirror each other: Cambridge, both teachers who became agents in France despite uneasy French accents – Harry's was so broad Mancunian that Maurice Southgate wouldn't have him on his circuit, while Francis's first potential wireless operator regarded his Belgian accent as too dangerous to be anywhere near. They both dropped to unsafe circuits, yet manifested a serene ability to replace them with their own, to be willing to interact with Gaullist and Communist alike, both possessing energy which they exhaustively dedicated to criss-crossing vast, difficult terrain to help establish resistance in vital places, such activity, in both cases leading ultimately to close brushes with death.

In Harry's case it meant having to flee to Switzerland in November 1943 after a dramatic kitchen fist-fight with an armed German Feldgendarme. With a bottle of Armagnac as his only ineffective weapon, Harry remembered his *King Lear* and tried unsuccessfully to gouge his opponent's eyes out – then escaped but was shot at. One bullet penetrated a lung, another grazed his heart, four others hit his side, shoulder and arm yet he managed to swim across a fast river and crawl through woods and fields to safety.[2]

> 'Harry is underwritten yet his achievement was one of the most important in France. His idea of *negotiating a sabotage* of a strategic installation, thus avoiding the use of bombing raids and their inevitable civilian damage, was the result of innate intelligence, brilliant lateral thinking laced with a pacifist's humanity It was something we ought to have done on a large scale. I know people tried to do it; Harry was successful.

'Before the Battle of Britain was fought over our heads in July 1940, there came the evacuation from Dunkirk in June and the trains, laden with survivors, often stopped on the embankment where our playing fields ended, near Kent House Station, and the boys ran across to them with mugs of tea. When I saw that I went to Sidney Gammon and said I felt a school must have the confidence and trust of the parents and they're not going to feel good about one of their teachers being a conscientious objector. I've got to go. And he said, "Thank you. I can only accept your decision."

What firmed things up so completely was that the boys had seen me cry.

'Called up, I had to register as a conscientious objector. The tribunal, under the chairmanship of the historian H.A.L Fisher, took place in Fulham although in August I'd already joined a farming commune in Lincolnshire.

My arguments were simply that human beings cannot solve their problems by war. We were not going to prevent fascism by fighting it with aircraft and guns; we had to find other ways of opposing an undesirable political situation. But of course at that time the reality of the camps, the Holocaust, were yet to materialise, the purely European war was just beginning and one could argue that we declared war because Germany attacked Poland and we couldn't do a bloody thing about it and didn't!

The argument involving the killing of an individual never came into it. I didn't personalise it like that but I did say killing people wasn't a solution. I was given every encouragement to say what I wanted to say and in terms I wanted to use. I wasn't in any sense cross-examined.

Although there were lawyers on the tribunal, they weren't there as lawyers. I think the tribunal chairmen had a good deal of choice as to who served – generally people with a fairly important social role of some kind or another – and that meant every time they brought in people from churches because the religious appeal was the most easily acceptable for acquittal.

Yes, I was confident. I was a privileged person speaking with privileged people. There were others who couldn't express themselves but the tribunal tried to help them. Other tribunals were much less imaginative but they all depended very much on the character of the chairman. Fisher was obviously a wise man who handled everything in a sensible way.

My questioning and opportunity to speak out took two hours. They then went away and they certainly spent time discussing my case before coming back and announcing their findings.

Fisher said, "You're not moved by a religious obligation. You've thought it all out carefully and you've come to a reasoned conclusion. We accept you are sincere but conviction based on reason is not the same as having an absolute compulsion – which is what the legislation is made for. You're a democrat not a religious objector and the democrat is obliged to follow the vast majority. If you're a democrat you believe in the vote and you believe that the majority of votes make the decision." My application was denied.

I couldn't reply. At that point I was convinced he was right and wondered how on earth I was going to operate!

I then appeared before an appeal tribunal which was chaired by a delightful old trade unionist who simply said, "We don't want to put this chap in prison; that's going to cost us a lot of money. He's farming, let him go on farming, that way he won't involve the country in the expense of his incarceration, so we'll allow him to continue to do what he's doing." That was pragmatic and sensible, just as Fisher had been academically wary.'

Contact with his family in Radlett had gradually lessened, even with his father:

'I was hooked with Rosalind and I went and stayed with her when I had free time but I took her to meet them and they thought she was marvellous. During my last year at University, when I was doing History, my father was teaching at the London School of Economics and that meant I had free use of the library. So we did meet and we did talk. His odyssey had taken him from anarchism to an almost right-wing patriotism via a deep concern for neutrality. I think the order of my father's priorities was art, music and then politics because his semi-diplomatic role, and indeed his status as a professor, had pushed him towards thinking about Belgium's future in the period between the wars. And that's when he became extremely interested in the nature of neutrality and he constantly wrote and talked about it. But believing in Belgian neutrality meant he couldn't make much impact in England as a military ally. He published in *The Times*, the *Observer*, the *Spectator* – I don't think he ever wrote for the *New Statesman*. After the invasion of Belgium and the fall of France he was terribly saddened and only sustained through his war work and art.

He didn't approve of conscientious objection, but he came to the first tribunal and offered to testify in my favour and said that he was sure Fisher believed I was perfectly sincere and it wasn't a question of running away from anything. So, in that sense, my father was satisfied that it was the only thing I could have done and that mattered to me.

One fact that might have weakened one's conscientious objection was the extraordinary attitude of the privileged British upper class. The Radlett Literary Society invited me to talk to them, saying how much they admired my courage in taking the decision I had. An Edinburgh undergraduate came and saw me and she was doing her thesis on the history of conscientious objection. She'd made a good study of the First World War and the cruelty and brutality exercised and I said the contrast was fantastic because "I am weakened in my objections by the generosity of the people who were supporting the war but were also supporting me!" It is much to the credit of the British that that attitude went on through the days of threat of invasion; they weren't foolishly optimistic – they just shut their eyes to it and said, "No, we're going to oppose that." There was no panic, just huge tolerance and Dad's Army.

'While I was teaching, I'd been attending the Peace Pledge Union about once a month and there I'd met Roy Broadbent and Dick Cornwallis who told me they were starting this community at Collow Abbey Farm, near East Torrington, Lincolnshire and would I like to join them. Again, I had to earn a living, I had no money, teaching was a closed door, I had to have food and lodging, so I said yes.

I joined in August. At the end of the harvest I'd taken the senior pupils to camp in Dorset. At the end of it I saw them off on a school bus and caught the train to London. At Clapham Junction we were stopped by an air raid and we arrived in Victoria too late for me to catch my train for Wragby at Liverpool Street, so I slept in a surface shelter which had a solid concrete slab for a roof. I was exhausted and slept soundly. In the morning I discovered that the blast from a nearby bomb had lifted the concrete slab and laid it *across* the shelter.

I found Roy and Dick were fairly advanced in their planning – they had the land, farmers who were going to help them and they wanted about twelve to live in that situation. They'd already decided that everyone, male and female, should have 15/- a week. Everyone was a pacifist. The old farmer who helped us – John Brocklesby – was a pacifist and a Methodist preacher and he welcomed the chance of having his land farmed by people he was helping to buy it.

In four quick months I learnt to drive and start a tractor, to milk and feed cows, to herd sheep, harvest sugar beet and potatoes, to muck out and spread dung. I loved the learning and the acquisition of new skills.

I'd expected to be able to tolerate the life but I didn't bargain for John Brocklesby who taught me everything – about sheep, time, nature, fleecing, the way to help ewes when they were delivering their lambs – all that came from him; something new every day. I think he encouraged me because they had a large flock of sheep and no one on the farm was taking a special interest in it. In fact, too many there were more concerned with their souls than working the land. Later I bought a rather lovely elderly mare and rode her round the sheep with an adorable collie. I spent a lot of time at the markets at Market Rasen and drove fifty sheep there most market days. When you were selling the sheep you had chaps who came round and felt their backs and said, "That's 50lb, that's 48lb" and I'd say, "You're underestimating". I'm sure the local farmers knew the chaps were trying it on and therefore respected me. You'd get about £25 a sheep.'

Sheep would help with a recruitment test in his SOE training and he knew how to bargain when it came to feeding starving Maquisard youths in the wartime Alps. Francis never denied the role of chance in his life or of being someone to whom things tended to happen: 'They arrive on my plate. As did Nan. She turned my agreement to join the commune into the wisest decision I ever made.'

'Roy Broadbent came from a very rich Newcastle family and he had money. He and his wife Dee were conscientious objectors and it was they, with Dick Cornwallis, the son of the British Ambassador in Turkey, and his wife, a friend of Rosalind's, who set up the commune. Roy was also an artist and a lot of his designed furniture stood in London parks and he did quite well on that.

Dee told me her sister was coming for the Christmas celebrations at the farm which didn't mean much to me. On the day, I had to wash myself for the party. We had no running water and no bathroom, only a metal tub before the kitchen fire. Splattered with blood from killing a goose – which none of the others would dream of attempting – I had third use of the water by which time it was . . . it had been a wet and foggy day into the bargain and we were all covered in mud. I was asked to keep an eye on the goose and started to wash. The outside kitchen door opened direct on to the Urals, so I yelled at someone entering from the icy yard, "For God's sake shut the bloody door!"

The reply was a low gliding sound – "Just as soon as I can" – and in walked this glamorous and beautiful young woman, dressed much better than we were used to in the countryside, understandably, with well-groomed hair: Nan. She tapped me on the shoulder:

"Be careful," she warned, "the goose fat is burning."

All I could say was, "It's not something I know about."

The goose was moved around and the vision disappeared upstairs calling for her sister.

I was completely thrown. In my world it wasn't normal to have a very beautiful woman come in when I'm sitting nude in the bath with a tide of sludge slopping round me. I got out, dried myself and dressed in the best clothes I had, which wasn't saying very much.

We had pre-meal drinks, a good goose, I think fine wine, and settled down for an evening's singing. What immediately drew us together was we both knew four or five songs with all the words which no one else did. That was fine – we were a duet, we recognised each other and we'd immediately found things we enjoyed doing together.

Then it came to one of the guests having to go home and I said I'd take him. Nan liked the idea of coming too so off we drove on a foul Lincolnshire winter's night to Bardney. On our way back the fog came down thicker and thicker and we clung to each other and made love in the car and couldn't move until daylight . . .'

5

Their wedding took place on 15 March 1941 at the Register Office in 'dreary little Caister', Lincolnshire. The couple, with clear and mutual determination, wanted no fuss and only Pieter from the family attended as Francis's best man.

> 'After lunch we made for a roadhouse just south of Doncaster that I'd booked for two nights, but on arrival we found I'd left my suitcase on top of a car with the result that at reception they were convinced we were "illegals" – not married – and they only had a room for one night. The following morning we were kicked out and found the Elephant and Castle near the station for our second night. Then Nan left for Leeds to look after her mother while I went back to the farm to look after two hundred expectant ewes in some possible danger. Because of my lack of thought I'd brought the tupping in too early and they were then having their lambs in bitter, bitter cold in early April. That meant going round collecting the lambs and bringing them to a protected area because, if the ewe dropped at night, her lamb was dead in twenty minutes. I didn't take my clothes off for three weeks – we had 1.96 lambs per ewe. It was hard graft but I enjoyed it. I'd sit up all night helping ewes to deliver and then go out and kill a sheep in the evening for food. Birth and death in the same day.'

It was Nan, small, slim, direct, Francis maintained ferociously, who proved the often unacknowledged 'rudder' in his long life; she, not wartime France, was his 'rite of passage'. It was she who 'helped me grow up'.

Born in Leeds, her father an architect, Nan was one of three children. A woman of sharp intellect and capacity, school, she declared, hadn't touched her. In Katharine Whitehorn's words, 'I don't know what sort of intellectual head she had and, frankly, I don't particularly care because that wasn't what one valued her for; she was *wise,* never mind brainy. She had emotional skills that were fantastic. She could *cope*. She negotiated lots of difficult times – war, Christine and the most staggering litany of medical conditions no woman should ever be asked to bear. She was a mother figure to us all.'[1]

'Nan, from early on, had quietly revealed a strong artistic turn and it was that that really put her under the shadow of her sister because Dee was already a Slade-trained artist and making things and Nan didn't think she could get that far so she was never motivated in her studies. Having done a two-year course in social work in Leeds Technical College, she went to Brighton for two years, looking after kids with special needs – one a man of thirty with the mind of a three-year-old. At the outbreak of war she was required to go to London, where it was rather like joining the Red Cross. Not there very long, she heard that her mother was seriously ill and needed someone to look after her. So back she went to Leeds. Then in 1940 she came in from the Urals for our Christmas party.

Apart from a feeling that Elsie, her mother, wanted to keep Nan to herself and could be guilty of inventing the seriousness of her illnesses, Nan was adored by both her parents and I'm sure they didn't think that she was going to be less happy with me than without me. It was difficult to tell. They were undemonstrative people in the main and Nan's anger over her education she never blamed on her parents. But I must tell one story about Elsie.

As the girls grew up I made a point of taking each one of them for an evening out in Paris as a kind of recognition of them passing into womanhood. Nan then said her mother and a friend, both about seventeen, had saved up hard for a trip to Paris. All their money was in cash and they'd travelled to London where their purses were stolen and they'd had to go back to Leeds. So I said, right, we'll take Elsie to Paris.

We started with a meal at the Tour d'Argent and I said, now you'd like to go to a nightclub, wouldn't you? She cried YES! We took her to the Nouvelle Eve – the kind of nightclub designed for the tourist – glossy and all the girls six feet tall.

The music played and we sat with Elsie and we watched the girls stripping and the principal figure hadn't even buttons on her nipples – she was totally nude. Then Elsie leaned across to Nan and whispered, "Look dear, she's got an engagement ring on." Sitting there, taking everything in, her eyes popping out of her head, it was what she'd dreamed about forty years before! She'd slid her shoes off under the table and when we got up to go – half past three in the morning – she picked them up and swept to the door as if to the manor born. Elsie I loved.

'After the lambing I was able to wash and dress at night. They loaned me a van and we went down to see John and then on a far from happy little tour to introduce Nan to the family.

My mother never forgave Nan for our being married without telling them and they rarely communicated. On the other hand, my father loved Nan and called her Helena, after Helena Fourment, Rubens' mistress. He understood but never showed his affection and respect for Nan in front of his wife. He showed it outside and Nan would say, "He's always very nice to me, but in front of the family he just keeps quiet."

It was at Radlett that we heard of Pieter's death.'

He had been killed in action having abandoned a promising career on the professional stage to join the RAF and consequently his name is honoured on the walls of the Royal Academy of Dramatic Art. His death would drive his brother and father into totally diverse fields of action.

All that is known is that Pieter was returning from a bombing mission over Kuhl. The plane, a small three-crew Blenheim, had been caught by enemy fire and the pilot badly injured. Pieter, as a sergeant, was the next in command, and he ordered the tail-gunner to jump which he did. Pieter, as part of his training, had been taught to fly but not how to land the aircraft. He tried and it crashed and exploded in flames on the runway in St Ives, incinerating himself and the pilot.

His fierce need to be a pilot, where, alone in his fighter, he could be 'responsible only to himself', had been denied owing to a slight sight defect and he'd therefore trained as an observer, part of a three-man bomb crew.

Always having been convinced that his brother Francis was better looking, precocious and somewhat masterful, he'd nevertheless grown in time into tall, Rupert Brooke-like beauty, become a good actor, a 'beloved womanising, carrier-on', and most importantly for those close to him but especially for his father, blessed with a new emotional, gently teasing, untidy intellectual assurance. He had become his own person. From this, in his last months, grew a closeness that made his death hard for the family to bear and for Emile pain he could only assuage through a wholesale commitment to Christianity.

Hugely aware of family, Pieter had written on 10 May – the date of the second German invasion of Belgium:

> 'I don't know a bit what to say. When you see this unintelligible letter you will, all of you, read between the lines and believe my sorrow, rage and hatred, when I heard this morning's news. Please, don't go on feeling like you are doing at the moment, it won't do anybody any good. I know, as regards myself, that I shall quieten down in a day or two; my feelings at the moment are too strong to last . . . don't let Jeanne worry too much; stop her hating anyway. Take care of yourselves both of you, look after each other and don't let what happens outside affect our home.'[2]

During a visit to the West End during the Blitz he could draw no comfort from the thought that some enemy towns were equally reduced to ruin and wondered whether civilisation would ever survive the wreckage. Like his father he could think all hatred useless; hatred did not bring back the dead, nor did it cure the sick. On the other hand, 'the job must be done, but it is a dirty job. Shall we ever get clean again?'

His last letter to his mother ended, 'I'm happy because Spring is here, as I've never been before. I've found a priceless jewel among the ruins of a war-torn earth.

God! What hopeless sentimental drivel! I'm as sentimental as your loving husband. Still, I like it, it's good fun. Daddy also finds comfort in sentiment, doesn't he? I'm afraid I need it horribly.'[3]

> 'When my brother first trained as an actor and went on the stage, I was rarely there, unhappily. I never managed to get to anything he did in the West End and then he'd stopped and joined up. The period when he and my father grew close together was very, very short and a reason why Pieter's death was such a tragedy for him.
>
> Like John Lloyd, Pieter joined the RAF. I just had to accept that that was what he had wanted to do. We all made our decisions. He was dead and that was it.'

Silence.

'Francis was very unemotional about the death of friends, colleagues, family,' explained his elder sister Elisabeth. 'For him it was far more important to remember them for what they were than to weep. Yes, it could sound hard but it was unhypocritical. If you're a Christian why were you crying? You believed he was in a better place.'

But Francis allowed an edge of real bitterness to show finally: 'The criminal use of outdated aircraft for combat purposes we knew not of.'

> 'Eventually they had a ceremony for my brother in St Albans Abbey and I thought it was terrible. They had the coffin brought in and everyone was weeping and Jeany, the young woman who had relieved us both of our virginities, was there looking ill and fed up so I went across and took her by the hand and said, "Come on, you've got to catch that train." Nan didn't look much pleased.'

By this time Nan was pregnant, suffering from morning sickness and having to make breakfast at six in the morning for a dozen workers without running water or electricity or gas. The water had to be boiled for twenty minutes to be safe and it came from a seventeenth century well about 25 yards from the kitchen. The house was fantastically cold with gaps in the walls everywhere.

> 'We didn't discuss whether we should have the first child but Nan was sure she didn't want any contraception and Niki was in a sense our gesture of belief in the world, and we wouldn't have had our child without that joint belief. We never stopped trying to have children.'

If one contributing factor in Francis's decision to become actively involved in the war had been the death of his brother, a second was undeniably the arrival of their first child in January 1942. At the birth Francis was not allowed near Nan – 'I'd upset the balance' – and a healthy 9lb baby girl was born by breech delivery before joining the commune on cold comfort farm.

But the bleakness wasn't the problem over the next few months; the war was. With the German invasion of the Soviet Union and the entry of America, it had become no longer a European conflict but a world war; now *everyone* was at risk. With the bombing of London everyone knew what violence meant: Germany had to be opposed by force.

'I looked at my daughter and I knew I couldn't not act.'

'Nan agreed and said, yes, we weren't really conscientious objectors in the total sense if we were thinking this way, and we were very mindful of H. A. L. Fisher's argument at the tribunal – if you're a true democrat you can't really reject the vast majority. Nan was a socialist and found it impossible to be an absolutist in pacifist terms. It wasn't a question of me compromising a young lifetime's belief; the conviction was that we could no longer remain pacifists, not that pacifism was wrong. I've never ceased to be a pacifist. We didn't *dispute* because we were both entirely in agreement, but we did talk it all through. We were both children of *The Angel of Mons* and also, politically, we'd met in an extreme situation and continued to agree on every step.

One of the strongest arguments we used was that if Niki were desperately ill, and the medication that would save her life was being brought across the Atlantic in a warship, would we accept the medication to save her life? To that and other invented scenarios we knew perfectly well that there was only one answer – however and whatever happened we would accept anything that would save our child's life.

It was the time and the times were changing. You had to argue with yourself and take a position in relation to a war that'd broken out and argue too with those dependent on you. If Nan had said, no, I want us to stay and continue to be pacifists, I would have accepted it. Our partnership as far as I was concerned was paramount and I couldn't break our situation without her agreement. That was our style for sixty years. In fact, it wasn't that way with Nan at all and I think she would have been extremely disappointed if I had taken any other decision.

We were also pretty fed up with the community. We were living and working with a dozen conscientious objectors, some of whom thought that all you needed to do to make a plant grow was to kneel and pray; they didn't pull their weight. I had to kill sheep for the community to eat and I said anyone who's not prepared to help me can jolly well do with not eating meat. But there were still those who said, Oh no, I couldn't . . . Another area of disappointment was during Nan's pregnancy. Her sister and the other women accused her of jumping the gun and having a baby before they had, implying that there was a pecking order in which the women could have babies! We didn't think of asking where that idea came from. And our disillusionment set in. Fundamentally, I didn't then and I certainly still don't believe that human beings can live in a communal way.

Believe me, it was not an easy or purely cerebral decision. After all,

I was about to *abandon* a wife and child to loneliness and possible danger and enter into a situation which would prove *doubly* demanding on her in ways I as yet knew nothing of. Pieter had signed on knowing there were married men crowding the recruiting offices understanding the situation even less than he did . . .

But Nan and I could talk and we agreed a lot about the need to be permanently loyal and that it was probably impossible and even undesirable, but we agreed too that we had to be very careful on that count. Obviously we were both going to encounter the problem at some point but we talked at length about living together and what a partnership meant. There we really didn't have differences.

'The decision having been made, what to do next? My major concern was to get involved in something with no long training because the war might be over before I was ready and then I'd feel a bloody fool. So I got hold of Harry Rée, who was in the Field Security Police looking after secret military schools, and asked him what I could do about my dilemma. He said he thought he could get me an interview with an organisation which could use my French and we both thought that that meant North Africa. It was the eve of the invasion of North Africa and it was obvious that the three French territories were going to be very important and the desert a place where the war was going to enlarge. But we didn't know or think anything more than that. The name SOE was never mentioned. I didn't hear the initials "SOE" until after the end of the war; to me it was MOI (SP).'

SOE – Special Operations Executive – formed after the fall of France in 1940 and the signing of Marshal Pétain's ignominious armistice with Nazi Germany, had begun serious operations in September 1942, and although Winston Churchill had called on his newly created Secret Army to 'Set Europe Ablaze', its real task was to help European, and especially French, *résistants* prepare for eventual D-Day landings, baulk the German reaction and achieve their own liberation through guerrilla activity and sabotage.

As a paramilitary organisation it did not believe in large uprisings: the Germans were too well trained and armed and their reprisals against civilians inhuman and too numerically vicious.

Right from the cradle the new organisation was seen as *secret, separate* and not even answerable to Parliament. In a letter to Lord Halifax at the

Foreign Office, Dr Hugh Dalton, the Minister of Economic Warfare, spelt out its vision:

> 'We have got to organise movements in enemy-occupied territory comparable to the Sinn Féin movement in Ireland, to the Chinese Guerrillas now operating against Japan, to the Spanish Irregulars who played a notable part in Wellington's campaign or – one might as well admit it – to the organisations which the Nazis themselves have developed so remarkably in almost every country in the world. This "democratic international" must use many different methods, including industrial and military sabotage, labour agitation and strikes, continuous propaganda, terrorist acts against traitors and German leaders, boycotts and riots. It is quite clear to me that an organisation on this scale and of this character is not something which can be handled by the ordinary departmental machinery of either the British Civil Service or the British military machine. What is needed is a new organisation to coordinate, inspire, control and assist the nationals of the oppressed countries who must themselves be the direct participants. We need absolute secrecy, a certain fanatical enthusiasm, willingness to work with people of different nationalities, complete political reliability. Some of these qualities are certainly to be found in some military officers and, if such men are available, they should undoubtedly be used. But the organisation should, in my view, be entirely independent of the War Office machine.'[4]

Luckily the new organisation soon had a head worthy of the challenge in the wiry, brilliant figure of (Sir) Colin Gubbins, who had written two short pamphlets, 'The Art of Guerrilla Warfare' and the 'Partisan Leaders' Handbook', after watching the success of Michael Collins's gunmen in Dublin in 1919. In these pamphlets Gubbins lays down the basic principles of guerrilla warfare – surprise, swift and sudden attacks, then immediate withdrawal; never 'hold ground', always plan the line of retreat; mobility; be sure of exact intelligence and clear knowledge about the ground where they will operate – usually near their own homes – so that they already know every path, lane, every hollow; if it is far from home then only use reliable guides.

Another vital pamphlet which would prove fundamental to SOE training was 'How to Use High Explosives' by (Sir) Millis Jefferis, with its simple tips on how a saboteur could attack, with ease and profit, motor car or lorry or bus axles, railway engine pistons, tramline or railway points, telephone junction boxes, electricity substations . . . if you wanted to ruin a whole shed full of engines, always cripple the same part of each one otherwise the one could be mended by cannibalising another. He details which kinds of bridges are or are not readily breakable with small charges, where those charges had to be placed, how their size was to be worked out, how they were to be laid, tamped, hidden if need be and fired . . . the advantages of a stout hammer – in those days many machines rested on cast-iron bases, which would crack if hit hard, thus rendering the machine unsafe to use.

From its Baker Street HQ in London, SOE sent through its sections to any country under Nazi occupation – including France, Belgium, the Netherlands, Denmark, Poland and Yugoslavia – agents, arms and explosives and its own elaborate codes and radio communication. Links with de Gaulle's Free French in London were fractious but real and SOE's supplying of equipment and aircraft helped lead to France gradually building up its own Résistance and renascent military networks.

The separate Gaullist section was called RF but SOE ran its own French operation – F Section – much to the irritation of de Gaulle who believed no decision should ever be made concerning his country without his approval; both sections, however, sent more than four hundred agents into the field, 10 per cent of them women, where their mutual trust and respect in the field ignored the posturing of politics.

F Section was headed by (Col.) Maurice Buckmaster, ex-Eton, ex-French reporter, banker and senior manager in France of the Ford Motor Company, a man whom it was said, 'brought the optimism of a sales director into Baker St.'. He'd joined the British Expeditionary Force and had fought in France until the retreat to Dunkirk. His job was to form an organisation to supply and train French Resistance members in occupied France and to gather intelligence. He personally took part in the agent training – they were his boys and, later, girls – and firmly believed all his geese were swans. He had the habit of giving his agents a personal gift before they left on their missions.

His valuation of Francis would border on idolatry.

The staff of seven, which would grow to thirty, amazingly so small, worked from a flat in Orchard Court, Portman Square, within walking distance of 64 Baker Street, 'facilities blessed with a black bathroom which gave the offices a slightly louche reputation'. At Orchard Court agents returning from the field were debriefed, cover stories for those about to leave rehearsed and clothes and equipment scrupulously vetted by the formidable Vera Atkins, assistant to Buckmaster and in charge of welfare and preparations for the field. A civilian until the last months of the war, 'she was regarded by many people as the critical force in French Section. In Baker Street's years of almost chronic crisis, Vera was the woman never seen to lose her head.'

Later, during his recall from the field in November 1943, Francis, extremely security conscious, became acutely aware of the casualness of the place; agents, although they were supposed to be kept apart, bumped into each other, and got to know each other's names while files were left on desks as the officer dealing with the agent left the room for whatever reason.

> 'Everyone was an amateur at the job, no one was a professional really and as amateurs they didn't watch everything they did. I was to learn it was a bit like being in the unoccupied zone in France, supposedly free, but where agents got trapped; there some used normal means of communication, which were recorded, and they seemed unaware that such intelligence would certainly be seized if not handed over to the Germans when they occupied the whole of France. I never believed that we amateurs could ever play clever buggers with the German security services; they were the pros.'

The man in charge of recruitment and supervision of training programmes was a dapper thriller writer (Major) Selwyn Jepson, who never used his real name and was known (if anything) as 'Mr Potter'. He'd arrived in SOE via the Buffs (the Royal East Kent Regiment) and the Directorate of Military Intelligence. 'A particular flair for "understanding people" gave him an important advantage in the delicate area of interviewing potential agents, not least in having to decide whether they were capable of undertaking difficult and dangerous missions which could cost them their lives. He had to feel his way without actually revealing the nature of the work the agent would have to undertake. He was looking for prudence rather than impulsiveness. Prudence, after courage, was the secret agent's most useful quality.' With excellent French, he could both test the French of the interviewee and discover in what region it had been learnt.[5]

He lived to be ninety, still writing, and with Boris Karloff and Sir Alec Guinness as neighbours.

*

As SOE was a secret organisation, recruitment could not be public. In fact, it relied almost entirely on the old boy network, on 'who you knew' – whether in the armed forces or universities but usually through that indelible artery of privilege – public schools drawn from The Headmasters' Conference.

> 'Yes, recruitment for all sections was carried out amongst the privileged and on a personal basis. University dons were used. Tom Henn became a Brigadier in the Intelligence Service and he was a Senior Intelligence Officer to Robertson in Italy. I met him in London and I'm quite sure he would have been consulted on anyone they recruited who'd been known by him.
>
> The problem of recruitment is explained both by M. R. D. Foot and W. J. M. Mackenzie in their books. You needed a lot of people as quickly as possible having competence and skills which you didn't know about except language, and so it was quite extraordinary that they made relatively few mistakes. And the ones they did make were by and large in recruiting people who were used to a very comfortable, wealthy life – and that was what went wrong with PROSPER – which we'll come to – people who liked to go to a smart, black-market restaurant and got themselves noticed. That was not the way to exercise security; that way other people died.
>
> Instructors at Beaulieu in the New Forest, the final training ground for agents, tried to rectify such imbalance; caution and precaution in the field had to be a way of life, of staying alive, obvious rather than needing to be taught. I think I told you the remark Pearl Witherington made to me after she'd been three weeks in France and was dealing with a very tough group. I said how are you getting on and she said fine, the blokes are easy – what I don't like is having to go into a restaurant on my own. A polite English Kensington girl, she was famously able to adapt herself whereas a lot of others weren't.'

Soon after landing she was in a safe house in Riom and she remembered during that time inviting Francis up to her room, 'against all regulations', where they sat on the floor trying to keep warm in the winter sunlight streaming through the window.[6]

Nevertheless, the old boy network, privilege, in the England of the late 1930s and early 1940s, was an inescapable fact of life even if Winston Churchill inimitably had his own name for SOE – 'The Ministry of Ungentlemanly Warfare'.

'True to his word Harry got me the interview with Selwyn Jepson who was a nice guy. I met him in a bare office in the Northumberland Hotel and we talked together in French for three-quarters of an hour. He didn't say anything at all about the actual set-up and at the end he said, "All right, I think we've got a job for you – you start your training 1 August." And that was it. I went in a conscientious objector and came out an officer.

'We had talked about my "famous father", about me having been a conscientious objector and everything you and I have gone over, and he wanted to know the reasons why I wanted to participate. I said one of the main reasons why I *hadn't* wanted to participate had been my fear of receiving foolish orders to kill people or get people killed from people who didn't know what they were doing, and so I was fairly anxious to get a job in which I had a good deal of the decision-making. That, I think, impressed him but generally I don't know why he took to me. Shades of Sidney Gammon.'

Later Selwyn Jepson wrote: 'It was one of the most interesting talks of its kind I have ever had. This was a man of the highest principles working on the land, put there by the Conscientious Objectors Board. We discussed at length the principle of warfare and the principles of Hitlerism. Cammaerts' motives were absolutely pure and, therefore, he was one of the most successful agents we ever sent into the field.'[7]

'Apart from possible use of French, I still had no idea what I was signing up for except that I was involving myself with military service and therefore submitting myself to a discipline. I couldn't even tell Nan what it meant – at that stage I wasn't being silent for security reasons, it was more a case of not knowing anything. Talk about ignorance: the first time I wore my uniform on a visit to Radlett, a private saluted me, I smiled, nodded and forgot to salute back.

The main difference, of course, was the decision to take part in world conflict *violently*, abandoning my reluctance towards violence and particularly towards death or serious wounding of people who might be completely innocent. What made me a pacifist was something I had to give up because facing the way the world was developing meant I couldn't stay away. And that meant changing decisions I had taken – i.e. not to allow myself to be put in a position where I would do things of which I would be terribly ashamed. As it was I accepted that and I did things of which I am terribly ashamed.'

6

The description of SOE's increasingly coherent training methods as 'a set of sieves each with a closer mesh than the one before' is clean and apt.[1] Three stages were involved at secret 'schools' held in country houses catering for different national groups. F Section's first course, lasting three weeks, used Wanborough Manor, south-west of Guildford.

Mentioned in Domesday Book, the tiny hamlet of Wanborough nestles on the northern slopes of a chalk ridge, the Hog's Back, leading eventually to Stonehenge. The manor house itself, with its brown and red brick, black wood and tall chimneys, reflects its mid-seventeenth-century origins. In the royal blue haze of the Surrey countryside it is hidden, silent, remote: ideal.

The course focused on physical fitness, Morse and radio signalling, elementary map-reading and initial acquaintance with firearms and explosives. The local villagers believed what was going on was 'commando training', though where women fitted into this was best not dwelt on.

'My particular group had no women students. Roger de Wesselow was the officer in charge – quite an impressive person when you realised a man without prejudice was having a look at you and deciding what you were worth.' A devotee of Gubbins, de Wesselow, ex-Coldstream Guards, believed in leading from the front and, over sixty, never failed to take part in the early morning cross-country run over the Hog's Back.

> 'The only part of the training course, at any of the schools, that I felt I wasn't particularly good at was climbing ropes and crawling everywhere – I was big and heavy and the relation between my arms and my body weight had always been a problem. They did timing on an assault course and I was very slow, but I finished it.
>
> In the evenings when work stopped we climbed over the Hog's Back again to a pub in the village on the other side but there was no one observing

how many pints we had or how it affected us. If they'd wanted to know that they would have done it in Scotland, where both the senior officers were heavy drinkers and there was a bar, because there was no pub within miles and we had to cross a lake anyway to get to any human habitation.

The whole experience was new and easy, but that didn't mean one didn't make mistakes. I did a stupid thing during explosives training – we'd been taught to use a detonator with plastic explosive [SOE helped to invent plastic explosive and improve German and Polish time fuses] and we were given the task of cutting a piece of angular metal. But I put the explosive under and laid the metal across it and there were a dozen of us in a sort of sandpit. I set it off and this heavy metal went shooting miles up into the air with no direction and the sergeant who was teaching us screamed for everyone to get flat on their faces – the whizzing iron could have sliced our heads off. We survived. I learnt.

Out of the dozen to fifteen who started at Wanborough there were only three of us who went through to act as agents.'

If at any stage in the training process an agent's nerve did fail, or it became clear to the staff that it would fail in the field, or any other strong reason against his dispatch appeared, a nice problem in security arose, for the agent was bound to know by sight at least the people on the course with him and if he had reached Group B he might dangerously know too much about clandestine techniques. Unsuitable candidates were therefore sent to SOE's 'cooler' at Inverlair in the remote Scottish highlands, sometimes for years, until it was safe to release them back into some other part of the war effort.

Every potential agent had a 'conducting officer' sent from their country sections, the best of them resting or retired agents who could advise out of practical experience. From parachute jumping to explosives and field work, they shared the whole length of training with their charges, which often gave them a better chance of assessing them than was necessarily open to the course instructors.

The subsequent career of Francis's conducting officer, John Macalister, collided with his own in an alarming way:

While I was in France he went to Nan for comfort and sadly fell in love with her. He found in her company something that relieved his fear. He was desperately afraid and he couldn't live with his fear on his own. He felt shame that he was conducting people who were going to be sent into the field and maybe to their deaths. So he thought he ought to go. He was arrested on his way to a train bound for Paris from the middle Loire Valley two or three days after landing, held for a time in Fresnes prison and murdered later in Germany.

What makes this doubly ironic is Macalister's conduct in the light of his assessment of Francis in October 1942. 'Intelligent and very discreet; vis-à-vis family most anxious that they should not suspect nature of work on which he is engaged. His wife knows nothing. He has mastered technique of maintaining secrecy without arousing curiosity when dealing with friends. Letters most discreet; completely reliable from security point of view.'[2]

'I enjoyed Wanborough physically and mentally. Everything we were doing was learning and just as I'd enjoyed learning on the farm, so I enjoyed the unexpected there. It was totally new; basically a psychological test. As to why we had been selected and for what we still knew nothing. They just said, your next course is on the west coast of Scotland and that was it. We didn't go home, we went straight to Euston Station. There was no gap. I think the idea was to keep things moving. At that point you still couldn't see the need for absolute secrecy and you could quite easily have gone from Wanborough and gossiped anywhere about what had happened; fatal.'

The next four weeks at the Group A special training school at Arisaig, on the western coast of Inverness-shire, were unequivocally paramilitary. Colin Gubbins himself had found the site – not far from his Hebridean home – and the Admiralty had declared the whole Sound a prohibited area. It was wild, bleak and in fine weather incredibly beautiful: but in bad weather not so, yet perfect for containing the myth of commando cover.

Francis trained at Meoble Lodge where the day started with everyone pairing off and picking up a good-sized log, about 1 foot in diameter and 6–8 foot long which they carried everywhere.

'It was 90 per cent physical, a question of stamina and outdoor training. You were walking long distances up to your ankles in tussocks of humid grass; it was roadless. With the help of a poacher we learnt how to live off the land and from small boats how to poach salmon in the Sound.' There was a professional forger who taught surprising things, e.g. reproducing signatures perfectly with the aid of an egg, or the art of extracting a letter from an envelope without opening it and, even more difficult, of putting it back again.

> 'We were taught how to avoid skylines. We kept our own pistol throughout the course. Map-reading again, this time memorising routes so as to be able to make our way by day or night without a compass and instruction in the reading of foreign maps. There was basic infantry tactical training, cross-country work, fire and movement, ambushes and the storming of a house. Railway sabotage was part of the course. There was a funny little railway line up the west coast of Scotland which was suitable for it and we were taught how to place a charge and how to derail a train – the enemy would send an engine ahead of the train to be blown up so you had to be careful that you didn't lose your explosive, taking care to delay the mechanism. Through no fault of his I was to lose one of my very best friends in France through this activity. The actual blowing up of engines in sidings, etc, came later, at the Explosives School in Hertford, where we were shown how to wreck an engine – via the piston box.
>
> There was small arms training with German and Italian armour and we certainly fired British and American pistols, rifles, machine guns and sub-machine guns. You had to know how to strip, reassemble, load, fire and maintain all the weapons you handled. Stripping and loading was done in total darkness as well as by day and firing both in the calm of a small range or, more practically, shooting at snap targets at the end of an obstacle course were *de rigueur.*'

Taught by two officers from the Shanghai Police, students were shown a new style of using a pistol – with a two-handed grip, knees bent and firing from waist level. Now common everywhere, this 'quick on the draw' method was invented by SOE, it being said of one of the officers, Bill Sykes, that he had been 'the fastest draw in the Far East', holding the record for drawing from a shoulder holster, cocking the gun in the withdrawal and hitting the target.[3]

The other officer, Donald Fairbairn, imposed a still more deadly survival skill on his raw students, the art of silent killing, the extreme version of unarmed combat. A fusion of ju-jitsu, karate and Shanghai waterfront practice, it nevertheless did little to disturb Francis's pacifism: 'For me it was simply part of our physical education and it wasn't rubbed into you that this was killing – it was self-protection. It didn't cause any sort of squeamishness at all. The day you decided to participate you accepted all the implications, one of which was that you might have to kill someone; it was now part of your consciousness.'

At the end of the four weeks the instructors' remarks read:

Cammaerts has worked extraordinarily hard and has shown great keenness in all branches of the training. He should make a first-class leader and organiser. He is well above average in all subjects, and probably one of the best we have had here. Very quiet and unimposing, he does not strike one at first as being particularly outstanding, but after short acquaintance, proves himself to be a top-notcher. He is an extremely good W/T Operator and is very keen to become proficient, but may be wasted if used for this job.

And the Commandant's Report:

An excellent man. Good all round. Should make a leader. He is highly intelligent, very keen and completely reliable. Definitely one of the best types we have had. Very pleasant and popular.

'We went straight from Scotland to Ringway, Manchester, for forty-eight hours and learnt to jump out of an aeroplane. I did one jump and found it an extremely agreeable sensation though others jumped from balloons which made some of them very sick. By now, you suspected, it would mean jumping from an aircraft to do what you were being trained to do and it might equally mean going to somewhere where ships didn't help. That seemed to finish the idea it would be North Africa.

I then went for a quick hug to Harrow-on-the-Hill and that was the first time I'd seen our flat. It was now October – getting dark and foggy – and I walked from the station past the school and heard some little voices singing "Forty Years On" and I felt "We're there!" – the house was just beyond that and we had about three or four days before I went to Beaulieu.

I hadn't realised how impractical "home" was. It was a big ground-floor flat with large rooms but the real problem was that the shops were in South Harrow and Nan had to walk all the way down the hill, stand in the queue for the butcher's and the fishmonger's and the office where you could get the orange juice and olive oil.

But much worse was the enforced silence. Nan understood that what I had become involved in was something which didn't allow me to say anything and that was terrible for someone so close to take. We were both

> caught up in it. I wasn't told, you can't speak to your wife; I was told the whole thing was secret. And *that* was the point at which I began to reflect on why the silence had to be; something out of the ordinary must be involved.

Clarification came at the Group B set of 'finishing schools', in eleven country houses, clustered around Beaulieu Manor in the New Forest. All pretence of commando training ended – students were being readied to drop into occupied territory.

'Beaulieu was the place where I think a couple of gay young teachers had taken me when I was a young schoolboy – just round the corner from where I'd snapped Queen Mary at Buckler's Hard which was a royal landing point.'

Within each school five departments covered agent technique: clandestine life, personal security ('following or being followed'), communications in the field, how to maintain a cover story and how to act under police surveillance.

If teaching up until this stage had been concerned with both fuelling and honing aggression – Nazi philosophy and practice had to be defeated – it was, after all, why he had volunteered for service in the first place. From now on it would be partly defensive, dealing with the ordinary, the day-to-day, the nitty-gritty of *survival*. Axis police services were explained and the way in which they meshed with the police systems of the occupied zones. Uniforms had to be understood, how to deal with police controls (be matter-of-fact, brisk, polite, dull) and utter care taken over documentation. Without warning, students would be hauled from their beds in the middle of the night and interrogated by men in Gestapo or Abwehr uniforms:

> 'That was pretty useless. You couldn't have them doing the necessary – pulling fingernails out. You could have had someone who was very severe and asked really hard questions – but that was not what it was like. Those likely to know exactly what happened under such circumstances were hardly likely to have survived.
>
> Psychologically and from a practical point of view it was emphasised, correctly, that whenever you moved anywhere you had to have a cover story to say where you were going, why, and what you were going to do. This was an essential part of security and it had to be as near the truth and as simple as possible. Asked where you were going you'd try not to

be definite – I'm going to the cinema, theatre, a shop to buy something . . . but don't involve other people – that put them in danger. Never publicly recognise another agent in the field. In August 1943 I found myself face to face with Yvonne Cormeau, George Starr's wireless operator, on a crowded train near Toulouse. I had to look straight through her.

To avoid obvious strain in pretending to be someone else what was paramount, as I've said, was that your cover was as close as it could be to your real state. The closer it was the less you had to "live" it. Of course, I wasn't an "engineer" in France, or a "doctor", but I made damned sure I'd've talked with engineers or doctors. The secret was just don't get recognised.

Although we were not coached on the political situation in France, most of us were very aware of the realities including, yes, Pétain's anti-Jewish policies as well as of the history of politics between the Front Populaire and the Nationalist Government

I'd talked about this a lot as a practising pacifist. As pacifists we had to consider what the opposition was like. Originally it was a question of Spain, Guernica then, quickly, Germany and her camps and Italy. We were for peace but what were we up against? *The Week* was a huge contributor to the realisation that there was a sort of half-conscious treason going on in the rest of Europe in relation to Mussolini, Hitler and the Balkans and gradually one's concern focused on what it was like in the German-occupied areas whether in Poland, France, Holland, wherever. We were not ignorant.'

At the end of detailed fieldcraft training, each student was tested in 'schemes' lasting forty-eight or seventy-two hours – losing those tailing them and making contact with a supposed Résistance member, or 'double agent'. Francis, in one of his schemes, found himself in Bradford:

'I was told to make contact with a man who was a bank manager and discuss with him the chances of setting up an organisation in case the Germans invaded. Well, for starters, invasion was no longer a concern but this had been put up so I went and met the chap and we agreed to have a game of golf together and on the sixteenth tee I said – there's no one around, can I ask you a question? It all went fine till they sent the acting Gestapo officer afterwards to arrest me and put me through a "savage interrogation" where a dear old Irish police captain questioned me. He said, what are you doing here? I said, I'm a conscientious objector and

> I've come to buy some cows for my brother-in-law in Lincolnshire. What's the telephone number? I gave it to him and he went away and rang up Roy. I've got your brother-in-law here and he says he's a conchie and he's buying cattle for you. Is this true? Roy said, of course it is, and the Gestapo officer came back roaring with laughter saying it was the best cover story he'd ever heard – cattle!
>
> But I never saw the report of it. And that was the end of Beaulieu.'

Perhaps because the course was so rapid, misjudgements could be and were made. The Commandant's final report on the full General Course read:

> [Cammaerts] is well above average in intelligence but more intellectual than practical. He is very serious minded and should prove a most reliable worker. His main faults are that he is almost too studiously minded and rather lacking in dash. He lacks drive and has a somewhat negative personality. For these reasons he is not suitable as a leader but should make an excellent second in command to an important man. Therefore he should make a good propagandist. He carried on his scheme most efficiently but without brilliance.[4]

But this can be laid alongside Leo Marks's exhilarating portrait in his fine book *Between Silk and Cyanide*. Marks was SOE's brilliant and innovative cryptographer and Francis had gone to him for further coding tuition:

> To briefing officers, every agent was a problem. But Francis Cammaerts was a problem agent. Officially I knew nothing about him. Nothing, that is, except for the mandatory details every country section supplied with a 'body for briefing'.
>
> He was a Buckmaster agent, would be known in the field as Roger, and was due to go into France in the March moon. Further information would be irrelevant to the teaching of double-transposition. If it hadn't been for the grapevine operated by the Brotherhood of Briefing Officers (BOBO), I would never have known about Francis Cammaerts's extraordinary past which set him apart from any agent in our combined experience.
>
> None of us quite understood what he was doing in SOE. He was an ardent pacifist who refused to join the armed forces as all human life was sacrosanct and it was wrong to take it under any circumstances. After a

year as a farm labourer he volunteered to be dropped behind enemy lines. Whatever the truth of it, he'd convinced Selwyn Jepson, SOE's chief head-hunter, and Maurice Buckmaster, a tribunal of one, that he was an excellent prospect as both saboteur and organiser, and they'd recruited him into SOE.

I was quite unprepared for his physical impact. Buckmaster had cornered the market in giant agents, and this one dwarfed even Rabinovitch whose Orchard Court chair he was straddling with equal discomfort. There was nothing plodding about his eyes as they assessed the merits of his briefing officer. Nothing plodding about the way he wrote out the text of the message he was about to encode. It was when he started to encode it that he began living up to his reputation. He paused every five letters as if counting heads in a classroom. Eventually satisfied that all were present and correct, he appeared to form the letters into a crocodile, which he led in slow procession across the courtyard of his paper. There was another pause as he seemed to rebuke some letters he'd caught pulling faces at each other. And that was only the first transposition. By the time he'd reached the second I could have strolled to the nearest church, said a prayer, and waited for an official acknowledgement. Instead I glanced at his code-card. His poem was in French.

The BOBO's explanation that Cammaerts was a plodder wouldn't help me to unplod him. Yet the longer I watched him at work, the more I began to suspect that he wasn't plodding at all. I asked him to stop encoding for a moment, I was going to take a gamble with Cammaerts which might bring him to a permanent standstill.

I showed him the mathematics of double transposition.

Feeling like a spiritual AA, I did my best not to talk down to him. Sensing that maths wasn't his subject (it turned out to be history), I explained as simply as I could what happened and showed him the relationship between the code-words when the transposition was complete. His questions showed he'd understood every word of it, and I didn't lose him at all until I forgot that I wasn't trying to turn him into a cryptographer.

As if to confirm that he'd seen enough, the man with a need to know resumed his encoding. He didn't spurt or do anything spectacular but cruised towards the traffic-lights, waited till they changed, and proceeded quietly and steadily to pass his driving test.

There was a lesson in all this. The more intelligent the agent, the less likely he was to respond if he were taught the mechanics of coding mechanically. I'd been slow to realise that what Cammaerts had really been doing was coding with character, testing the logic of it all, trying to satisfy himself that these alien procedures were soundly based, taking nothing and no-one for granted, least of all his various instructors.

I realised that he was asking me a question. He wanted to know if maths were my subject, and I told him that I didn't have one.

He looked hard at me and smiled.

It may have been the quality of that smile or the penetration of that look, but I found myself feeling very sorry for anyone who made the mistake of writing this man off.

Unless he happened to be German.[5]

'After Beaulieu and during the Christmas holidays I had jaundice, which dragged on for three to four weeks. I was furious and the whole thing was very unpleasant for Nan. She told me, "People who have jaundice can't be lived with." The pressures were already there.

The flat was just above the old Northolt Racecourse which was packed with anti-aircraft guns firing all night, for the hill was used as a direct primer for German bombers. Although her brother Finn had a room, she stuck it until the V-bombs started, then she went back to Lincolnshire.

Of course, thousands of other women were in the same position but at least they knew what their menfolk were doing and could share gossip; except for her child, she literally had no one she could talk to. Given her love of people how she would manage over a long period was difficult to imagine.

Finally, I was sent to the Explosives School at Brickendonbury Manor, between Hertford and Hoddesdon, for training in sabotage and demolition techniques. Apart from the joy of realising a boyhood dream of learning to drive a real railway engine on real rails, the course was enormously valuable because it dealt with steam and hydro-electric power stations, transmission systems, engineering factories, steam and electric railways and road transport, all of which would form a part of my initial brief in Provence. The course was run by George Rheam, "a large man with a large mind", the inventor of many industrial sabotage techniques and an instructor of genius. He had that rare combination, accurate hands and a highly imaginative brain.

He was an exacting teacher with the gift to foresee the sorts of problem his pupils were likely to encounter on the ground and has been called "the founder of modern industrial sabotage".[6]

After Hertford I was asked if I would care to go in and out to Vichy France and I said no. The Armistice treaty with the Germans had allowed the Pétainists to retain an army of 100,000 men and, although there were a number of officers who came out and worked with us, there had been suggestions to London that there were still others willing to help and that would be my job. I didn't want anything to do with it. It ranked in my mind with the kind of "stupid order" I'd always been determined to resist. I turned it down because I had quite specific views on playing *any* kind of game with the right wing. What we had to deal with now in France was the left and the centre if you like – not what might be done with people who might want to turncoat.

I wanted to be involved in a France which was revolutionary. France was politically familiar. I wanted to be associated with a rebellion. People in South Africa said to me years later – you've had nothing to do with a genuine revolution at all; for me Résistance was as much to do with revolution as apartheid.

The real agony was waiting, during bad winter weather, for clear moonlight. It was decided that I would be taken into France by Lysander rather than dropped by parachute because my jaundice had weakened me. In turn that, together with Belfast and Beckenham, formed essential parts of my first cover – a French school-teacher seeking the warmer climes of Provence in which to recuperate from jaundice. Provence was also my proper destination where part of my brief would be to look into the state of a huge network, CARTE, which appeared to be in trouble.

Then, at last, on 21 March, I was driven down to Chichester but we were turned back because of heavy cloud. So another night of helpless wordlessness at Harrow. The following night the trip to Tangmere, near Selsey Bill, was repeated and this time everything was fine – at last moonlight – and I was away. The parting from Nan had been awkward and jerky.'

7

March–April 1943

The rail descent into France was fraught with the kind of daily danger Francis had already experienced in Paris and he would have a similar taste of it within days; he needed to the full his alert intelligence to survive. He was an illegal operative; every man and woman within an inch of his body could be an enemy or informant. The collaborationist government of Marshal Pétain was his enemy and under Germany now governed the whole of France. His friends were few and as yet unknown. What he needed in every sense of the word was *contact*.

'I never saw the doctor who got me my "fiche d'admission" again in France but in 1968 I was having a meal in Nairobi next to a lady who suddenly asked, "Didn't you stay one night in a flat in Paris, March 1943?" I said, "Yes". She grinned, "It was mine! I'm working for Médecins Sans Frontières."'

At this stage Francis had no idea of the sinuous facts behind Marsac's arrest. Instinctively he obeyed the golden rule of all clandestine work – if someone is arrested or 'burned' get out, move, disperse. At best you had forty-eight hours to avoid the probable consequences of betrayal – resulting from the torture or 'turning' of a colleague through a promise of his or her life in exchange for collaboration. It will happen to him again within days.

The journey to Annecy meant crossing the German-imposed demarcation line between the northern occupied and the southern non-occupied zones of France at Châlon-sur-Saône. The potential hazard of an identity check turned out to be only a formality, the Germans and Italians having on 11 November 1942 overrun the south in retaliation for the Anglo-American invasion of North Africa three days earlier.

Francis stuck to his pre-arranged cover – fantasy has the vicious habit of proving fatal – and prudence now informed his every move:

> 'I didn't eat because I wanted to save my food coupons. Another basic rule I quickly used – look bored when travelling, if in doubt don't speak, mumble if spoken to; don't look like someone on his way to blow something up, look like someone who's suffering from jaundice. At Annecy I caught a little bus for the last eight kilometres to St Jorioz, a picturesque place halfway down the western side of the stunning lake, surrounded by snow-clad mountains the like of which I'd never seen before, all set against a blisteringly blue sky.
>
> The bus was crowded with what seemed like students but they were gossiping out loud about all sorts of things which might well have been illegal, i.e. possible Résistance matters. We weren't very far from the Plateau de Glières which had already had its first Résistance disaster at the hands of the Germans; it wasn't a non-active area. St Jorioz was tiny and my worry increased when the five or six young men, looking not a jot like villagers, got off when I did and made straight for a nearby villa. This was later pointed out to me by Mme Cottet, who with her husband ran the central Hôtel de la Poste, as the headquarters of Peter Churchill, Odette and indeed of the CARTE organisation. It was public, far from silent, full of mysterious comings and goings, unsafe.
>
> Churchill's courier, Odette Sansom (LISE), wasn't about so I went to the villa and they showed me to the Hôtel de la Plage where I'd been booked in and which was quite a long way down from the main road on the edge of the lake but much too easy to find.
>
> Again I didn't like the look of things; again I had to wait.'

Prior to SOE and RF involvement in 1942, fledgling Résistance groups already existed in the south-east as well as elsewhere in France though occupying themselves more with propaganda than sabotage. This was not due to any lack of will but to a severe lack of weaponry and explosives; a defeated army swiftly runs out of the means of striking back.

CARTE, based in Antibes, had the appearance of such a group, but on closer inspection revealed itself, unlike the Communists and the Gaullists, to be totally lacking in any political or organisational rigour. It was the plaything of a painter, André Girard, a noisy, persuasive patriot with his feet 'firmly anchored in the clouds', a hater of Hitler, de Gaulle, Pétain, politics and the British, a lover of America: a fantasist who claimed he could raise a force 300,000-strong nationwide yet was never guilty of a single act of sabotage. CARTE properly belonged to the high-living, surreal world of the Riviera, to an unoccupied-zone mentality where the 'citizens' took their politics from a German controlled magazine, *Signal*, and where the war, already costing £15 million a day, didn't exist. In Peter Churchill's words, 'What a stupendous warm-hearted bouillabaisse it all was!'[1]

Churchill, an ice-hockey international and freelance writer, himself no stranger to self-indulgence, of imperfect memory – he would forget the difference between French time and GMT – and blessed with a conceited intelligence, had been sent to the Côte d'Azur in August 1942 in the wake of the loss of thirty-one groups in the south-east stretching from Toulouse to Grenoble and Marseille to the Italian frontier. The groups, created and magnificently coordinated by Captain Francis Basin, had collapsed on his arrest. Thus SOE could only see CARTE as a ready-made alternative complete with army; Churchill was to be the liaison officer between London and CARTE while at the same time running his own group, SPINDLE.

But gradually it became obvious that Girard was a liability and no messiah. His demands were preposterous – 'even to equip CARTE's projected sabotage teams with explosives would absorb nearly 4000 tons of stores. SOE's available airlift could not carry a tenth of that amount.'[2]

CARTE, moreover, was splitting itself apart. Genuine *résistants* in the group, led by Henri Frager, fiercely resenting the lethal combination of autocracy, inaction, ambition and inefficiency, at last instituted a civil court martial – *un lieu d'honneur* – where Girard was indicted before a French general as being unfit to retain his post and CARTE passed into the more capable hands of Frager and Marsac and the circuit renamed JEAN-MARIE. London needed to know what was happening and the almost comical attempts to pick up Churchill and Frager began.

But before Girard escaped to England and later on to his American dream, leaving most of his family in prison, an example of his suicidal ignorance of security would lead directly back to St Jorioz:

> 'In fact Girard and his numerous talkative friends never got beyond the initial stage of drawing up lists of their members on forms devised by Girard containing six paragraphs of personal description – name, address, appearance, telephone number, experience, specialities, capabilities, discretion, everything. These forms – in clear – not coded – were as a

> rule kept in Girard's study; sometimes his supporters carried them about openly.
>
> Over two hundred of the most important of them were being taken from Marseille to Paris by André Marsac in November 1942; he fell asleep during the long journey and when he woke up his briefcase with the forms in it had disappeared. An Abwehr agent had taken it. CARTE's downfall was thereafter only a matter of time.'[3]

In fact the German security forces waited four months until 21 March 1943.

Did Marsac report the calamity? Did Girard know of it, did London, did Peter Churchill? If Marsac did then the subsequent lack of circumspection and ingrained inattention to detail was collective and par for the course; if he didn't then his inaction was criminal, putting everyone in appalling danger, not to mention those at the pickup field in Compiègne.

What dispersal did take place at the beginning of 1943, however, appears to have been more to do with the break-up of CARTE itself than with Marsac's accident. The decision to relocate the new *réseau* (network) in St Jorioz, well away from the Riviera, meant everyone moved there. But old habits die hard and in this case proved fatal. Peter Churchill and the beautiful Odette Sansom lived as man and wife in the Hôtel de la Poste – as on the Riviera, Churchill could never resist hotels – while, 300 metres away, the Marsacs took over the Villa Tilleuls which also housed Roger Chaillan (Bardet), Marsac's sinister deputy. Couriers and *résistants* came and went, while across the lake Henri Frager and his wife and two or three others took a villa at Talloires. Such proximity was a disaster waiting to happen.

Fundamental to guerrilla/Résistance work was the avoidance of a perceived headquarters: always minimise risk by reducing open contact. One person who saw the danger was Peter Churchill's wireless operator 'ARNAUD', Captain Alec Rabinovitch, a young, giant Russo-Egyptian Jew, boxer, student of entomology and ferocious curser.

The agent, his wireless operator (or 'pianist') and his courier formed the basic unit in SOE work, all having been stringently selected and trained. Most couriers were women, it being rightly assumed that in a country where since October 1942, men were increasingly being rounded up for initially voluntary but soon forced labour in Germany, women could and did move about more freely.

In this particular trinity, if Churchill always 'assumed the leisurely manner of the connoisseur' and Odette was 'of the moment', Rabinovitch was a tough 'who clearly believed nothing and nobody'. He would snarl at Churchill, 'I don't like fucking mountains, they fucking well interfere with my transmissions!' Dismayed at the turn of events he removed himself to Faverges, a village 10 kilometres away.

With Churchill and Henri Frager back in London, Marsac in Fresnes prison in Paris and Odette and/or Roger Bardet in charge, St Jorioz was vulnerable and the Abwehr moved in. Already, for Francis, all this was aeons away from the charcoal skies of wintery Britain.

'During the two or three days I was in St Jorioz, I first met, at the headquarters, "ALBERT" – Auguste Floiras – who was to become my pianist and the best and most reliable friend I had in my whole stay in France. Then I had lunch with Odette and she told me about negotiations going on with an Abwehr officer who had introduced himself as "Colonel Henri".'

The colonel was in reality Sergeant Hugo Ernst Bleicher, in his early forties, eyes benign behind his spectacles, a man, in the words of Odette's biographer Jerrard Tickel, unblessed with the homicidal chastity of the SS. He had brought Odette a letter from Marsac and explained, 'It was I who arrested Marsac in order to save him from the Gestapo and in order that I might make a certain proposal to this brave and patriotic Frenchman. Only he can save Germany from destruction. Remember I am answerable to the army not the Nazi Party.'

Odette ploughed on. In the letter Marsac said Colonel Henri was wholly trustworthy and that she should listen to his plan. Colonel Henri wanted her to give him a transmitting set and code whereby he could get in direct touch with the War Office in London. On her side she wanted to know if Marsac's letter had been written under duress. So she suggested that Henri would allow her to send a man with him back to Paris, that he would take him to the prison and let him talk to Marsac alone. He would then report back to her and she would decide what to do in the light of his report. 'The man she will send will not be worth arresting in view of the importance of Henri's proposal. One does not catch flies with vinegar.'[4]

The man to accompany Colonel Henri back to Paris, complete with food parcel, would be Roger Bardet, Marsac's deputy.

> 'I couldn't believe what I was hearing. I said to Odette that of course they had the experience and I couldn't go against them but to me it felt like a trap, an impossible fantasy at that stage of the conflict.

Later that afternoon Arnaud cycled in from Faverges and through him London was informed. He later told Odette he couldn't work with me, that my appearance was too English and my accent atrocious; he looked very Jewish and therefore in greater danger than I was. But that changed. I would soon discover the south-east of France was full of refugees – all with different accents and shapes and the German police had no idea who was who and what was what.

The next evening I met V. H. Hazan, Jacques Langlois and Jacques Latour – all active *résistants* who had backed Henri Frager in the overthrow of André Girard. They'd come down from St Gervais where they had a training school in the mountains and each one complained about the situation in general, the lack of security and the untrustworthiness of Roger Bardet.

As in Paris it all felt badly insecure so I decided, CARTE being beyond repair, I'd get out, follow the rest of my brief and set up a group of my own. This meant the next day, guided by Michael Taperell, the son of a former British Consul in Antibes, making for Cannes.'

Bardet returned from Fresnes prison and testified to Colonel Henri's absolute integrity and brought a second proposal. If Odette could arrange a Hudson pickup at one of three airfields, Henri would get Marsac out of prison and himself fly with him and his wife, Bardet and Odette to London. There she would introduce him to Colonel Buckmaster, head of SOE F Section, and between them they would work out peace terms on behalf of the German High Command acceptable to the British War Cabinet.

London's response to such lunacy was immediate and unambiguous. The signal read:

HENRI HIGHLY DANGEROUS STOP YOU ARE TO HIDE ACROSS LAKE AND CUT CONTACTS WITH ALL SAVE ARNAUD WHO MUST QUIT FAVERGES AND LIVE BESIDE HIS MOUNTAIN SET STOP FIX DROPPING GROUND YOUR OWN CHOICE FOR MICHEL [PETER CHURCHILL] WHO WILL LAND ANYWHERE SOONEST STOP ENDS[5]

It would become tragically obvious that only two people were capable of responding properly to such orders to disperse – Arnaud, who had begun to suspect that Roger Bardet was collaborating with the Germans and therefore should be shot, a job he was keen to carry out himself, and

Francis, who had already moved on to Cannes, safe for the moment at least.

'I was installed in the house, amidst olive trees, of Adolphe and Thérèse Glise on the road to Le Cannet, north of the town. They had given up their café-restaurant when the German occupation occurred – they didn't want to be involved in serving German soldiers. Through them I made my first contacts with what would become hundreds of non-military French men and women who would prove fundamental to any success that might be achieved.'

Very carefully Francis picked his way through the debris of disillusionment and demoralisation left by CARTE's failure. Many of the group had been arrested, gone to ground or, as in the case of Girard's wife, been sent to a concentration camp; above all there was no contact with London.

> 'There was also a small sympathetic restaurant where I could eat, make contacts with one or two local activists like Henri Bochenek, a young Jew, and his sister who had a furrier's business. During the next four or five weeks I travelled to Antibes and met Mme Berthone, a wonderful woman, and her son Pierre, a very charismatic young man. They had been close to CARTE but became highly critical of its methods. I also met a neighbour of theirs, Pierre Agapov, a radio mechanic who had already worked with Résistance groups and with Arnaud. In between trips to Juan-les-Pins and beyond Nice to Monte Carlo, I spent time with Pierre Agapov as I had to know whether I could trust him to be my Number Two. I was feeling my way. I had to work slowly from people who were recommended and who would in turn recommend others, then help them set up their groups and run them as leaders. This became my unchanging method.'

Such care earned Francis his 'impeccably secure' reputation.

> 'Henri Bochenek let me try out a small bungalow he owned on the outskirts of Cannes. There I was joined by "Albert" as my pianist and so began a marvellous relationship which will only end with his death in 1970. He was small, humorous, straight and sincere, a very loveable man, who enjoyed life. Resister from the start, he'd distributed underground newspapers from the Préfecture in Marseille where he was a clerk before leaving for England to be trained as a wireless operator. Returning to work for CARTE,

neither Frager nor Churchill had given him much to do. He was quiet about his wife and sixteen-year-old daughter, Paulette.

Regular contact had to be established with London. Cannes was useless for radio with high mountains within a few kilometres and, besides, Albert considered the people of the coast "infected by money" and having no sense of politics. He suggested we move up the Rhône Valley to Montélimar, to the house of a good Freemason friend and operate from there.

Then, at the end of April, I received a fleeting visit from Arnaud who told me that Peter Churchill, on his return to St Jorioz, Odette and others, had been arrested by Bleicher.'

The facts are simple, the decisions they made incomprehensible.

Acting on the signal from London, with incredible physical determination Odette, Arnaud and Jean Cottet from the Hôtel de la Poste had finally found a dropping zone for Peter Churchill in the Semnoz Mountain, high behind St Jorioz – 'An Alp all to yourself!' Peter Churchill's reason for returning into such obvious danger was to feed a need for action with the Maquis on the Plateau de Glières, east of the lake, and help revenge the earlier massacre by the Milice and Germans of a relatively small group of Résistance workers who had decided that the Glières was a good place to set up camp; they were wiped out. In the event Churchill's arrest had the fortuity of denying him a second chance in 1944 when, with Maquis groups growing all over France, the Plateau de Glières was again regarded as suitable and some seven hundred men decided to stand and fight rather than melt away; again they were annihilated. The previous massacre had led Odette to travel all the way to Compiègne to inform Peter Churchill of it before he'd left for England.

In London he had been expressly warned to keep away from Odette until she'd slipped Bleicher, but there she was to receive him on the Semnoz and they both made for the Hôtel de la Poste. Odette's reasons for not having quit the hotel and crossed the lake were the time it took her to meet and convince all her French colleagues to go into hiding and the difficulty of paying them all when she did find them. After the Semnoz they were both immediately arrested at the hotel.

This is neither Peter Churchill's and Odette Sansom's story, nor the place to recount the savagery of their subsequent treatment at the hands of the Germans and their bravery, but what pains is their style of living, their non-contact with ordinary people, but above all their carelessness. A few messages were found on the captured pair and Churchill was carrying a pocket book, *in clear*, containing the telephone numbers of three of his Riviera sub-agents . . .

'You cannot rely on your addresses not being given away; people under torture can reveal anything. But they didn't even move anywhere and they were therefore picked up at the hotel where they'd been staying before, knowing that the man they'd been talking to was an Abwehr officer who had already arrested their No. 2! That kind of stupidity to my mind was unpardonable. Lots of people lost their lives because of it.'

Subsequent raids on the old 'haunts' of Churchill and CARTE after Marsac's arrest and the destruction of the St Jorioz *réseau* harvested victims in Marseille, Toulouse and Lyon – including, it is presumed, the person of Georges Dubourdin, Francis's fellow Lysander passenger. Francis and Arnaud agreed on one thing:

> 'Roger Bardet was certainly actively informing the Abwehr. In fact, he came looking for me. I let it be put about that I had gone back to England via Spain. He had a photograph of me so I shaved off my moustache.
>
> He was arrested after the war on suspicion but was not condemned. No, I was never asked to be a witness. Sometime in 1944, during the latter part of the Résistance, he'd behaved in a heroic manner and that is why he got off. Like a number of people who were double agents, or collaborators, when they saw the way things were going they joined the Résistance to save their skins.
>
> Arnaud had obviously escaped arrest and been ordered to return to London through the Spanish escape route over the Pyrenees. All I could do was offer him brief hospitality and equip him for his further journey. I never saw him again.'

Rabinovitch returned on a second mission to build up a *réseau* for D-Day. He was caught by the Gestapo and, being Jewish, treated with particular bestiality. He was later sent to the extermination camp at Rawicz in Poland and there put to death in March 1944.[6]

> 'Arnaud had given Albert a radio set but he hadn't got the crystals – they are what makes the radio resonate on a personal frequency – although before he left he gave me a contact with George Starr at Agen. So I took the train there, went north to Riom, where I met Maurice Southgate and a radio operator, Guy Jones, who had actually used Nan's parents' house

in Leeds during training. There I was given the crystals and the real work could start.

From the moment of landing in France, for my own good, but especially for the safety of anyone I came in contact with, no one would ever know my real name; I was "Roger".'

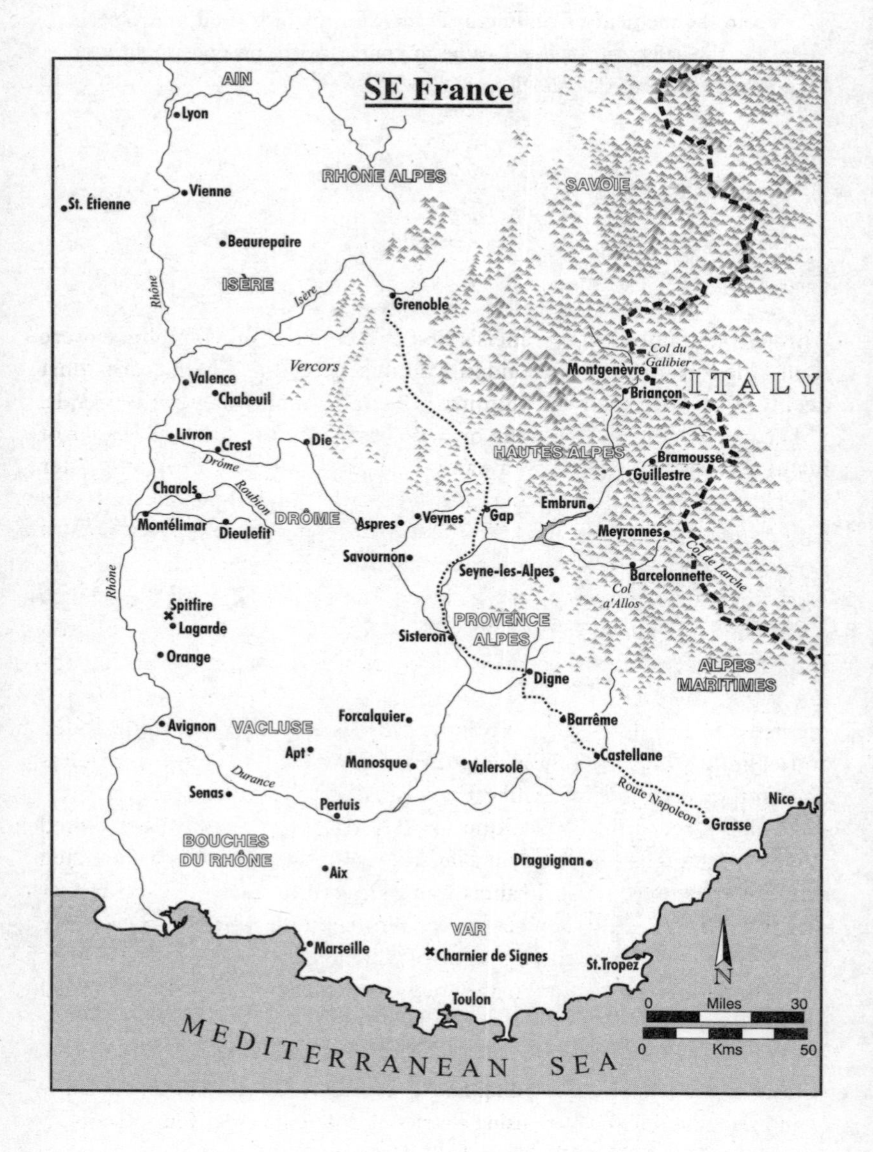
SE France
AIN
Lyon
RHÔNE ALPES
SAVOIE
Vienne
St. Étienne
Beaurepaire
ISÈRE
Rhône
Isère
Grenoble
Vercors
Col du Galibier
Montgenèvre
Briançon
ITALY
Valence
Chabeuil
Livron
Crest
Die
Drôme
HAUTES ALPES
Bramousse
Guillestre
Charols
Roubion
Embrun
Montélimar
Dieulefit
DRÔME
Aspres
Veynes
Gap
Meyronnes
Savournon
Col de Larche
Seyne-les-Alpes
Barcelonnette
Col a'Allos
Rhône
Spitfire
Lagarde
PROVENCE ALPES
Sisteron
Orange
Digne
ALPES MARITIMES
Forcalquier
Barrême
Avignon
VACLUSE
Apt
Castellane
Manosque
Valersole
Durance
Senas
Route Napoleon
Pertuis
Nice
Grasse
BOUCHES DU RHÔNE
Aix
Draguignan
VAR
Marseille
Charnier de Signes
St.Tropez
N
Toulon
0 Miles 30
0 Kms 50
MEDITERRANEAN SEA

8

May 1943

Through no fault of his, Francis's first two contacts in Montélimar were soon killed as a result of London's double-checking. Their deaths hurt deeply. They were active, committed, brave men and they were friends.

Having left Pierre Berthone on the coast to be the first cell leader of his new circuit, JOCKEY – a name Francis would first hear only after the Liberation – he and Albert moved quickly up the Rhône Valley to Montélimar and there made contact with the two men – Raymond Daujat, thirty-five, a corn merchant, General Secretary of the Agricultural Cooperative, rugby lover, leader of the local Résistance group, and his close friend Roger Poyol. Poyol's two brothers, Gaston and Marcel, immediately provided shelter for Albert to begin his incredible work. In fifteen months' 'flawless activity' he would transmit 416 messages to London – an F Section record – each and every one coded and sparely phrased. The average survival rate in 1943 for a wireless operator was six weeks. Unlike Francis, Albert was never caught.

Francis's recruiting technique for JOCKEY has already been noted and because of its simplicity a safe filigree of contacts was established through successive trust. Francis was wary and excessively careful over security. On his clear advice the leaders kept his identity secret. He knew where to reach them; none of them knew how to reach him. Telephone use was forbidden and no written messages were ever carried physically.

> 'I never used hotels or boarding houses because you had to fill in a form and sign it and if you were using a series of different names your description was fairly easy to follow and the Germans and French police knew that lodging houses were profitable spots. As were railway stations – it was

often more sensible to get off at a small station and cycle to the main town, thus avoiding the probability of main station checks.

Each cell consisted of around fifteen members; if there were decidedly more then another group was created. These were not orders, they were our agreed, inviolate, iron procedures.

A "cell" was an isolated unit with minimum contact outside. Other groups might make contact deliberately – say through shared political belief – a *département* might have ten to fifteen groups, all of whom knew each other – but my cells were not like that because in terms of safety and security the isolation of cells above all avoided multiplicity of arrests.'

Francis insisted 'it would be wiser' if every man automatically worked out for himself a good reason for every action. In case of snap controls or surprise arrests, that material always travelled camouflaged, that no one spent more money than they had been seen to do previously and that everyone learnt to remain as unnoticed as possible.

'It was not my duty as an agent to give orders; I was there to advise, support, keep them in touch with what was happening elsewhere. If you gave orders and they were disobeyed you had to take sanctions to ensure they didn't happen again – that was something I simply wasn't entitled to do. As far as I was concerned the first priority was security and that was achieved through conviction not orders. The reason de Gaulle banished George Starr – a brilliant agent – was because he gave orders and when George, at the liberation of Toulouse, marched at the head of the troops, he made a mistake; he should have had his chief French leader walking there instead.'

During his search for Albert's crystals, Francis had already set up 'fall-back' positions west of the Rhône with fellow agents George Starr at Agen and Maurice Southgate at Riom, in case vital help should be necessary, and he now began to work eastwards and slowly involved hundreds of men.

'Starting in small places and meeting the villagers, what was apparent even from those first steps was that it would ultimately be possible to set up a series of independent units, reliable teams, able, willing and in a position to attack rail and telephone communications, and, when the appropriate supplies came, to sabotage hydro-electric power and interrupt bauxite production in the upper Durance Valley. The Germans had no copper and they had to use aluminium to transport electricity. Bauxite, vital for aluminium, was then shipped from La Ciotat on the south coast to Norway, essential to the German war economy. It was insisted that this was one area, plus targeting transport and communication networks, by which we could reduce German efficiency. They were both part of my original orders of mission.'

Throughout France the idea of 'resistance' must never be restricted solely to military commitment alone. 'Engagement', whether active or through the supposed passivity of people who put their lives, children and property at risk by feeding, clothing and sheltering *résistants*, equally meant 'resistance' and knew no barrier of class or age.

'Years after the war a friend, Dédé Rochat's daughter, who had been a ten-year-old at the time, told me how, at school, other children were boasting their parents were *résistants* – sometimes falsely – and she could not say that an English officer was sleeping at her house! How children of that age could instinctively understand what was necessary I even now find incredible; as far as I know they were never tutored; they knew.

Wherever I stayed I told them I was English because the penalty for putting up an Englishman was you and your family were executed. So I never felt justified in accepting hospitality in a home without them knowing I was English and as I never used a hotel or lodging house that meant a lot of people knew I was English. But it was two-edged. For them the fact that I was English was an immense encouragement; they were tremendously excited by meeting and being the friend of those people who were prepared to stick it out with them. That's what it amounted to.'

Francis's step by step method willingly embraced all:

'In Avignon I established an active cell with a couple who were to remain close friends until their deaths at the end of the century – Louis Malarte, a fine dentist, and his brave wife, Myrose – whereas cells at Crest, Beaurepaire, Chazelles-sur-Lyon emerged from Roger Poyol's activities as a "*coquetier*", i.e. someone who collects rabbits and poultry from farms; a brilliant cover. The rabbit skins he subsequently sent to Elie Marion at Beaurepaire and he in turn sold them on to the hat-makers in Chazelles. So my first three teams in France were due to the hat industry and a trail of rabbit skins!'

While it is true that at this stage in the war there was no severe pressure of time, Francis's activity was nevertheless phenomenal and in time his antennae would reach out from the Drôme to Grenoble and in due course even wider afield to the Alps, Antibes, Cannes and Marseille. By bike, on foot, by occasional car or charcoal-fuelled lorry – 'buses were not plentiful' – some fifty groups were readied, between May and August, to receive weapons instruction, clothing, food, guns and explosives. Each team marked parachute dropping zones, safe houses, or depots for secreting arms and materials. And this was achieved despite the fact that he was physically conspicuous, well over six feet tall, with huge feet – in fact he was affectionately nicknamed 'Grands Pieds'.

Fairly Nordic in appearance, with his upright bearing and sloping shoulders, he was in many ways a dead ringer for Charles de Gaulle – 'especially from the back'.

'He had extraordinary gifts as a clandestine operator, which enabled him to overcome his bodily handicap for secret work by flair and daring. Above all he had those intuitions of danger which seem to preserve natural clandestines from traps the less wary fall into.'[1] His cover story changed with the demands of the job in hand and was always kept simple; he never slept in the same place two or three nights running. He now inhabited a world where agents could be and were caught through simply having looked right instinctively, on crossing the road.

> 'As long as my cover was secure, I didn't find it an undue strain maintaining a false identity. I don't remember the pressure being something that I felt acutely, but there were close shaves. Later, at the end of August, beginning of September, Louis Malarte in Avignon needed to deliver some weapons and explosives to north of Marseille where a group had specific work prescribed but nothing to do it with and as my second-in-command Pierre Agapov and I had a "doctor's" car we offered to take them down. Halfway into the trip we were stopped at Senas by SS troops. This worried us a lot because usually you were stopped and checked by the German version of the military police, a species infinitely dimmer than the SS. We were ordered out of the car and told to put our palms on the roof, US style, while they went through our papers. Then they started to slash open the material of the back seat. Pierre, who spoke very good German – an ambivalent virtue as it will turn out – asked what on earth they were doing. They said an American bomber had been shot down and they were looking

for the crew. Pierre roared, you mean you think we've sewn them into the back seat? The Germans laughed. They didn't open the boot which was not locked and stuffed with weapons. They just told us to get into the car and drive off.

Another way out of a problem was to spit blood. The Germans were terrified of TB. Once I got out of a train at Avignon and there was a rather heavy control check going on and they took a long time looking at my papers. So I coughed, bit my lip on the inside and spat blood on to the platform where it could be seen on the hard surface; my papers were smartly returned.'

What is necessary to convey is the sheer physical effort the region covered by JOCKEY demanded. The Isère and Drôme valleys led first to the immense limestone fortress of the Vercors plateau, all sawtoothed ridges, vertiginous gorges and dense forest, goat-tracks and one road; as outside, you walked, you climbed. Further high climbing brought you to the two divisions of the Alps and the high Italian border:

'George Chardonnet, a coal merchant and cousin of Dédé Rochat, one of the leading members of the team at Beaurepaire, lived in Grenoble and was a close friend of the civilian leader of the Vercors – Eugène Chavant (CLEMENT). He introduced me to Clement and I walked with him from St Martin d'Hères 1000 feet up into the southern part of the Vercors and there I met a man who is now General Costa de Beauregard (DURIEU) who at that time was a former regular officer. He had been running a youth cadre for the Vichy army but was busy in fact converting it into a *Résistance* group; it was to become one of the most famous in France.

Durieu explained to me how the Vercors might be used in resistance terms – with which Clement entirely agreed. He was talking of the "Plan Montagnard" whose tragic realisation would lead to the massacre of the Vercors, at which I would be present. I decided to support what they were doing and to ask for materials to be sent there but it never became part of my circuit, it belonged to the French Military Resistance.'

Francis's cells set-up potentially controlled all the principal routes south and the subsidiary lines of communication – the Durance Valley, the Drôme Valley and the main mountain roads at Digne – Manosque – Seyne-les-Alpes – Forcalquier – Barreme – Castellane and north to Mont-Dauphin – Gap – Embrun and Briançon. JOCKEY therefore covered in the first four months an area larger than Yorkshire, Lancashire, Derbyshire, Nottinghamshire and Lincolnshire combined.

> 'Radio action was always detectable and obviously we didn't want to be caught operating in the same place for long periods of time. To minimise risk Albert moved to at least ten different locations during the time we worked together. Detectors could not only establish where you were but also the personality of the pianist – each had his or her own style, or "fist", when transmitting . In Digne, because our contact was a distinguished doctor – Paul Jouve – who had a small hospital of fifty to seventy beds just outside the town, we tried to operate from there. But the nurses got too interested in this patient climbing regularly on to the roof to attach an aerial and we had to get out. Albert moved to Seyne-les-Alpes, 40 kilometres up in the hills on the way to Gap, and that was where I started to set up teams on the subsidiary lines of communication and from where I first visited the Vercors.'

Two aims drove Francis during those early months – first, training eager groups in weapons use and sabotage with inadequate or even non-existent materials, until supplies finally began to fall from the skies in August, meant that maintaining morale was of paramount importance. The second, equally vital, was the preparation of dropping zones for those supplies. *Résistants*, by their very nature, wanted to fight, anxious that an Allied landing, be it from the north, south or outer space, should not catch them without arms. Francis in this equation was The Enabler, the link with the source of all they wanted. Unfortunately during that period Baker Street was busily concentrating its efforts in the north and north-east. Local trust in the twenty-seven-year-old held fast, but, on his side, it had to be earned and nurtured with patience, tact and, above all, imagination.

The three early dropping zones (DZs) Francis set up were at Beaurepaire in the Isère Valley, Eygalières, near Avignon, commanded by Louis Malarte, and a third, Valensol in the valley of the Durance. They were at strategically chosen points, distant from each other, and thus allowed arms to be distributed throughout large areas. Later, for very good reasons, the mountains became DZ territory:

> 'Virtually once you got above the tree line it was common land – free for hunting and parachute dropping and much less of a problem in relation

to night-time activities for the groups. But in a place like Beaurepaire the summer grounds were often agricultural land and it was part of a team's job to make sure that the owner, or resident, knew what was happening and was friendly. I was never told of anyone refusing us. We'll come back to DZs and some of their problems when the drops really start raining down – but one huge difference between high and low land was that there were zones in the mountains where fires could be lit without attracting attention, often in snow, and so much brighter for the pilots to spot. On the plains people regularly rushed out and waved torches about when they heard an aircraft!

Selection of DZs was by word of mouth. Leaders proposed places to me and if there was any doubt I'd go and visit the spot. I then sent the geographical details and any information crucial to the aircraft's approach at the right level to London and it was the RAF who had to approve them in relation to nearby mountains. Again I never had a ground rejected.'

This early phase of the story began with two untimely deaths and ended with two more. On 18 June Francis was joined by two SOE officers – one, Cecily Marie Lefort (ALICE) to be his courier – but it would be her fatal ignoring of advice and subsequent arrest that would necessitate the rapid dispersal of JOCKEY's centre of activity further east, away from Montélimar.

But if Alice's folly was peculiar to JOCKEY, and still ten weeks away, it was the betrayal and arrest three days later, on 21 June, of Jean Moulin, the most important and powerful force in the Résistance in France, that sent shock waves through the whole anti-German movement.

Jean Moulin (1899–1943), born in Béziers, was the son of a republican Professor of History. Having just missed active service in the First World War, he trained in law and began a mercurial career in public service.

'He had a quick, clear, decisive brain, having learned at his father's knee how to order his thoughts and keep them in order. He had sparkling eyes, a lively manner, broad shoulders, medium height, grace of movement, and an almost absurdly youthful appearance. But above all he had charm: simply to be in his presence was a delight. He got through paper work fast and neatly.'[2]

An early marriage failed. Through the rise and fall of the French Popular Front he served in the Air Ministry as *chef de cabinet* to the Minister and during the first eighteen months of the Spanish Civil War had his first taste of clandestinity – browbeating a right wing official into selling a dozen aircraft to the republicans. In January 1939, though loathing the Pétain government, he was made Préfet of the Eure-et-Loir *département*, the youngest Prefect in France, holding down a position of immense administrative control. Denied call-up he was marooned at Chartres.

On 10 May 1940 Germany invaded the Low Countries and on 14 June the Wehrmacht entered Paris. Ahead of them millions of terrified refugees – including several hundred thousand disorganised troops – poured west and south through the Eure-et-Loir towards the imagined safety of the unoccupied zone of France, continually harassed and strafed by German aircraft. In its turn, Chartres was bombed. With intense energy Moulin set about saving the water supply, put out fires, organised fuel for bakeries, made sure the wounded were nursed and the dead buried. Needing to discredit him, M. R. D. Foot reported, the Germans: 'found a pile of mutilated corpses, most of them women and children, and on 17 June required the prefect to sign a declaration that they had been mutilated by French West African soldiers. No evidence was produced. The corpses looked to Moulin like air raid victims; he refused to sign. For seven hours he was interrogated and beaten up; he still refused to sign. He was shut up for the night, first with a woman's corpse, then in a stone hut with barred windows from which the glass had been blown in. He felt he had made protest enough, lay down on a cast-off mattress on the filthy floor, picked up a sliver of broken glass, and cut his throat.'[3]

Luckily he was recognised by his Prefect's uniform and his life saved in the French hospital. Within twenty-four hours he was back on duty but for the rest of his life he bore a huge, jagged scar on his throat which he always covered with a scarf. Impressed, the Germans dropped the charges.

Moulin said of himself, 'Since 17 June 1940 I have been a dead man on leave.'

Marshal Pétain's self-appointed government, as much as the Nazis, drove him into active resistance. In November, for ignoring a decree barring anyone from public office who had been returned by a Popular Front vote, he was put on half-pay – i.e. sacked – and he retired to Béziers.

There, appearing to be a quiet connoisseur of modern art, he was in fact extremely busy under the sobriquet 'Joseph Mercier', sounding out the possibilities of resistance.

During 1941 the failure of the Germans to destroy Russia meant that the war was not going to end early. With nerve and efficiency Moulin went irresistibly about his dream. With the utmost respect for difference and with patience, he set about assessing options, seeking out people keen to heed the virtually unknown General de Gaulle's national rallying cry to arms of 18 June from London.

By the summer he had detected four main groupings – Liberté and Libération Nationale (the two would fuse into Combat under Henri Frenay and were anti-Communist), Libération and the Communists. The Americans would support any anti-Communist movement, but, importantly, Frenay, like Moulin, believed in de Gaulle – whom the Americans considered to be quasi-Communist! After the collapse of the Ribbentrop–Molotov Pact, the Communists could go back to fighting the Nazis – whether to divert German energy from the Russian Front or through genuine patriotism it didn't matter to Moulin; what was necessary was unity. Neither Gaullist nor closet Communist, what burned in him, a civilian, was the dream he had of a restored Republic and to that end he would organise rebellion with as much care as, in Chartres, he had maintained order.

By the end of October, representing the fragile unity of the groups, he was in London. There the new head of SOE F Section, Maurice Buckmaster, failed to enlist him and RF, the Gaullist section of SOE, secured him. This delighted de Gaulle as F Section's (i.e. Britain's) independence of action continued to rile the General, who believed nobody should operate in France without his knowledge and consent. Despite that, the Foreign Secretary, Anthony Eden, insisted SOE would continue to operate independently and that French Resistance bodies should not plan any general uprising before the Allied invasion. But it is probably Moulin's belief that military resistance was possible only in the long run that convinced the General rather than British diktat. De Gaulle and Moulin took to each other immediately.

By 4 November the General had signed a directive for Moulin to take back to southern France as the delegate there of the Gaullist Committee of National Liberation and of the General himself. Among the groups this produced active suspicion: was Moulin de Gaulle's man? Was it, in order to defeat the Germans, necessary to accept the direction of de Gaulle? Was this a move to ensure de Gaulle's control of post-war France at the expense of the socialists, the communists . . . ?

For fourteen months Moulin criss-crossed France clandestinely.

The groups that had sent him to London felt generally that the main task of *résistance* lay in propaganda but Moulin could see that beyond that would come the need for action. Already random Germans were being killed leading to swift and vicious retaliation, the execution of forty-eight hostages for the death of one German officer being the normal tariff.

The envisaged Secret Army had to have a shape, a command structure, however lean, and General Delestraint was appointed by de Gaulle as its chief. Unfortunately, he knew nothing of clandestine work and as a result would die in Dachau. Having missed a rendezvous in Paris because he'd forgotten the password, he had absent-mindedly signed his real name when registering at an hotel . . .

By contrast, Moulin was a master, continually on the move, always with a woman friend following a little way behind him when he worked in towns, carrying a full set of papers to cover a different false identity for him. He never let anyone know where he stayed, meetings took place in cafés, well checked out, or in an empty flat. Nothing was written down: he could contact people, they couldn't get hold of him. Foreseeing the need for arms he organised these and their dropping zones . . .

The politics of *résistance* took a huge twist on 11 November 1942, the day the Germans retaliated for the Anglo-American invasion of North Africa by overrunning the unoccupied zone of France. Priority thereafter was a matter of concentrating totally on ending German occupation and Moulin had the task of creating a *national* resistance council – the Conseil National de la Résistance (CNR) – to oversee and direct resistance work throughout the whole of France. Already he had founded a Study Council whose task it was to work on the problems that would come with the post-war setting up of a Fourth Republic and to smooth the abrupt transition from liberation into everyday peace. This would eventually be achieved with immaculate precision, but Moulin would not be alive to see it.

He had, furthermore, been nominated by de Gaulle as chairman of the CNR where fierce doctrinal differences called on every skill as a diplomat Moulin possessed, and more; only red herrings and useless talk angered him. Gentle, patient and intelligent, he realised that the courage and patriotism of the early party leaders of the *Résistance* were at the root of their work and therefore made them jealous of their powers. As Georges Bidault, the future CNR president observed, 'He was above political parties, but also in agreement with them, understanding their basic permanence and their value in victory.' Raymond Aubrac, a future Commissaire of the Republic, put it more roundly: 'Civil war, that other occupied countries had known, was not inevitable before the arrival of Jean Moulin but by June 1943 it was no longer possible.'

On 27 May 1943, the original CNR, consisting of eight delegates from the main resistance movements, including the Communist-dominated National Front, one from each of the two principal trade unions and six from political parties, including again the Communists, held its first meeting. Everything went smoothly and the most important piece of business was the passing of a resolution supporting de Gaulle against General Giraud who, much admired by the Americans and leading the Vichy army in North Africa, was trying to set up a less ardently republican focus in Algiers; its publication spelt the end for Giraud.

Twelve days later, on 21 June, Moulin chaired a southern zone meeting of military chiefs at Caluire, a suburb of Lyon, the fiefdom of the infamous Klaus Barbie. As the meeting assembled, German police burst in, there was no rear escape, everyone was arrested and only one man – René Hardy, the railway sabotage chief – escaped. Much later it emerged that he was in touch with Barbie. Tried after the war for having betrayed the meeting, he was acquitted. Lax security was a possible explanation for the disaster; someone, it transpired, had called out the rendezvous in the street and, heard by a Gestapo officer, this was followed up. None of the arrested broke his silence for the vital forty-eight hours.

'Moulin was beaten, all over, very severely indeed, for several days on end. Eventually he signalled – he had said nothing and by now could no longer speak – that he wanted pencil and paper; they were brought. He drew a cruelly lifelike cartoon of Barbie, his principal torturer, and handed the pencil back. They got his name, eventually, from someone else, wrote it down, and showed it to him – he could by now no longer hear, but he could just see "Jean Moulins". He signalled for the pencil again and crossed out the final "s".'[4]

In the words of his sister Laure, 'He reached the limits of human suffering without revealing a single secret and he was the one who knew them all.'

Driven to Paris, where the SS, furious with Barbie for having ruined a promising interrogation and being busy with a wave of Buckmaster agents' arrests, wanted him off their hands. Dying, he was put on a train to Germany.

'It is not quite clear when or where he died – probably on the train, perhaps in or near Metz – probably on 9 July, possibly a day or two earlier in Paris or in Frankfurt. Nobody wanted to take the responsibility of answering for him.

Nor is it even quite certain that the ashes that are buried in his name in the Pantheon, where France buries her greatest heroes, are authentic. What is quite certain is that he earned his place there. It was he who unified resistance; who concentrated the scattered energies of the French into the sole channel of anti-German activity; who saved France from the civil wars that ravaged Poland, Yugoslavia, Greece; who gave the battered nation back its self-respect. He never blew up a train, or knocked down a bridge, or even carried a pistol; he made sense of the work of those who did. As André Malraux said at the ceremony of the laying up of the ashes in a splendid invocation to the dead and to the young, 'He made none of the regiments; but he made the army.'[5]

For Francis:

'He was a very important man. By June 1943 80 per cent of France had deserted Pétain and backed de Gaulle. Moulin was hugely responsible for that miraculous turn round as was, of course, the German invasion of the Soviet Union and the entry of America into the war after Pearl Harbor. In the early formations of resistance each little group had different political leanings; fundamentally, Moulin brought them all under the umbrella of de Gaulle.

I heard of his death at Beaurepaire. Groups felt that they had lost "contact" and what you needed if you were going to do anything in *résistance* was communication and what I and other agents offered was communication. Terrifyingly, his tragic arrest and gruesome death made that easier. Recruitment jumped.'

9

June–November 1943

With the area of the new skeleton network now defined – i.e. bordered by the Mediterranean, the Rhône Valley from Marseille to Vienne including the line of communication on the west bank of the river, a line from Vienne to Briançon passing through Grenoble and down the Italian frontier – so too were JOCKEY's leaders in place. In the Isère, Georges Berruyer, in the Drôme, Raymond Daujat, in the Vaucluse, Jacques Latour, in the Bouches-du-Rhône for the region between Marseille and Tarascon, Jacques Langlois, for the line running eastwards from Marseille, Henri Vian, and between Nice and St Raphael, Pierre Berthone. The first names are used deliberately – it was a network irrigated by personal trust.

At the break-up of CARTE in St Jorioz, Jacques Latour had gone to Paris and discovered the untrusted Roger Bardet acting as Henri Frager's right-hand man. Frager was ultimately arrested by the Abwehr sergeant Hugo Bleicher at a rendezvous arranged by Bardet. Alarmed, Latour turned down a senior position in the Lille–Paris–Cherbourg area because of his deep distrust of Bardet and returned south. What had convinced him of Bardet's treachery were his accounts of his escape from custody. He had maintained that, while being taken for interrogation in a Gestapo car, he'd succeeded in knocking the revolvers out of the hands of the two men guarding him before escaping into the Métro – hardly the character previously known to his nearest and dearest.

> 'I communicated with Latour through Louis Malarte. Those who were clean from CARTE all knew Malarte and he already knew Latour's father. I never had any doubts about him; my only worry was Bardet.
>
> I never spied on or double-checked my leaders and we've talked about my security methods – none of us could do any work if we were arrested.

If I found they were doing something in an indiscreet fashion I'd tell them – you're putting us all in danger – but I would never have taken measures to find out if they were doing it – that I would have regarded as being absolutely against the basis of our working together. If I had one skill it was in not making errors in my recruitment. You could not afford to make them because everybody was in everybody else's hands. Of course I made a mistake with Agapov and we'll be looking at the fallout there.'

This instinct for people, antennae sensitive to nuance, was constantly being tested. In midsummer Raymond Daujat asked Francis if he wanted to meet Fred, an American officer who turned out to be an OSS (the Office of Strategic Services and the American equivalent of SOE, the forerunner of the CIA) agent. Francis agreed as long as the man knew nothing of who he was. They called at his house, for in the field you never arranged 'meetings': that was far too dangerous.

Five foot ten, squarely built, tough-looking, thirty-five years old, with dark, short hair brushed back, Fred spoke French with a hideous accent and claimed to have been sent from the UK to organise 'all the Maquis groups', boasting that he was 'the eyes and ears of the USA'.

'There was a wireless transmitter on the kitchen table and I asked him if he realised there was a German listening device, a "gonio", within 100 metres. He didn't know the slang and said the Gestapo didn't worry him, he had friends there. We quickly realised this wasn't a man we needed to know but we stayed and listened; everything he said showed absolutely no inclination to distance himself from German Intelligence. As we left I said to Daujat – "he's deadly dangerous because he's so stupid. He may not be a double agent but he doesn't know what he's talking about. He's got no idea of security so for God's sake tell all your chaps to keep away from him."

Before I was recalled to London, Daujat told me Fred had been seen driving around in a petrol-driven car with guns showing through the window. Daujat later gave me the names of *résistants* Fred had been involved with and they had all disappeared. In London I told them about Fred and said he should be recalled because stupidity was as deadly as collaboration. The last I heard of him was post-war when I was serving in Berlin and I had a letter saying – "Fred's on holiday here. Shall we kill him?"'

It does a cardinal disservice both to Francis's work and to his desire to give a balanced account of what was achieved in the south east of France if solely the leaders are mentioned by name here. Yes, resistance started in the towns, among intellectuals, disaffected army groupings, in the old political parties, unions and religious associations. Yes, the Forced Labour Service, Service du Travail Obligatoire (STO) – originally called SOT until the Germans realised that the acronym translated as 'stupid' – transported tens of thousands of young men to Germany as forced labour and so created the '*réfractaires*', the rebellious ones, who took to the hills and in so doing provided early manpower for active resistance. But from 1942 it was the peasantry, rural folk, who occupied a preponderant place at the heart of the *Résistance*. France is 75 per cent rural. It was the peasantry who made guerrilla activity possible, whether by the Allies or the Maquis, in disorganising the German army. Without those thousands of '*compagnards*' safety, information and camouflage were impossible. They were known by their first names, too.

For example, at Beaurepaire on the eastern Rhône Valley plain – Lucien Séguin, specialist in false identity material; Aimé François Brazier, a daring driver of a taxi-ambulance who would transport supplies and clandestines in broad daylight; Jean Colas, 'on the whole a grocer' but a brilliant organiser; Prosper Ponçet, farmer, his wife and three sons, always involved in actions as well as stocking and camouflaging materials and hiding men in his buildings; Paul Rônat, tradesman, who would be elected mayor at the Liberation; Gaston Bruyat, carpenter, whose wife Josephine still can relive the nightmare feelings she experienced every time Gaston disappeared off into the night. On 4 August 1944 she'd had to cycle into the country and collect her husband from hiding because the Germans had ordered immediate delivery of four coffins. It had been one of Beaurepaire's tragic days, with vicious reprisals which would traumatise the town but, not knowing for which possible friends they were intended, Gaston was forced to work through the night; Camille Truchet, works chauffeur, who took part in all the drops as part of the reception team; André Rochat, farmer, one of the most active members of the team whose farm was a permanent safe house for men falling from the sky and for *résistants*, and whose children would never forget the weight of ever present danger and the very heavy secret they'd had to live with. These survivors, male and female, are just some of thousands.

'It was only after the war when I went and visited and looked up old friendships that I got to know their real names – I'd only known them by their field names. Many, of course, were not from the area – they were refugees like myself and so I'd lost contact completely. Even now I get letters from their children saying so and so worked with you during the war – do you remember him and others? And I have to write back, "Unfortunately we didn't know each other's names . . ."'

Beaurepaire was special – it was the first place Francis, as Roger, cycled into to meet Elie Morin, the contact man to whom Roger Poyol sent his rabbit skins, and said he'd like to set up a group in the town. He was told that the man he needed to see was Georges Berruyer, a brilliant leader in his own right. This Francis did to immense profit. Beaurepaire was the site of their first arms drop and where they experienced the unforgettable thrill of hearing an aircraft as it rumbled heavily out of the moonlight – 'for us!' – the sound at last evidence of others' concern. It was the lucky ground he hit after having to bail out of a burning aircraft the following year . . . it was there that he learnt of the death of Jean Moulin . . . but, above all, it was the place he returned to every month to send messages, activate orders from London, arrange weapon instruction and, after fifteen-day stints in Marseille or Nice, to eat. 'Oh the tomatoes, the mutton, farmyard poultry, the cream cheese of Beaurepaire – no wonder I recovered!'

That was part of a salutation he sent from Botswana, on the South African border, to the citizens of Beaurepaire on the fortieth anniversary of the Liberation, it ended thus:

> 'You knew, my friends, that my presence under your roof meant death and torture, not only for you, but for your dearest, young and old. You knew I looked an Englishman and that the Gestapo had my photograph and that my accent was hardly Dauphinois. You lived under the menace which shadowed all who resisted but despite that you always received me with open arms, lodging, a place at your table and, if I felt depressed, knew how to console me with good humour and warm friendship.
>
> Twenty-five kilometres from where I am, men are fighting for their freedom and dignity just as once we struggled together. Here we are fighting ignorance, disease and drought. I salute you all and as soon as I return to Europe I will come and embrace you.'[1]

As he moved away from the main lines of communication into the very small towns and villages, two clear facts of rural resistance immediately stood out. Firstly, clandestine work without local backing could not be wholly disguised because all strangers were noticed and, secondly, when the time came small groups would be able to carry out very effective action against movement on the winding mountain roads and rocky escarpments, the nature of the landscape for the moment discouraging regular German patrols.

'The first point was not as negative as it sounds. The advantage of small communities and having cells based there was that not only did people know each other well and could therefore make decisions about their ability to participate but they also knew the ones who might betray them. Everyone knew everyone. They knew there was a certain number of people you had to be careful about – but that increased the workable trust.

There were no "meetings" of the group. In time we'd meet at parachute operations and occasionally for the distribution of materials but never all together; weapon training could be with a single young man who didn't know how to handle the weapon; real names were never used.

That way groups of four or five men camping out in deserted villages, in shepherds' huts or under parachute tents near a reception ground, could build up bases, with stores of materiel, food, clothing, etc, for road ambush work after D-Day. There we could train them and arm them as they became more "*résistant*". They could also be formed from the original political and racial refugees who had fled from the north, hid in the south and sought local help. Little groups of Jews, socialists and Freemasons had moved into the hills, the safest place to be. The Freemasons had gone underground and their inbuilt organisational secrecy was as solid as that of the Communists. Groups were formed, too, from the original youth cadres or, of course, from those who fled from STO. On STO being made compulsory, the flight into the hills doubled.

Then the problems of feeding them arose, of training them and getting through the winter. Summer in the Alps was fine but far from funny come winter with skimpy clothing. Desertions were few but there were many young men who went home simply because they couldn't keep warm. All fifty groups had to be visited regularly.

It wasn't a quiet life. Mobility in terms of bicycle, bus, lorry and train applied to all refugees – we were all of us moving around – and in that way clandestine movement didn't stand out. Everyone in the camps had an uncle or cousin in the country and, since the people in the big towns were hungry, they too came out into the country to find something to eat.'

The persistent lack of receptions lasted until August. Much vital information about the south-east was transmitted back to London during that period but the sense that by early winter supplies needed to be forthcoming and that groups couldn't be expected to wait all winter doing nothing taxed ingenuity.

One answer to the problem was a stream of 'mosquito bites' – or armed sabotage. Groups set to work changing the destination labels on German goods trains so that, although the trucks arrived intact, they were hundreds of kilometres from where they were supposed to be. Sand was poured into oil containers, cables sliced, telephone lines ripped down. The damage was often minor and could soon be repaired, but it had a sure nuisance value in spoiling the quiet of the German occupying forces; above all, it served to satisfy the impatient spirits of the *résistants* whose energies would be badly needed at a future date.[2] It was no mean feat to block all lines to Italy in July for four to seven days, thus impeding troop movements or to put twenty locomotives, twenty tankers and 150 greaseboxes out of action along the south coast.

London, obviously impressed by the rapid, safe setting up of JOCKEY, took it upon itself to send two officers to Francis – neither of whom he had requested. As his courier, Cecily Margot Lefort (Alice), already mentioned, would complete his basic unit of agent, pianist and courier.

Forty years old, born in Ireland, a skilled yachtswoman and married to a French doctor, Alex Lefort, an equally passionate sailor, Alice had lived in France since the age of twenty-four and was thus fluent in French. At the occupation the couple had fled to England, and left their home on the Brittany coast at St Cast, west of Dinard, with its tiny beach beneath the villa, available to the Résistance to use as part of the VAR escape line for downed British airmen and others needing to get out of France. In England she joined the British Women's Auxiliary Air Force and then SOE.

On 16 June she was flown to Le Mans with two other women – Noor Inayat Khan, a pianist, and Diana Rowden, a courier – where they were met by Henri Déricourt (GILBERT), the Air Movement Officer for F Section and a double agent. Déricourt, it is reputed, was paid £5000 for every agent he betrayed.

> 'Alice ought never to have been sent to France. She was a shy woman who was just completely lost. The reason she'd come to France was to see her husband, a doctor in Paris. My first reaction was to send her home as quickly as I could. It was a delicate situation. If I'd had an excuse I would have used it but I wasn't going to say to her after three weeks, you've got

to go. I was twenty-seven she was forty; she had a lot more experience of France than me. All I did was to try and help her avoid doing certain things, one of which was very important – never to go to Raymond Daujat's house, it was watched.

She carried messages, helped with the coding for Albert which was a long job but, whereas I was constantly on the move, there was quite a lot of sitting around in her life and the need for simple human contact might have been the reason for her going against advice to Daujat's house.

Baker Street made mistakes and she was one of the most serious. Like my conducting officer from training she looked forward with terror to the next day; they both anticipated failure.'

The second officer, dropped in the Sologne two days later, on 18 June, was a young French subaltern half her age, Pierre Raynaud (ALAIN). He had escaped to England and been trained by SOE. His reception group, whom he considered completely safe, were all arrested within days of him leaving them.

On 22 June he established contact with JOCKEY and handed over 200,000 francs. Money sent by plane to an agent was written off. It appeared in no accounts record; it was 'lost' and often that was indeed what happened to it.

The money was much needed. Despite Francis's innate cavalier attitude to finance, expenditure now demanded respect. Several leaders were full-time, paid agents each receiving 2000 francs a month (£20) – but the largest outlay remained travel and transport. Often this involved the tricky purchase of motorcycles and petrol – almost solely under the control of the Germans – and the black market had to be played.

As the months passed and the reality of war made its presence felt, another heavy item of expenditure became apparent – when an agent was 'blown', the family had to be supported. Francis was already pressing for a system whereby the families of his casualties both before and after D-Day would be maintained; there was an imbalance. If a soldier in the French army was killed his widow became eligible for a government pension, but the dependants of Francis's agents, who were engaged in subversive activity under a British organisation, were not. They, like the groups, had to eat. Every franc helped.

'Pierre Raynaud was very young and formerly extremely right wing. Before France he had refused to work for de Gaulle in London – I only found that out in the course of time. He was a woman chaser and every time I sent him anywhere as a sabotage instructor – Charols, Beaurepaire, Crest – he'd try to seduce the leader's wife. When I left for London in November I put him in charge of the Drôme because Raymond Daujat and Roger Poyol were really in charge and they could keep an eye on him if he misbehaved. But they were both killed and he became responsible for the circuit there. On the other hand he was hard-working and he was there when the massive drops started and his work in the south Drôme while I was away was very valuable. Afterwards his wayward tendencies grew and there were problems.'

On 1 August two men were talking on the bridge over the Roubion at Charols, some 13 kilometres east of Montélimar. It was easier to talk quietly in public. The tall man's mind was habitually razor-sharp but not totally calm. 'When I'd left England in March Nan was pregnant with our second child. The doctor had said the birth would be at the end of June. It was now a whole month late. The promised BBC personal message hadn't arrived. All my friends were listening daily and what was worrying was I felt sure I wouldn't be told if something bad had happened.'

Another unspoken practice in clandestinity demanded that you did not get involved emotionally with colleagues; that you avoided loading those you worked alongside with the responsibility of personal matters; in the field all knowledge was dangerous. The two men bent the rule.

Half to reassure Francis, half to unburden himself, Albert told the story of his wife and young daughter, Paulette, arrested and already passed on by the French police to the Germans and thence to Ravensbrück concentration camp, north of Berlin. He had had no word of them. His two sons were also on the run in the Drôme and on the coast . . .

An unbreakable bond was sealed.

'On the 10th I was with Roger Poyol and his wife when the message came – "*Josephine ressemble à son grandpère*", (not "*grandmère*", the reversal was deliberate); the doctor had made a mistake of a whole month! I asked Roger for a bottle of his *gniole*, a ferocious, homemade *marc*, and seated on a stone in the yard, I baptised my daughter Joanna (Jay) born on 1 August, the very day Albert and I had talked on the bridge at Charols, by drinking the lot.'

Finally seven containers were dropped near Beaurepaire early in August; inadequate in number though they were, as they were methodically collected the adrenalin surged: 60–80 centimetres in diameter, 1.5–2 metres in length, when packed with arms and explosive materials they weighed up to 200 kilos each. Four men could just carry them by passing two battens top and tail to create a litter for moving each one at shoulder height, sometimes knee deep in snow. In future drops, when the numbers of containers vastly increased, many did not fall within a convenient area, but they all had to be found, collected, together with their parachutes, and hidden before dawn. It was the leader's job, or Francis's, to account for every package and container dropped.

The explosives were immediately used against the hydro-electric plant at L'Argentière in the Durance Valley. Targeted for attack from the very outset, the assault on aluminium production succeeded but only after brusque intervention by the legendary Paul Héraud, who, seeing the Manosque team's nervous inexperience, took over the operation then disappeared back into the Hautes-Alpes.

'Such interactions were never a problem in the circuit or seen as interference, political or otherwise. It was in the nature of the courage certain groups had and others hadn't; some were shy of doing anything "noisy". At that stage I had no idea of how important Paul Héraud would be in my life.'

Power supplies were interrupted and a number of railway turntables and locomotive sheds on the line between Grenoble, Valence and Lyon blown up before the supply of explosives ran out; then it was back to 'mosquito bites'.

The lack of supplies was galling. Four drops between August and October furnished only 33 containers and 6 packages, while a further operation in November, when Francis was in London, only added 11 containers and 5 packages to the total. From January to August in the following year the numbers would rise to 80 operations, 1848 containers and 1199 packages, for a combination of reasons, not the least of which was the efficiency of Francis's anger and appeal in London.

As soon as further containers arrived serious sabotage was resumed. The Germans, thrown by the growth of sabotage in a hitherto peaceful area, knew the man who directed operations to be a certain 'Roger', a name beginning to take on the dangerous potency of legend and a danger to them but also for those suspected of being in touch with him. Such a one was 'Alice'.

On the evening of 10 September, against orders, Alice called at the house of Raymond Daujat in Montélimar. The Gestapo arrived immediately and

Daujat, who was in the garden with Alain, escaped with him. In her panic and inexperience, Alice hid in the first place she could find – the coal cellar. It was too obvious. Arrested, she began her long journey to the horrors of Ravensbrück, having betrayed no one under interrogation.

Alain, who knew that Francis was visiting a Résistance leader in a village in the Drôme, hurried to him and Francis, although Montélimar was now blown for him, returned. But nothing could be done. They had no chance of hijacking any train that was taking Alice to Lyon. To stay would only further endanger the lives of his friends in the area. Sadly, he left . . . and, as with Paris, as with St Jorioz, burned, the instinctive and agreed reaction meant dispersal. Relocation was vital and rapid decisions to protect his helpers were made. Alain found temporary refuge in the village of La Paillette, while Albert moved up to Seyne-les-Alpes, between Gap and Digne, surrounded by awesome peaks, with the deep green Vallée de la Blanche opening up beneath it; the beauty masking the corrosion of occupation. There, peripatetic Francis too found a safe house with the Turrel family who remained his hosts, on and off, until the Liberation.

M. Turrel, a local grocer, was described with obvious respect by Xan Fielding:

> M. Turrel, fat and jovial, in a waistcoat three sizes too small for him, looked as carefree and contented as an actor in a documentary film and with a wife of peasant passivity . . . they were typical of the hundreds of thousands of 'small' people all over France whose role in the Resistance was unspectacular but beyond measure valuable. Without any of the vainglorious conceit that characterised some of the self-styled 'chefs', and with no thought of reward or glory, they had placed their home at our disposal since the beginning of the occupation, thereby endangering their lives far more than any number of an armed maquis band. Yet neither their expressions nor manner betrayed the slightest sign of the precarious existence they were leading.[3]

Built as an act of devotion to his wife, his house, uniquely, had a bath . . .

Famed, too, as a mule centre, those who used Seyne had much to thank the sure-footed beasts for as they carried packs of munitions and food regularly into the peaks. 'In Seyne the mule is king!' and the equal obstinacy and stubbornness of the local Seynois transformed such traits into virtues.

*

As his reorganisation consolidated into its new security, Francis met the man whom he declared to be 'perhaps the most important man I've ever known' – Paul Héraud, Commandant DUMONT.

'To a man those I recruited said – you've got to know the Boss! I said, fine and I set off to meet the Boss and I walked with him and that was it. The whole Hautes-Alpes structure involved Paul Héraud and that's important because it was totally different from the rest. There you had a leader of ALL the Resistance before armed resistance existed and who then became the commander of the armed resistance. There you had this marvellous, great montagnard, who taught young people to enjoy and appreciate the mountains and who was a skilled artisan. He was a cabinet-maker with one apprentice in a small way in Gap and having, unusually, left school at eleven, had taught himself his own arts skills and had an enormous respect for wood. There must have been people who gave him a hand when he was very young but he never spoke of it. He always talked about the present and the future so I learnt very little of his past but he also had a self-awareness that was very very strong. Why everyone wanted to follow him, I think, was simply because he inspired respect due to the fact that he appeared to have no side, no warts at all. I walked with this incredible man in the mountains quite a lot. He possessed a knowledge of worldwide religions greater than any university don. His understanding of Islam, Buddhism as well as Christianity was extraordinary. He had no religion of his own but an immense interest in human beings' need for religion; maybe there was some significance in him being a carpenter! Our conversations lasted for hours in the mountains with me desperately trying to keep up with him – he might have been small but he was the mountaineer. He had no heavy emotional ties; he was very much a loner, but adored by everyone.

He had a team of people which included Georges Bidault, who at the Liberation became the mayor of Gap, Serge Barret the Secretary-General of the Préfecture in Gap, who became Préfet of Algiers, and his good friend and deputy Etienne Moreaud. Moreaud was an engineer employed by the electric utility company Energie Alpine and the ingenuity and courage of Paul, combined with Moreaud's knowledge of the vulnerable points of transmission lines, led to often spectacular results. In December 1943, for example, the pylons near Pertuis were dumped into the Durance river. But besides the personalities there were centres like Montdauphin and Guillestre that were better than any of the groups I ever created and his cell structure extended from Briançon, near the Italian border, to the frontier of the Drôme.

As a sergeant of engineers he had done military service but, like very many Frenchmen, he was overwhelmed and shamed by the 1940 defeat and at the Armistice he joined the Groupes Francs, the activist arm of Combat, saying to people who felt like he did – we're not going to accept this. So the Hautes-Alpes was very active. The Gendarmerie provided the Résistance with all its transport – if you wanted to go anywhere there was a gendarme who'd take you on the back of his motorbike – and that was the whole *département*!

The following year Paul made me the head of SAP – Service d'Atterrisages et Parachutages – the French Landings and Parachute section – because, he said, all the stuff that's arriving was arranged by you so you might as well look after it, which was the kind of wisdom he had. In fact, what he'd done in his clarity was to make an English SOE agent the head of an organisation which was part of the Secret French military, the BCRA – Bureau Central de Renseignments et d'Action militaire! Cool actions like his gave the lie to the deep suspicions surrounding contact and cooperation that festered in London and Algiers.

Paul Héraud was quite simply the greatest man I have ever met. For two years the Germans knew that he controlled resistance in the Hautes-Alpes and dared not touch him. When I slept at his flat we simply booby-trapped everything before going to sleep. It was well known that entry to his flat would blow him and everyone else to bits.'

The necessary swift dispersal to Seyne-les-Alpes caused deep concern in Baker Street, following on as it did from the collapse and destruction of the huge PROSPER network around Paris, commanded by Major Francis Suttill, which had resulted in large scale arrests of SOE agents throughout the north. Buckmaster was desperately keen not to lose the best man he had in the south-east – if Francis were to be arrested then there was the danger that *réseaux* in the south-east would be 'rolled up', as had happened in the north. The strategic importance of the existence of JOCKEY to the single land route into Italy could hardly be overestimated. However unwilling, Francis had to be recalled to report fully on the situation in the south. Longing to see his wife and new daughter, he nevertheless felt that, so soon after the Alice fiasco, leaving the groups he had so assiduously assembled smacked almost of abandonment.

If several signals from London were ignored, one came finally that could not be:

> GO TO PARIS NOVEMBER 12 STOP MEET BISTRO PLACE CLICHY SUNDAY MORNING MAN WITH FIGARO NEWSPAPER[4]

The leaders of the unwieldy PROSPER network had evinced some of the same careless, high-living habits of CARTE and compounded the idiocy by meeting daily in the same place over a black market meal, forgetting that every restaurant had its Gestapo spy who understood English.

> 'You just didn't act like that; you had a moral responsibility to others and the relations of others.'

Swiftly they were followed, arrested and some turned – including the chief wireless operator Gilbert Norman (ARCHAMBAUD); several hundred further arrests followed. But if the 'turned' agent was dangerous enough, even worse was the undetected existence of the double agent. And the man in the Paris bistro with his copy of *Le Figaro*, towards whom Francis made his way was a close friend of the PROSPER leaders and who had not been arrested – Henri Déricourt (Gilbert).

Formerly a circus trick pilot, then a civil and French air force transport and test pilot, he had been in Aleppo, Syria, when it was overrun by the Allies. After a mysterious journey through France, he escaped to Glasgow in August 1942 and, unlike Jean Moulin, opted for F Section rather than the Gaullists. Not all the security forces were keen to give him a clean bill, however, because his journey from Syria to England might have exposed him to pressure to become a German agent . . .

Trained by SOE, he returned to France and his ostentatious wife, and, as SOE's Air Movement Officer, organised Lysander and Hudson flights between the Loire Valley and Tangmere in Sussex. Being hand in glove with the Sicherheitsdienst (SD) in Paris meant they watched most of Déricourt's arrivals and departures; he even allowed them to read mail being carried, including private letters to wives and sweethearts.

Although Déricourt dealt with the SD and Sergeant Bleicher worked for the rival Abwehr, their respective flats were only divided by a party wall in rue Pergolese in Paris.

Contact was duly made in the bistro and the sturdily built, fair-haired man instructed Francis to board a certain train to Angers, in the Loire, where he would be met and taken to the pick-up point with the other passengers. In the event, they included the then unknown François Mitterrand, future President of the French Republic.

> 'Déricourt's operation was smooth, quiet, unfussy and absolutely on time. The way he handled his passengers and the way he herded the cattle in the field where the plane was due to land I could only but admire. The operation took place without interference. The security was perfect – which was not surprising when you knew the facts.'

Francis complimented Déricourt on his organisation and asked for a contact address because, when he returned to France, he needed to be able to send extensive written reports which he could not do through the already hard-pressed Albert. But Déricourt looked him straight in the eye and warned, 'after tonight I never want to see you again'.[5]

> 'I thought that was just security and, when he was arrested in 1946, I volunteered to testify in his favour because he had probably saved my life.
>
> Then I was handed his file and saw that two of our dearest friends had been arrested and executed after one of his operations. No shadow of a doubt he was a traitor and he never paid for it properly. My "escape" was luck again. I had a lot of luck in France – which, like any and every agent, I always needed.
>
> Looking back at it now, knowing what he was operating, it seems he felt friendly towards me and didn't want me to get involved. I don't think he had any of the sort of conscience I'd expect someone like that to have. I think he was an adventurer, greedy, determined to hold as many trumps in his hand as he could. I don't think he was cruel or wanted to damage people although, yes, people died because of his activities. I'd call him a completely heartless deceiver who enjoyed the kicks involved; that was the way he was going to get the best out of the war.
>
> By November 1943 he must've known he was in danger of being on the wrong side and he might have done a number of things I don't know about to protect his skin because, in fact, he was pulled out, taken back to London and there he never got what he deserved.
>
> The shrewd Vera Atkins, Buckmaster's assistant, saw through him and wouldn't hear a word, except of criticism, against him. For her Déricourt was interested only in Déricourt.'

In April 1946 he was arrested in Croydon on his way to fly a civil aircraft back to France 'with a substantial quantity of gold and platinum for which he had not troubled to secure an export licence. Viewing what appeared to be his excellent war record, the magistrate let him off with a £500 fine; the fine was paid for him by a private acquaintance never connected with any government. Déricourt went on flying for many years and was reported killed in an aircraft accident in Laos on 20 November 1962.'[6]

In Lyon, before the German occupation of the southern half of France began to take its grip, Denise Domenach Lallich, aged fifteen, started a diary and through its sharply observant pages, peppered with schoolgirl slang, we grow up with her under German rule. Her text, like her intelligence, is uncompromising – 'uncritical obedience is the virtue of an imbecile'.

Her father knew Germany well and warned his children that certain French admiration for the German youth culture of cleanliness, industry, discipline and sport hid a dangerous sub-text of anti-Semitism. Many in the family disagreed but his simple answer to the deeds of Munich in 1938, laced with irony, said it all: 'Come back in a year's time, by then they'll have had time to hone their weapons.'

Soon this truth became obvious – news died in the hands of government propaganda – and the fifteen-year-old could cry:

'I've still got ringing in my ears the voice of Pétain announcing that he'd asked for an Armistice with the Germans! And from that day I began to loathe him! Then the Italians join Germany – oh the macaroni bastards!'; by October 1940 – 'we now have coupons for nearly everything – bread, meat, sugar, oil, butter, flour, soap, coffee, coal . . . it seems there's a French General in London who thinks like us!'; 12 November 1940 – 'Italy declares war on Greece – 'I'm going to buy a Cross of Lorraine for my bracelet – it's the badge of the partisans of de Gaulle!' . . . 'in the street we hate the Germans and despise the Italians. I'm an Anglophile and a Gaulliste!'; December 1940 – 'only one-page newspapers – it is bitterly cold – I'm sure my teeth're going to chatter until the day I die! We are forbidden to buy clothes without permission from the Préfecture! Long queues.'

Refugees excited real pity – 'many children are separated from their parents and have no idea where they are. They have flown from Belgium, Luxembourg or the north of France . . . The charity of the French is amazing – even poor people go without things themselves to help and come back every day to assist . . .'

She belonged to active Catholic student organizations and read the clandestine papers of groups such as Franc-Tireur, Libération and Combat. Churches were good places to rendezvous. She visited relations in the country, she kept rabbits, and, as her father had foretold, anti-Semitism was rife: April 1941 – 'Germans invade Yugoslavia and Greece – they are going to suffer like us – it's a good thing there are the English – our last hope . . . what about America? . . . Britain invades Syria . . . A friend reports that Boulogne, Calais, Brittany are Gaullist . . . there's an escape route through Spain.'

November 1942 – the British and Americans embarked for North Africa . . . the Nazis overran the unoccupied zone – 'Pétain takes control of all the services but Germans everywhere in lorries, trains, aircraft'; Giraud and Darlan go over to the Americans – 'French soldiers kicked out of their Barracks', the French Fleet is scuttled at Toulon – 'a disaster – why die – why not go over to the Résistance!!'

Stalingrad – 'every day the Russians resist the Nazis is a victory over the darkness that envelops this part of the world.'

Gradually Denise exchanged propaganda for direct action. She and other students violently opposed STO as boyfriends began to disappear: 'Not a Single Student for Service in Germany!!'; students were helped to join the Maquis of the Vercors and of the Ain . . . to the Milice (see pp 129–30) – 'dim, failures, blown up out of all proportion in importance by their black uniforms, thugs!' – was now added the presence of the Gestapo . . . despite the heavy curfew she acted as a courier to the Maquis on the other side of the Rhône, sometimes using the innocence of her young brother to get documents past the police controls on the bridges, never thinking that the Germans would ever hurt a small child . . .

After October 1943 arrests multiplied: 'the curfew sounds at ten o'clock in the evening and no one gives us passes because the reprisal troops, Mongol-types, shoot anything that moves . . . one grows quickly in that moment when one doesn't die . . . several of my friends have been caught in Cours Gambetta and shot three days later . . . bodies and ruins accumulate since the Normandy landings'; 15 August – 'the Allies have landed in Provence . . . but one can't rejoice, the deaths fill us with despair . . .'

Her tiny portraits of different Résistance groups and of bewilderment at all the activity – the savage German retreat, Maquis fury, aircraft, cannons, horror and terror – are brilliant. On 23 August 1944 Paris was liberated and she wrote: – 'Now and again joy at the Liberation intoxicates me, then, suddenly, I have the feeling I'm dancing on corpses.

I hope I will know how to be happy, but I know I will never again be innocent.'[7]

In her story, which rivets with its everydayness, Denise talked of the kind of people and their resourcefulness that Francis, as he flew back to his world of family silence, could not help feeling he was abandoning.

She would inscribe a copy of her diary to '*Francis Cammaerts, homme de courage et de l'honneur*'.

They never met.

10

November 1943–February 1944

Arriving in Harrow, Francis was met by his small daughter, Niki, who solemnly took him by the hand and said, 'Come in, you're going to be with Nan in her bed.'

'That was deeply affecting, a moment of intense pleasure and then the new baby but overall the visit was awful. The huge pall of silence crushed us. Between us the predominant emotion was one of caring. That I should be there after those nine months and not be able to say a single word about anything that had happened or might happen in the future was bad enough, but after a few weeks trying as hard as I could to get back to the Drôme and not being able to tell her why was far worse.

She didn't ask any questions because she already knew a lot that had been told her by others and she couldn't even tell me that. It was double, terrible.

Our lovemaking was entirely desperate, due not only to the fact that I was physically incompetent, virtually impotent – partly the reward for hundreds of bruising miles on a racing saddle – but also, I think, mentally. Not to be able to say a single word about anything important meant that intimacy was threatened. How could you be close when you couldn't say a word about what was occupying all of your mind and the whole of your emotional concern? We couldn't chatter!

All we could do was to hug each other wordlessly, as one does relatives at a funeral; we could only cling. We were constantly inventing little things to do in order to pass time without talking. I did some of the shopping, we took the girls out but the weather was bad . . . Cling – what a word.

'Virtually every day was a working day, catching the tube from South Harrow to the blacked-out offices in Baker Street – the whole thing having an appearance of mad normality But there was no doubt that for both of us it was a source of relief

There were frequent debriefings – I knew a lot about what George Starr and Maurice Southgate were doing in circuits close to mine. I talked to a few future agents about rationing, identity permits, ration cards, I went on a course for S-phone use which proved useless and I was invited to Lincoln, Kent and Northamptonshire to meet about a hundred aircrew who were going to be used on special operations. They needed to hear someone who'd been on the ground to tell them what it means to be down there as opposed to being in the aircraft. I explained the problems that were posed if they flew in too high and didn't allow for the strength of the wind at ground level which affected all arrivals. They were good meetings full of intelligent questions from people anxious to provide good service. It wasn't a question of being unaware of the problems through bad training – these were men who hadn't done it and that involved rear gunner, dispatcher, the whole crew – not just the pilots.'

There is little doubt that Francis's keenness for all this was but a facet of his fierce pleading for more drops, more materials and the right materials. Those urgent needs he had set out in a report sent by Lysander on 16 October to Baker Street, 'in part repetition of lists already sent in July':

1. Money. Preparation for winter is very costly. Have informance service comprised of a number of whole time men who have to be paid. Officers in maquis have greatly increased expenses and life is not cheap.
2. Ration cards. These cost 2000 francs each. Very urgent need for all with hidden identity. Send two hundred at least twenty J 3. (i.e. for teenagers)
3. Extra detonators. In all my reception there has been a shortage.
4. Limpets. For use on oil and petrol tanks.
5. Fire pots. For ammunition wagons.
6. Torches and batteries for receptions. (Not easy to find good ones.)
7. Accumulators. For all radio work, very important for use in emergency.
8. Radio accessories as ordered. Very important for Albert and internal system which is for use in emergency when all else is out.
9. Extra sets for Albert. Very urgent.
10. Receiving sets for messages at least twenty of earphone type.

11. Can you send five-metre transmission sets for telephonic use over short distances, would be very useful in mountains.
12. Personal needs. WINTER CLOTHES for Albert and self. Overcoat, Ski clothes, woollen underclothes, pullovers, stockings, ski boots. My clothes, all but ski outfit, are at my flat.
13. Soap. Unobtainable and essential for maintenance of self and clothes. I ordered 4lb at least with each delivery have not received an ounce.
14. Two deliveries without provisions, this is hard luck on teams – is there a reason?
15. Bicycle and lorry tyres as ordered.
16. S-phones and Eurekas.[1]

A respect for the personal clearly ran alongside the technical needs, as did vision – the second paragraph of the report in question read – 'PLEASE SEND BY RETURN this directive also instructions about care of families of those who are killed or wounded, particularly in case of my disappearance.'

In October 1943, together with other French leaders, Francis had sent a report back to London via Spain, prophetically stating, '*if the German order of battle was not substantially changed, and if the resistance was properly armed, then a landing on the Mediterranean coast could get to Grenoble in seven days.*'

> 'The authorities who considered our report shrugged and said we were a bunch of amateurs who didn't know the first thing about military logistics. Then, later, in January 1944, they did send a military Mission – "UNION", very high-powered, three colonels US, French and English – to have a close look at the numbers of Maquis and their military potential, and they reported, "Seven days, nonsense, forty-eight hours!" That didn't do us any good because forty-eight hours wasn't possible, but what gave us all the greatest pleasure was that in August 1944 the southern landing arrived in Grenoble on the seventh day – the whole of the Alps was clear of German troops, who couldn't operate at all; their only lines of action were the south coast and the Rhône Valley!'

Francis had men ready and restless; what he did not want was to betray their expectations. As their enabler, London had raised those expectations; they had to be honoured. No respecter of persons where his network was concerned, he pressed his case remorselessly both with his superiors and with theirs. He was listened to even by Military Intelligence who tended to regard the upstart SOE as 'amateurs', and to the end of his service Francis returned the compliment by holding that body in a field man's disdain. Of course, the general military and political situation bore directly on the problem of supplies, as did the availability of aircraft and containers, but what was clear was that, as a result of him being in London at that time, and for which Francis claimed no credit at all, the flow of materials increased before Christmas and most of the dropping zones in his circuit were receiving arms and explosives fairly regularly in the New Year. With effect from 17 December he was promoted to the rank of captain.

Much was happening everywhere while SOE leaders fought their war-long battle with Bomber Command for more aircraft.

In Tehran on 28 November 1943, Churchill, Roosevelt and Stalin, for the first time sat around the same table to determine strategy for the war they were waging together. Churchill's plan for an invasion through the Balkans was vetoed and Operation ANVIL – the invasion of Europe via the South of France – affirmed, though final dates remained fluid. The Western Allies' main effort was to be devoted to north-west Europe and ultimately to Normandy and Operation OVERLORD, leaving eastern and central Europe entirely in the hands of Stalin, enigmatic and still flushed from his triumph over the Germans at Stalingrad. Alone, Churchill found that worrying, and, in the light of the subsequent Cold War, he had every reason to.

After Christmas, Churchill, ill, took off to Marrakesh to recover and there met many dignitaries from de Gaulle down; everyone urged him to send more aid to the Résistance and he promised to help. In January a high-level meeting of his ministers, which included Brigadier E. E. Mockler-Ferryman, head of SOE's London Group, and Emmanuel d'Astier de la Vigerie, de Gaulle's representative, whom Churchill liked, was told in no uncertain terms that Churchill wanted deliveries of arms increased especially to the area lying between the Rhône and the Italian border, from the Mediterranean to Geneva – JOCKEY country.

The very next week six sorties flew into south-eastern France. 'Churchill, sensing that a beefed-up Résistance army could replace ANVIL – in which case no divisions would have to be transferred from Italy – further added, "I want the March deliveries to double those planned for February".'[2]

One major agreement between Roosevelt and Churchill after the Tehran Conference was that General Eisenhower would leave Algiers and take up the duties of Supreme Allied Commander in London. As D-Day planning advanced, de Gaulle was excluded. However, the US had to talk to him over plans for ANVIL as he led the Free French and, as co-President of the Committee of National Liberation, had moved to Algiers in May 1943 where the FCNL met. His co-President was General Henri Giraud, Commander-in-Chief of the non-Gaullist French troops in North Africa, a conservative, unimaginative career officer whom de Gaulle found uncooperative and a serious impediment to his own ambitions. With customary lack of political finesse the US backed Giraud. Nevertheless, de Gaulle, through the legacy of Jean Moulin, could count on the Résistance in France, and, after a mutually respectful meeting with Eisenhower, where de Gaulle's complete grasp of the military and political realities behind ANVIL, plus his own immense, prideful need for French involvement, gained the respect of Eisenhower and led ultimately to the eclipse of Giraud in March 1944. Algiers thus became firmly the twin supply terminal with London for the coming struggle in France.

Under the code-name MASSINGHAM, SOE had existed in Algiers since the Allied landing in November 1942, and after the beginning of 1943 Eisenhower wanted SOE and OSS, the American arm, to work closely together. At first it was an unequal marriage – SOE had already been operating out of Cairo and Gibraltar and initially had all the planes, ships, containers and contacts with Europe. 'OSS differed from SOE in that it contained an Intelligence component (SI) as well as an operations section (SO). In England SI activity had been curtailed because British Intelligence was unwilling to accept a parallel operation by what they considered naïve newcomers.' However, by July 1943 SI intelligence gathering was already considerable.

Once the OVERLORD and ANVIL decisions had been made, focus shifted from the Balkans to France and both OSS and SOE began to cooperate more fully with the French and the way was open for French Intelligence under Jacques Soustelle, and the French 'Action Service', under Lieutenant-Colonel Constans (SAINT SAUVEUR) to link up with MASSINGHAM. This was greatly helped by the mutual admiration between Constans's man, Willy Widmer, and Lieutenant-Commander Brooks Richards, head of SOE French Section working into France from Algiers, which led directly to better coordination between Algiers and London. Nevertheless, the clash and interplay between the different intelligence services would feature heavily in the south-east from this point on. But mention must be made of a brave success and it means returning to the previous year, to November 1942, the month of the Allied landings, TORCH, in North Africa.

After the German occupation of the 'non-occupied' zone in southern France by way of retaliation, there could be no pretence of 'freedom' under German rule. What was abundantly clear to a sixteen-year-old schoolgirl in Lyon soon became so to everybody, even to Vichy government leaders who decamped to Algiers.

Eisenhower, the commander of TORCH, immediately found himself in difficulty. As he telegraphed Washington, 'Without a strong French Government of some kind here we would be forced to undertake complete Military occupation. The cost in time and resources would be tremendous.'

His solution was to instal General Giraud, de Gaulle's enemy, as Head of Government. Released from captivity under dubious circumstances by the Germans, the dithering man got lost in Gibraltar. However, an even worse candidate, Admiral Darlan, Pétain's second-in-command, was in Algiers visiting his sick son. A quisling of some dimension, he became a chance alternative for the Americans.

But, encouraged by a few French generals who wanted the Allied landings to succeed, a brilliantly organised group of some forty Gaullist *résistants*, all between eighteen and twenty-two, armed with only 'comic opera Lebel guns' and armbands, on the night of the landings were determined to cut off any orders to resist the Allies and to imprison Darlan, and they succeeded spectacularly. Although there were heavy casualties in some of the other TORCH landings, in Algiers not a drop of blood was spilt.

Darlan and other astounded chiefs were released through the good offices of the American Vice Consul. In an effort to maximise any 'gift' of Algeria and Morocco that would have to be made to the Americans if the TORCH landings were successful, and to strengthen his own position, Darlan, 'the dauphin of Pétain', had ordered French troops to resist the Americans landings at all cost. The Americans appointed him High Commissar of the French State and he thus became the 'Overseas Pétain' and senior xenophobes, chauvinists and anti-Semites flocked to join him. The American gesture horrified every liberal thinker in France and Britain; every existing or potential *résistant* felt betrayed. Would resistance in France now turn to communism as the only possible salvation from the detested 'national revolution' of Pétain? What drove American thinking?

'The problem of the American attitude was that fundamentally there was no diplomatic corps and the people who dominated the information on Vichy and on France were Admiral Leahy and Robert Murphy and they were simply seduced by the French haute-bourgeoisie. They thought they were marvellous and everything else was terrible. Before America came into the war Leahy was the US Ambassador to Vichy.'

For a young Jewish medical student, Henri Rosencher, who had participated in the exultation of the night of 8 November, all turned to ashes in his throat. Algiers, liberated by the Gaullists, was, through the Machiavellian appointment of Darlan, handed over to Vichy by the Americans; resistance in North Africa had been duped.

Then the dubiety of Darlan's appointment was suddenly removed. A group of Gaullist aristocrats had drawn lots for the honour of killing him and the short straw went to the young Fernand Bonnier de la Chapelle, who had in fact been trained by SOE. A fervent Catholic, his conscience revolted at the thought of what he was about to do until he was granted absolution by the Abbé Cordier. The rest of the group guaranteed him police help in his escape and money, etc, for quitting Algiers.

On Christmas Eve, 1942, granted an audience with the Admiral, as soon as the orderly had left the room de la Chapelle executed Darlan, using three bullets. Unfortunately a French window which should have been left unlocked denied escape, the 'wrong' police were first on the scene and the young executioner was arrested. At dawn on Boxing Day he was shot without trial and his sacrifice felt by the whole French Resistance movement.

General Giraud replaced Darlan.

After the execution of Darlan and the murder of de la Chapelle, the replacement government of Algiers, influenced entirely by the Americans, spent a lot of time tracking down and arresting the very Gaullist resisters in Algiers who had made the Allied landing so easy. With the result about 150 French Resistance officers were spending their time trying to avoid arrest and capture and accusation by the newly installed Vichy-type regime when all they wanted to do was resist.

So they went to Brooks Richards in SOE F Section and said, could you help us take part in the war but avoid the present persecution?

Henri Rosencher remembered:

The English, full of regret, explained that North Africa was under the influence of America and, besides, they could do nothing without agreement with the French Authorities. The Americans were glacial and we left our meeting with them utterly crushed. So back to the English and, luckily, we met Brooks Richards, who would become our dearest friend. Being already our clandestine radio contact, he agreed to telephone Churchill to make sure we were protected. Two days later Churchill's response arrived. If we wear English uniforms, our security will be guaranteed – 'the French police will have no right over soldiers of Her Gracious Majesty.'[3]

Shocked at almost having become English because we wanted to fight as Frenchmen, we finally decided, with Brooks Richards, that we would stay French soldiers, officially attached to the Free French Forces (FFL), provisionally administered by the French Army of North Africa but put at the disposition of and under the command of 1st British Army, complete with identity discs and English pay books! But we insisted if we were given orders which we disapproved of, we retained the right to say no or to criticise.

So was born the 'Special Detachment' on 11 November and under British tuition we learned how to use Sten and Bren guns, commando knives, grenades, how to handle explosives, how to set primers, lay mines and set booby traps. Thus prepared, five days later, twenty of us set off for Tunisia as an advanced guard of 'ghosts' into the critical no man's land between the Allies and the Germans.

As the desert war intensified, their contributions were incredible. Brooks Richards was their 'King', inventive, demanding where security was concerned, even insisting on morning parades, sending incessant groups of three to four men against enemy outposts or on 18–20-kilometre treks to observe and note enemy movements, convoys, artillery placements; with their blackened faces they became perfect guerrillas. 'No drink, no smoking. No pitched battles; observe or hit and then disappear.' The Gospel according to Gubbins.

When they were eventually accepted and sent, I think, to Italy, the Allied Command needed 600 people to replace their 150. I think it is an important story because on the one hand it indicates the kind of Vichy-type behaviour of the newly installed government and on the other the almost hysterical belief by the Americans that the Gaullists were worse than the Communists. My pain in all this is that there were a lot of people killed on the Résistance side. It was a terrible story which has been put under wraps like so many other embarrassing political facts. The Americans made a hopeless mess of their relationship with the new France and the French, so relieved to be helped to liberate themselves, were very forgiving. But the residual attitude to America that coloured the whole of de Gaulle's post-war reign was born in those mid-war years. I wanted that story told.

Henri Rosencher's subsequent war was packed with drama – Tunisia, Italy, Barcelonnette and the Vercors in France – his capture, deportation to Dachau, return after the war to discover he had lost his entire family, his attempts to deal with anti-Semitism, his vigour . . . but by the end he was a tormented soul. Friends and I tried to help and then he just disappeared . . .

The Emergency Action Messages Francis had briefed his groups about before leaving for London – that, in the event of them arriving, they were to immediately carry out all the sabotage they could – had to be acted on because they would probably mean that something heavy was involved.

'We'd already been disappointed when we realised autumn was far too advanced for something big to happen but when the messages came through they must've thought "perhaps we're wrong, it can happen now!" You don't send messages, as they in fact did, just to see if the chaps were awake. There had been the recent attacks on ports in the north, like Dieppe, so now there might be corresponding attacks in the south which would have made the messages significant. As it turned out they were not in the least so.

I'd been telling Baker Street what I'd done, been able to do and what we needed. My understanding is that the Action Messages were sent to test my honesty and that my organisation was as extensive as I claimed.

Immediately about twenty operations were carried out successfully and that fast response convinced them that I wasn't bluffing; tragically, I lost two of my best friends in the process.

It was during an operation attacking a military leave train in Montélimar that Raymond Daujat was killed. He went back to check a device that hadn't exploded and it blew up; as a result of the derailment sixty Germans lost their lives. Roger Poyol was assassinated in January because he was known to be close to Raymond Daujat; he was shot on his doorstep without trial or arrest and his wife deported by the Gestapo.

I was told in Orchard Court that they were dead but not how they had been killed. If anything was needed to make me even more determined to return, it was that news of their deaths.

'What prevented me going back was the atrocious January weather. I was willing to be dropped "blind", that is without a guaranteed reception committee, but eventually they got hold of an aircrew who volunteered, in spite of the conditions, to fly me back – luck again – and I could get away. The plane, captained by a Squadron Leader Cook, had a crew of six, and we took off from Tempsford on the night of 9 February.'

As the aircraft ploughed on through flak towards a waiting team south of Castellane, the young acting major felt convinced that if 1943 had been the year of mistakes as well as achievements, 1944 held anticipation of success in its days, uncertain but real. However, low cloud prevented the drop:

'The dispatcher told me we'd have to turn back, that we couldn't drop, and the mission was aborted. The next thing I knew was him saying we'd have to jump – the aircraft was on fire. It might have been anti-aircraft fire or icing – I don't know why aircraft catch fire – but this one did. As I jumped I could see that it was ablaze.

The amusing part of my second ever drop was that heavy clouds at certain points seemed to be going down and I was falling slower than them so I appeared to be going up! I explained this later to my French friends – "*si ça continue je trouverai le Bon Dieu!*" As I was descending I realised the huge canopy of the parachute fell more slowly through thick cloud than it would through clear sky. So I was going down very slowly and it was like being in a dense London smog virtually the whole time – I don't know how many minutes it took from 10,000 feet but it seemed an eternity . . .

When I came out of the cloud I had 25 metres to go! A potato patch is the softest part of a farm you could wish for and there one was and I hit it. In that filthy weather I could have landed in the middle of Lyon, not on a lonely farm. Luck again.'

11

February 1944–6 June 1944

> 'I rolled up my chute and, clutching my equipment, knocked on the door of the farm. A man's head appeared out of a first floor window wanting to know what the hell I was after at two in the morning. I said I'd had an accident but he was suspicious – you're five kilometres from the road. I said didn't you hear the aircraft? With that M. Dumas woke up his house – we've got a pilot – get a bottle of wine and make an omelette! I discovered I was near Hauterives, an hour's bike ride from Beaurepaire. Luck?
>
> The Dumas explained that they had been trying to get into the Résistance but their sons were prisoners in Germany and there was so much work to do on the farm; nevertheless, they joined the cell. The next day they loaned me a bike and I could get back to my work. The Dumas were what I'd learnt to expect from folk in the area. By February 1944 there was a nine in ten chance that in the region people would welcome one with open arms. One in ten might be frightened and send me away, one in a thousand would ring up the police. My treatment at their hands represents a perfect example of Harry Rée's dictum – "anybody who fails at this job is either a fool or a rogue!"'

Partly with their help the crew members were eventually located roaming the countryside – they had all bailed out and survived despite the Germans hunting them with dogs. Back with Albert and the crew settled, Francis was free to join in the excitement in his groups – it was palpable, everybody had been receiving parachute drops, already an indication of the change of pace that would mark the second half of his mission.

All of the airmen remained hidden for several weeks until they could be put on the escape route, except for twenty-one-year-old Sergeant

Len Gormal, the rear gunner, who, against explicit orders from his squadron leader, risking court martial from the British as well as death from the Germans, decided to get involved in local resistance activity:

> 'Much to my delight! Without knowing a word of French and dressed as a gendarme, he took part in a raid on the prison in Grenoble where the team managed to free four of their companions. He took part in several parachute receptions and was very active. Just before the chance came to make their escape via Spain – I don't think Len wanted to go – his squadron leader threatened him with court martial on their return until I told him you'd better put him up for a decoration if you want me to help you get back home.'

Returning to his flying duties, Len Gormal was shot down and killed twenty-four hours before VE Day.[1]

Francis's habitual modesty did not hide his nerve in all this from official note: 'Cammaerts, for whose capture the enemy was offering three million francs, ran the gravest risks by so sponsoring non-French-speaking uniformed personnel at a time when his own security was in jeopardy.'[2]

Speed was now of the essence. Told by London to prepare for Allied operations in his area – but in no specific detail – meant visiting every one of his groups and their dropping zones immediately. A possibly incomplete list of DZs in JOCKEY territory prior to 1 May certainly included:

Alpes-Maritimes	2 grounds
Basses-Alpes	10 "
Bouches du Rhône	3 "
Hautes-Alpes	10 "
Isère	3 "
Rhône	2 "
Drôme	25 "
Vaucluse	10 "
Gard	3 "
Ardèche	2 "

'When one realises that each of these grounds was controlled by a sub-*réseau* under a local leader, with a complete organisation for the reception and distribution of material, his achievement makes impressive reading. These DZs were spread over approximately 20,000 square miles.'[3]

JOCKEY was not the only circuit in the area. By now Francis had close contacts with most of the French Resistance and French military groups – Gaullist or Communist, it didn't matter; the enemy was Germany. In *The History of the Groupes Francs in the Bouches-du-Rhone*, Madeleine Baudoin freely testified to his importance in the area: 'The acts of sabotage executed by the Groupes Francs would never have been possible without the explosives furnished by the JOCKEY *réseau* led by Lt-Col. Francis Cammaerts, alias Roger.'

The swiftly darkening situation is well caught in a report Francis sent by Lysander in March 1944 soon after his arrival back in France; the tone is fearlessly admonitory, intolerant of delay. A few paragraphs read:

> 'RECEPTIONS. Have been too much concentrated on certain grounds while others remain unserved. Packing has been atrocious. Failures far too frequent. Number of planes sent must be indicated in message . . . I have lost two departmental chiefs within the last ten days at Antibes and Avignon and cannot yet say how far this will affect general result. Eurekas and S-phones will always be used where possible, but I must have more, for the transport from ground to ground causes too great a delay.'

After recommending colleagues for decoration he went on:

> ACTUAL POSITION OF TEAMS. In F (Drôme) resistance is strong; teams armed and equipped for all work given, but position is critical and very difficult. In G (Vaucluse) organisation seriously burnt by arrests at C (Avignon) will do what I can to re-establish general order. For the moment cannot count on much concerted action. In H (Bouches de Rhône) teams are ready but not equipped , can only give them a minimum, all depots and transports excessively risky. In I (Var) a new young movement may work very well, but not really ready – lacks equipment. In J (Alpes-Maritimes) have saved something, but situation after arrest makes it impossible for me to say how much will be done. In K (Basses-Alpes) have stocks; morale is bad but can handle the situation with what remains. In L (Hautes-Alpes) awaiting anxiously deliveries; if supplies come will work very well. In M (Isère) I only just touch must have delivery at ground asked for – resistance very strong, but state of siege which exists makes life very difficult.'[5]

The report then detailed sabotage on fifty-four locomotives across the region, on electricity supplies and the reduction of output to 10 per cent – all the work done by detachments who had no connection with D-Day groups.

But it is in the overall situation that the colours darken most. Strategically, the Germans had become increasingly nervous about the south-east of France. As the German High Command felt that no invasion would come via the Pas-de-Calais or even Normandy, according to Field Marshal von Rundstedt, to whom Hitler listened rather than Rommel, then the Allies would strike from the south if only in support of their offensive in Italy. Furthermore, the Germans were increasingly fearful of the havoc the Résistance and the French Secret Army could wreak on their troops and lines of communication if and when the landings on the Mediterranean coast took place. Therefore, by March 1944 strong reinforcements, especially of Waffen SS units, had been moved into the south-east, accompanied by more squads of SD and the Gestapo. *Résistants* to the Germans were 'terrorists' and measures against them were greatly intensified. Francis covered this in the report:

> 'GENERAL SITUATION. Passing very difficult days. Germans are attacking all, even slightly suspect. General acute disappointment everywhere, due to delay in Allied arrival. A strongly mounting current of Anglophobia everywhere, particularly among Resistance Movement. The SS have been charged to fight resistance using same methods as in Russia. Result is a reign of terror, farms burnt, shootings and hangings. In centres where *résistance* was strong a state of siege exists, elsewhere there is a general ferocious attack against the "*maquis*" and all who help them. *Barrages* (road blocks) and searches are general, for this reason transport is excessively difficult and dangerous. The only solution is to serve all grounds and to send to all areas supply of W/T sets, small receiving sets, Eurekas, S-phones, arms, munitions and food supplies. Due to very serious arrests at Lyon, Marseille and elsewhere, resistance in all its forms is hit hard.[6]

> 'A word about this word "*maquis*". Nowadays many people think the Résistance was the Maquis but it didn't come into being as a name until the turn of the year – 1944. Résistance publications used the term – which is Corsican for brushwood or scrub – to describe the young people in the

hills; in Corsica they were bandits, in France they were deemed "terrorists". In my cells we never used the word "*maquis*" until after 6 June 1944. The men were known as "Company X" – where "X" was the code-name of the leader. From our point of view it was a hell of a lot more dangerous to work from home in, say, Montélimar and go out and blow up a train at night, then return to work, than to sit in the woods and behave like a Boy Scout. No, that's a hard statement. There was no antagonism, and enormous sympathy for those on the run, especially in the winter when the Maquis had to endure terrible cold without adequate clothing. What has to be realised is that the year spent building up a cell of fifteen, wherever, so that they could fight well after D-Day, was a more dangerous time than the actual period of fighting. Where the Maquis had the edge on the *sédentaires* – a kind of "sleeping" reserve who could be called on to leave their homes if and when necessary, get what weapons were available and serve with already organised groups – was that they had the space to train in in a more realistic way; you could fire bullets in the mountains, in the towns you could learn to strip a weapon down but you couldn't pull the trigger. But they were all *résistants*.

In the Drôme there were long-standing "*mentalités*" of revolt. The Wars of Religion had been very important in the area; Montélimar had been at the centre of them, Crest as well, where they are still very proud of having resisted Richelieu. This anti-authority attitude of the Protestants had survived. In the mountains they all went after the chamois, even though it was forbidden. They needed the meat to feed their families.'

One concrete change Francis returned to was that with the increasing delivery of weapons and explosives, training, especially in the mountains, passed rapidly from theory into practice. The difference between kinds of explosive could be demonstrated, e.g. one of the chief uses of mine powder was to loosen and create big rockfalls, ideal for ambush. Plastic explosive on the other hand, was useless for that purpose because it was far too fast and merely blew stone to dust – but was fine for cutting railway lines. Powder could be stolen from the mining centres – London and Algiers tending not to parachute in powder for obvious reasons.

Better training with more weapons was equally possible but the big drawback there was lack of variety. Francis claimed never to have received a single mortar, despite his pleas in London and subsequently, 'with mortars you could fire over the top of a hill. Small mountain artillery

I don't think was ever sent. Stens were OK house to house but useless in mountain ambushes. We had Brens, which were much more useful, and rifles. We had some lighter American rifles later on which were better than the .303s which were heavy to carry up and down mountain paths.'

The sloppy packing of containers, above all in Algiers, often led to a 20 per cent loss of contents and drove agents spare, Francis reporting to London on one occasion that 'at last delivery, parachutes failed to open as usual, containers fell on house and crushed the back of mother of one of the reception committee this bloody carelessness absolutely inexcusable you might as well drop bombs stop relatives didn't even complain but my God I do!'

London passed this on to Algiers and demanded it be investigated.

The explanation came via Ray Wooler who supervised parachute packing for MASSINGHAM, 'The trouble was not careless packing by the Spanish Republicans we used in this work, but the fact that we had to use parachutes made in Egypt of Egyptian cotton for lack of parachute silk in the Middle East. These parachutes were far more prone to failure than the silk ones, but they were all we had and it was that or nothing, until silk became available in the required quantities from US sources.' But as late as July 1944 Francis was still reporting of deliveries from Algiers to both the Vercors and the south Drôme – 'half material broken or useless'.

Then, in the mounting pressure of early spring 1944, the Germans struck and JOCKEY came under immediate strain.

> 'Just as I had had to be very careful about going into Montélimar after the deaths of Raymond Daujat and Roger Poyol, the town was too dangerous, so too now was the coast; suddenly the Germans began arresting people.'

Various reasons for the betrayal included one of 'a thoughtless girl at Cannes who couldn't resist boasting to one or two old friends that she had new friends of importance'.[7] This indiscretion was followed up by the Gestapo with their customary antiseptic thoroughness and the arrests began – including two of Francis's earliest contacts, Pierre Berthone and Marc Taperell, neither of whom would return. Francis believed, 'the lack of security in the days when the coast was in the so-called unoccupied zone began to reveal weaknesses which the skilful Italian Information

Services had unravelled. CARTE (Girard), remember, had left all his stuff behind, the Italians had found it and they told me this after the Italian Armistice and so I knew that some of that documentation, not all of it, had been leaked to the Germans.'

On 4 April 1944, Pierre Agapov, Francis's No. 2, was arrested in Cannes, his place of birth.

'His arrest might have been from another source because he was certainly not involved in CARTE and so not on any of the lists. Nevertheless instead of doing what we'd agreed – staying shtum for forty-eight hours and not bargaining – he talked. He was not tortured and for that reason was tried after the war. The agreement I had with my fully employed agents was that, on arrest, we simply said, "This is my number and I'm a lieutenant or sergeant or whatever and you know that I can't say anything more than that", which was perhaps the best cover story. Anyway, he gave away Janyk, a Polish-born OSS wireless operator, possibly three others but certainly also Martinot, an American OSS sabotage instructor, both new arrivals, as well as Jacques Latour at Eygalières, which was definitely known to CARTE. Janyk, Martinot and Jacques Latour, as well as Agapov, survived their concentration camps.'

The threat from Agapov's arrest was acute.

'Although not universally popular he had acted as my second in command and knew the whole circuit. Everyone had to be warned instantly as he was then seen, early after his arrest, driving around with the Germans. My job involved a full rapid tour to ensure minimum damage was done.

Chazelles and Beaurepaire were safe. From the Hautes-Alpes to the Drôme nothing was touched. Only Marseille was fairly comprehensively "burned", but there security had been poor. Louis Malarte was by far the most important person in the Vaucluse. I had to advise him to leave his dental practice and shift to a different part of the *département*. It was his choice and he moved with Myrose to Forcalquier and, in turn, contacted all his own people in the Gard and the Vaucluse and recommended removal when desirable. This was the most important unit in the Vaucluse at that time – the Maquis Ventoux – controlled by Philip Beyne and a young lawyer, Max Fischer. They were a 150–200-strong, well-ordered unit and Louis Malarte joined them. A couple of helpers and I warned everybody and most of them were sensible and moved and the arrests stopped. We prevented distress going beyond what was probably CARTE information. People were safe, generally, because they retained their houses but slept elsewhere – it was quite a habit by then.'

This was testimony to and reward for the detailed care Francis had taken over security. Hardly anyone outside Cannes was arrested because no one knew how to get in contact with the rest of the circuit. Even Agapov couldn't contact his leader directly.

Part of the bargain the Gestapo had offered Agapov, so he pleaded later, was the same as they had offered Gilbert Norman of PROSPER – immunity for his friends' lives if he would betray them. 'This time they were unsuccessful, for there was no means by which anybody but Cammaerts could betray the bulk of his agents, since they were unknown to each other.'[8]

The assertion that a full personal description of 'Roger' was then circulated all over southern France together with a huge reward is puzzling – if it was why was no one successful in detecting or betraying him? For Francis the answer is simple: 'there was no mass circulation. Gestapo leaders kept the information to themselves – they wanted the money!' 'No, I avoided the coast and it was virtually abandoned until the landings. Sereni (CASIMIR) replaced Janyk from Algiers and we got on with building up to 6 June. He was excellent.'[9]

*

'Despite the tension I loved moving around the region. Southern France, for a young Englishman who'd never really been abroad, to be in the Ventoux or Briançon was breathtaking – beautiful and usually sunny. I never had a full winter. I'd left in November 1943 and came back in February 1944. It was very cold in February but I didn't go through the arctic suffering that a lot of my colleagues did. Yet the tension was there undeniably.

You asked about being afraid, fear. It's the most difficult thing to talk about. Obviously I was aware there could be the knock at the morning door, that there might be the arrest, that things could go wrong. I must have often been frightened but I didn't have any of the traditional symptoms – I didn't pee my pants. When I thought I was on the edge of death in Digne I felt no different from what I had been feeling a couple of hours before. I don't know why but I simply haven't experienced those symptoms which are talked about in fiction . . . fear wasn't something that changed any direction I was on. I've been asked this question many times and I really don't know the answer. I can't identify fear in myself.

Hours away from execution, all I felt was – what a pity. We were so tired we slept all the time. I always reject things I don't like. I don't want to worry. And I accept the argument that if you don't worry in a given situation that can put the onus on others to worry for you but a lot of people are profoundly affected by their imagination – I'm not. And that at times is and was helpful. Usually it's an advantage not to be moved by anticipation, by something that might happen.'

Francis agreed he liked talking about the war and there was little self-glorification when he did. But what often became obvious was a desire to describe things in their *ordinary truthfulness* which could sound like him underplaying achievements. Modesty could be a form of untruth.

'Emphasising the ordinary is my reaction against the interpretation of action by both the media and commercial writers and so on and very much a reaction against the change of balance between the activity of the individual and activity as a whole. My interpretation of the word modesty is it achieves a balance of the truths. It is the modest attitude to happenings, particularly the exciting events, that tends to be neglected in the eyes of publicity of all kinds. That I resent. In that sense truth is distorted.

A good example is women in the Resistance. The women agents are given a huge amount of admiration and publicity. The women who are just as important and were living through it get practically none at all. This creates an imbalance which I have always tried to rectify.

Let's be easy about this. After the Liberation, after the war, what has continuously irritated me has been the talk about resistance as if it was created by a few heroes and heroines. And they've tried to make me a hero whereas the most important thing was the heroism of the people we were living with. That certainly makes me angry and makes me play down my role because my role keeps on being exaggerated. And that for me is very, very strong.

For all my friends in France I was the Angel Gabriel, someone who came with something which was vital to them, cut off and informed by another force. They were sacrificing everything – children, partners, elderly relations, their land. The notion that we both owed so much to each other had nothing to do with father, mother, sister, brother . . . it had to do with something absolutely special – like something you and I have with former students. Who has ever defined love! That was a passionate love which was neither physical nor intellectual and yet eternal, can't die. Nothing can take it away.

One-quarter of all the arms parachuted into France after 1941 were dropped in the single month of May 1944.[10] Everything, everyone in the Résistance, moved quicker. Alliances, relationships, assumptions subtly changed, expectation ran through daily life. It is simply not true to say everyone outside the Résistance shared this unsure excitement. Apathy, non-cooperation, fear, equally had their place and the ratio of involvement to non-involvement varied from region to region and from town to country.

The political situation, vis-à-vis the Résistance, was hugely complicated, almost Byzantine, as de Gaulle grew in stature and effect and the Communists tried to avoid compromise. The major factor in this was that in March 1944, having rid himself and France of General Giraud, de Gaulle had begun to create the FFI (Forces Françaises de l'Intérieur) – *the army of the new France that was to be*. The role of the Résistance was clear – 'Local clandestine activities,' De Gaulle later wrote, 'had to take on, at the right moment, the character of a national effort; had to become consistent enough to play a part in the Allied strategy and lastly, had to lead the army of the shadows to fuse with the rest into a single French army.'[11] Easier said than done.

Regimentation involved accepting the mantle of French military rank and was accepted by most groups outside the Communist-led FTP (Francs-Tireurs et Partisans). Hardly any FTP units could align themselves with de Gaulle except in a purely formal way; their military and political dreams and loyalties were too diverse theoretically, though, rather like the expected clashes between SOE's F Section and de Gaulle's RF Section, such differences seldom materialised in the field.

The FFI was given a military structure under General Koenig and many of the gifted Communist leaders de Gaulle had incorporated into his staff were gradually demoted. In turn, Koenig was to all intents and purposes ignored by Eisenhower until after the Normandy landings. Nevertheless, resistance in the field ultimately took a huge step towards sanity with the fusing in June 1944 of all Résistance groups, including SOE F Section, under the EMFFI (Etat-Major des Forces Françaises de l'Intérieur). The willingness of all important F Section agents like

Francis to support de Gaulle before D-Day without marginalising the Communists undoubtedly helped; everybody genuinely involved in *résistance* wanted to get on with the war without bothering about 'exterior' *résistance* politics or personalities.

•

As overall pressure increased, the sending of messages absorbed the genius of Albert to its limits. Twice a week Francis would seek out his pianist to help with coding and the slog would start; it couldn't be rushed – messages of 150 words had to be put in groups of five letters. From where Albert was operating was critical. If he was at Charols and Francis was in the Drôme – pretty easy, well within cycling distance – but if he was in Seyne-les-Alpes and Francis in Beaurepaire . . .

There were now too many drops to report back on and the messages tended to confine themselves to critical information – especially drops arriving in unexpected places. Eighty per cent of what Albert was transmitting dealt with parachute operations and the other 20 per cent on anything unusual – but most important were contacts with other agents, or reporting any interference with or damage to transport and industry.

> 'Where was I in March, April, May – I didn't know half the time. Suddenly all the parachute grounds were asked to stand by in case of emergency need – that is if an aircraft hadn't found another ground it would use one of ours and unload before heading back – very demanding on groups who'd barely survived a vicious winter. It was almost impossible to know when or where emergency need would happen over the whole area. Then there were the dramatic surprises where five to six chaps were told they were going to receive one or two aircraft and ten arrived and between them they had to move the enormous load without any help – sometimes at a height of 2500 metres.'

In a broadcast to the BBC Foreign Service in August 1945 Francis recalled this hit and miss world of stand-bys:

> 'One day I climbed with Gilbert Galletti's team to a ground about 2000 metres up. Under brilliant moonlight I was told it would be little more than a two-hour climb. Four hours later, the snow up to our knees, we arrived. The mountain was beautiful at that height but I was too exhausted to care and too cold – I was only wearing Gilbert's old ski trousers, three sizes too large round my waist, and the wind howled. The planes arrived

but didn't see us. So after waiting around for another five hours to make sure they didn't come back, we began the equally exhausting descent, the cold further piercing our inadequate clothing, which took till dawn, when the men promptly went off into the fields to work! There was a team in Annot who made the same kind of trip four times a week for two months without receiving a single drop; that calls for immense patience.

But when materiel did arrive it was even harder. The pilots were incredibly courageous in dropping in places still surrounded by 1000-metre peaks and as a result containers could be spread over a distance of five or six kilometres. It often took a fortnight to collect them all, some having fallen into precipices. Ten tons of materiel to move and rarely more than six or seven men to do the work . . .

Don't think for a moment that the teams only restricted themselves to such hard but not necessarily dangerous work. They knew their valleys, they were the distributors and after 6 June they all took up their guns and explosives to attack the German lines of communication in the valleys. It was precisely between 6 June and the end of August that their work was hardest because the drops continued throughout the fighting; reception and distribution had to go on and when there was a pause, to sabotage and ambush and attack German forces. You others, comrades in the towns, never disdain the *compagnards*. If in doubt, think of the Vercors.[12]

'At the same time there were the newcomers to be organised. Although in 1943 we could have recruited lots of enthusiasts, then we had nothing for them to do. Now there was plenty. We had to select with care and train for action almost immediately. Over the whole of the south-east grounds were being used that had been untouched before. Some teams had been reduced because of the bad winter and others were swamped because of the labour demand. It was very confused – people being allowed to go away to keep warm and others coming in tenfold ready to kill. They all had to be fed . . .

Cutting means of communication could be counterproductive – certainly in denying access to one's own friends but also through fouling up access to food. South-east France is a very fertile area with plenty of fruit, olives and so on but that couldn't last right through the winter or any non-harvest period, and certainly not in amounts sufficient to satisfy the fresh numbers in camps. So as the Germans increased their activity on roads and rail, it was a problem we had to solve locally or we imported, stole and transported certain goods we couldn't get locally – for instance, fat for outdoor cooking. It was highly complex and the only way to succeed was with local people and their know-how. As with the weapons and explosives, we were constantly preparing to receive, receiving and finding places to store food.

The Germans had demanded from the Vichy government "x" percentage of agricultural produce to feed their own people and those in Germany, with the result the French farmers became very good at concealing their output and therefore their percentages. Sometimes they even destroyed their crops to avoid handing them over and with the local leaders they were unbelievably skilful in managing the winter problems.

In the Drôme Alain came into his own in this respect. We were in the centre of the transhumance country (the seasonal moving of livestock from one region to another) and thousands and thousands of sheep were driven through it twice a year. The drovers were professionals, they did nothing else, and they were allowed by the owners a percentage loss of sheep that dropped dead and they were always ready to let us have the "phantom" percentage loss. We're talking about a quarter of a million sheep (and the percentage) going up from the Gard to the Hautes-Alpes. Indeed, a slight increase from Market Rasen.

Another important feature of all this was that most of our food could be distributed over pretty short distances except in the very high mountains – where, in any case, there was not much danger of meeting Germans. There you had to move food up to teams waiting for drops using mules and horses, you didn't have to have trucks. No, it wasn't the food that was a problem – it was the need to negotiate with the producer and even then what we would have expected to be a major difficulty wasn't because the producers were only too ready to help – as we've already seen.

Our job was to keep people alive. There were no desertions or collapses. I don't think I heard of any inflated cells in the south where numbers became impossible and men had to go. They stayed and had something to eat. They didn't die of hunger. They may have been very hungry and at times only lived on grapes but they were supplied and they survived and that in itself was an extraordinary achievement by local people.'

In the blind, final days' build up to 6 June, two distinct action policies in the Résistance became clear – one was '*attentisme*', or 'wait and see', and the other '*action immédiate*', or 'quick action'. The Communists and all right-wing groups were for quick action, as was Francis, but the socialists, who formed the majority, were *attentistes*. A prominent socialist politician from Marseille told Francis – you should be helping the people of Marseille and when asked when were they going to use whatever he'd give them, replied, as soon as the Germans go!

In the large towns people, understandably, were *attentiste*: reprisals were too vicious. Those whose bases were in the country were much more ready to say, let's go on attacking. But there were new dangers in this. The increased number of SS groups spread the terrain for reprisals wider. Whereas before the Germans weren't likely to pinpoint a community within five kilometres of an attack for revenge, now it could mean 15–20 kilometres. Geographical position had to be thought out carefully and attacks launched where it would be hard for the SS to finger a local community. But often this safeguard didn't work because the Germans were becoming frightened. Confident of victory up to the end of 1943, now, because of the huge increase in activity, and the vast Europe-wide stretching of their thinning resources, they could see that things weren't going exactly as expected and panic grossly sharpened their cruelty.

The SS groups were dangerous but the ordinary occupying troops, one third German and two-thirds Poles, Hungarians, etc, having in most cases been forced into military service, were either old or of not very high quality young soldiers; few spoke French. They were the enemy encountered manning roadblocks or guarding the petrol pumps at local aerodromes, often willing to risk the black market game. For such personnel the idea of filtering up into the narrow defiles of the Alps seemed suicidal with the result that if the German command identified a problem – e.g. Barcelonnette or the Vercors – then it was SS groups which undertook the serious task of launching a major attack, using specially trained mountain troops from Austria or Bavaria.

Nevertheless, there were many country incidents complementing those in the main towns because if Résistance intelligence about German movements, etc, was good, theirs about Résistance activity was poor: they lacked real contact and overestimated numbers tenfold. Where air supplies were concerned they had little idea *what* was being dropped; they knew the planes were coming but not that the container contents were more often than not Sten guns rather than artillery – just as well they didn't.[13] They didn't have skilful information people. Except in one regard.

SS activity was aided in no small measure by the detested Milice – Frenchmen hunting and betraying Frenchmen.[14] They were an auxiliary, uniformed police force composed of 'scum of the jails, brutalised of the most brutal, cream of the offal'. Would-be gangsters, they were highly dangerous because they worked and lived in their home towns and villages and their local knowledge of people and places was real. 'They were often sadists as well, who enjoyed making nuisances of themselves by tiresome enquiries, were fond of threatening language, and enjoyed carrying out their threats. They might be found at work in any part of France and their presence always served to put agents on their guard – if it was realised in time.'

An American major, involved in the liberation of Lyon, testified to the fate of Miliciens still sniping from rooftops as people danced in the streets:

> The Germans had blown up Rhône bridges (although one was still usable for foot traffic) and all but two Saône bridges. When the French armoured cars began to cross on our bridge, we dashed across on the other, and aided them in hunting down the Milice.
>
> It would be interesting to record something of the hysteria that sprang up in Lyon. The Milice were hunted down and killed with mad displays of hate. The actual battle casualties consisted of one or two Maquis and one or two civilians, but for the next two or three days, simply pointing a finger at a person and yelling 'Milice' was enough to have him torn limb from limb . . . The FFI as quickly as possible regained some semblance of control, and the sporadic firing gradually died away.

*

'Sure, there were times of inaction, sitting down periods, because you had to avoid doing anything you didn't have to do. Apart from allowing oneself to think of family, how the hell was Nan dealing with her isolation – no doubt in ways and with powers I couldn't begin to imagine – you'd mainly enjoy friends; you weren't dealing with dim colonels in the mess, you were at home; books were few and the local press you didn't read with any interest.

Talking of books, back in what seems now the relative calm of July 1943, I was in Manosque and, knowing that Jean Giono, a writer I had revered both as novelist and thinker since my teenage years, lived nearby, I decided to visit him, touch the hem of his robe so to speak. In some of his political essays which I'd read before the war, he was advocating passive resistance of a very strong order and he was foreseeing the virtues of pacifism. But that was the extent of my reading. I hadn't heard of his position vis-a-vis the occupation.

Friends were horrified – you can't be seen near him! I found their doubts difficult to handle, but I was determined to go. As usual I just dropped in and presented myself as a student, saying, among other things, that his advocacy of passive resistance seemed to me not to have been sufficiently exploited. He let me go on for a half-hour then turned round and said, "Get out! Out!", obviously feeling guilty and not wanting to be associated with his past. Apparently he'd earned a lot of money contributing to the Vichy press. Whether or not he was a collaborator is a moot point but the fact that his writing appeared in the collaborationist press was enough for him to pay dearly for it in terms of his reputation – especially among his fellow writers. It was revolting behaviour; the end of a hero.

No, against ferocious, factional revolt you found yourself dealing with everything in a calm, almost banal, day to day manner and even the exceptions – the messages, recruiting, explosions and weapons to be distributed – were done in a very ordinary way and we're back to the word "ordinary". That was the intense pleasure I got out of it all. You weren't forced into a position where you had to guess what motivated people; we were ordinary friends deciding to do what had to be done in a non-hysterical state. I've spent a lot of time talking about this period in my life and the most extraordinary and the most valuable part of it was the housewife feeding us, lodging us, cleaning us, saying what would you like to eat, we haven't got much but . . . It threw everything into perspective. That was what made the ordinary an extraordinary experience and why I hate heroics – because it's wrong; what was right was ordinariness.

That's not to say any two days were ever the same. You stayed with friends, you got up and set off to another group – sometimes 100 sometimes 15 kilometres away. They would never know I was coming. Determined by the number of people I could reach, I might be on foot or have a motorbike, or bicycle, or use of a producer-gas vehicle.

Producer-gas was either chips of wood or, better, charcoal if you could get it. You had two cylinders way up above the roof of the vehicle and you filled both with either the chips or charcoal. Then you lit them. There was a sort of draught operation. Those cylinders produced a gas once the fire got going – which exploded – so you proudly had an internal combustion engine working much less efficiently than with petrol; very slow to warm up and start.

Once you did you had a huge pull-out choke which was absolutely essential. After 20–25 kilometres, in the mountains it could be as few as 15, you had to restock – draw up at the side of the road and put in more wood or charcoal. The wood was always damp and so it didn't work very well, the charcoal was usually fine but difficult to get hold of and you ended up always having to carry more wood or charcoal than goods. The ignition was electric via a battery and there was much cranking and pushing. In 1939, in England, you reckoned an ordinary petrol-driven car would break down at least once a fortnight; around Digne in 1944 we'd break down every hour. My God, I travelled hundreds of kilometres that way.

On these trips, in every area there was lodging. Sometimes I'd stay with the leader – as with Georges Berruyer at Beaurepaire – but that was what he wanted and he was the boss. I didn't have to check anything first. I was absolutely certain that what they told me was the truth and any real danger was signalled by a pot in the window . . .

If there were parachute drops and I happened to be there I'd stay and take part. Occasionally I arrived when they were preparing an ambush and I'd stay. The only arm I'd be carrying would be a pistol which for ambush purposes was next to useless. Ambush technique meant spending nine to ten minutes attacking – then getting out; you didn't hang around firing a pistol from 100 yards. If I went on an operation the leader was in charge; he decided the moment we went in and that was strictly stuck to. I think the groups were very happy I was taking part – on the drops they'd ask questions like 'is this the right speed to send the morse letter' – a prearranged letter flashed from the ground for recognition. There my presence helped.

I used the S-phone once – it was a device for conversation from the ground to the aircraft – but I never used Eureka partly because it needed two bits of equipment. As far as I was concerned all information was secret and I was therefore sceptical about such "open" devices. We were always getting our aircraft and so there was no need to use Eureka. But the S-phone was good because you could say "hello – go round again" or "bugger off quick!"

Normally containers were dropped from 300 metres or below but as I've explained, lots of our operations were in high mountain country and we couldn't blame pilots for staying further up. Often there were very strong winds which hurled them further than they wished. I've talked about fires in the really high mountains but the normal guidance was by little hand torches. The men who guided the planes in must usually have been marvellously careful and accurate because we had some curious drops from North Africa. It was different from there because the airmen were American mostly and had had very little practice and I've already castigated Algiers' packing. But the women who packed in England were very precise and very conscientious and sent little love messages – making the whole thing personal!

The landing places had to be flattish and were of three different lengths. One was a ground which one recommended only for the reception of materiel and goods – that could be relatively short as long as it was accessible to the aircraft and findable. Then you had grounds you recommended able to accept human beings – they would be at least twice as long. Finally, you had actual landing grounds which had to be four times as long and they had to have good altitude off the edges of the ground for take-off; all these factors had to be examined in the light of what you recommended the ground for.

I never carried a cyanide pill. I think I was given one and lost it. Anyway I never had any intention of using it. I've never been attracted by suicide in any form any more than I have by capital punishment because it can always be a mistake.

'In this second period of my work in France I was checked perhaps once a month by the Milice or city police. The Gendarmes I didn't worry about – the reason they were different was that they were part of the army and as French soldiers they hated the Germans and they weren't going to work very hard for them.

The elderly German officers we've already covered – they'd respect me if I was a teacher – and tall and blond and Aryan? They assumed their enemies were Jewish, dark and small, it being the South of France. If I was "working" for Ponts et Chaussées (the Highways Department) they wouldn't know what it was or what its staff were like. They wanted to see your papers and be sure you had the necessary ones for anyone on a bicycle on that particular road. And you weren't body-searched.

The number of checks by the Milice was low. There were less of them in the hills than in the towns but they were there and, like the SS, wandering. That is to say they were sent to areas where it was thought a special check was needed but obviously there their 'street cred' was of less value than locally in cities. They were young thugs, hooligans, very young and mercenary in the eighteen to twenty-three age range. Up in the Alps they didn't know much more than the Germans did, but back in Marseille they'd know what train you would have come on . . .'

In the days running up to 6 June, General de Gaulle issued a warning and instruction to the Résistance to execute every member of the Milice.

12

6 June 1944

As the first craft of the OVERLORD armada neared the beaches of Normandy on 5 June, at 9.15 on the same evening the BBC broadcast hundreds of Action Messages, their cryptic contents meaningless to casual hearers, but to *résistants* the length and breadth of France they meant one thing only – the uprising could start. For the French nation, '*Le Jour J*' had arrived, the painful shame of 1940 could be assuaged In their thousands the *sédentaires* left their homes, farms and families, and flocked to a Maquis rendezvous eager to expedite the injunction – 'make as much mess as you can!'

The most alert and efficient groups went into action immediately and in the next twenty-four hours 950 out of 1050 planned interruptions of the railways were made. JOCKEY's rail-cutting was as efficient and prompt as the specialist railway circuit PIMENTO's, a near neighbour – every train leaving Marseille for Lyon after D-Day was derailed at least once in the course of its journey.

But no *résistant* would ever forget 6 June.

> 'I was at Guillestre, in the Hautes-Alpes, staying in Gilbert Galletti's flat over a warehouse when the messages came through. Immediately we climbed up into the hills to his group, removed our munitions from their hiding places and got moving.
>
> Leader of the Maquis d'Eygliers, a Groupe Franc specialising in sabotage and directly responsible to Paul Héraud, his tutor and friend, Gilbert owned a haulage firm in Montdauphin and he and his brother distributed the sacks of wood and charcoal necessary to constantly fuel the *gazobois* vehicles in the area – a perfect cover. Burly, friendly, a father of four, he had picked up his sabotage skills from local mines, quarries and Paul Héraud

himself, and his degree of success was so impressive that after the war he was richly decorated by both the French and British governments. He was a very close friend.

I found that mountain people always needed to find and had found ways of surviving and therefore *résistance* was almost second nature. In the mountains if someone was on your side – fine – if not you had to be careful. People like Gilbert were natural leaders, to whom people turned in every sense and for most solutions; they were people who threw themselves responsibly into whatever they did and wholeheartedly. Like Paul he was completely attractive. They were both of that tradition which stemmed from the days of the French Revolution, of always being on the side of the extreme left, of the people, and were totally trusted.

The next morning, a kilometre north on the road to Briançon, at the foot of the hill the Montdauphin fort stands on, we looked back and saw Mme Galletti trotting down the road. We'd told her she'd be safer at her brother's with her children. Her place was on the main road and had been in constant use for a couple of years whereas her brother's flat was unknown. She said I don't want to leave my home – but we'd insisted. She'd gone about 500 yards when she stopped, looked back, turned and went home. She would not leave her nest; she didn't and was never arrested. And she was typical. The wives seldom took to the hills, they stayed at home. Thirty years of age, whatever danger was to come she'd face it out as she had up until then; a remarkable woman.

A couple of quick stories about Gilbert. He knew an engaging chap who was a professional thief and Gilbert used him after 6 June to drive a truck full of explosives through German barriers and do the distribution after. He was brilliant at it but hopeless otherwise. The next thing I knew when he was no longer ferrying weapons was that a man rang me up and said, this fellow has come and ordered several bottles of wine in your name. After the war I had four or five letters from governors of prisons in France saying we've got this friend of yours and he's given your name as a reference. I wrote to each of them and said, he's a great French patriot who did a marvellous job at a very critical time. But it was Gilbert's genius to have found a man like that for a job like that.

Then, sometime in 1943, Gilbert's youngest son, Bernard, was still crawling and we were eating a meal together when this eighteen-month-old appeared with a revolver in his hand. There was a deathly hush. Quietly Isabelle jollied him, took the Colt away and hid it in a high cupboard and for forty-eight hours that baby searched the flat relentlessly. He wanted to find that 'thing' that could make the adults shut up. He didn't cry or create, he just wanted to find it!

After a year's silence all the Action Messages had come in half an hour. What we now know through the release of documentation, post war, is that the success or failure of the Normandy landing was poised on a blade and Eisenhower's decision was to play every possible card. One of those was to tell the French Resistance to do all it could to interfere with general military activities and that is what we set about doing with relish – blowing up railway lines and electricity supplies. When Koenig, ten days later, sent his message – "stop it you're going too fast!" – it was too late as well as being exceptionally foolish.'

First-hand accounts abound of the day-to-day attacks mounted all over France and the following will perhaps be excused for not belonging to the south-east, but its value lies in its feel for guerrilla activity. Although the Germans here, distracted and delayed in the Creuse, were on their way back north to the Rhine, techniques for disrupting retreat were honed everywhere during June and July:

. . . in a few minutes an unending stream of armoured cars, motorcars, motorcyclists, lorries, and occasional tanks appeared. They all seemed to be in slight disorder and were in no particular formation; private cars could be seen with troop-laden lorries on each side of them, and motorcyclists appeared at irregular intervals. The speed of advance was exceedingly slow, about five miles an hour, and there were frequent halts to remove a tree trunk, investigate a supposed trap or reconnoitre the roadside. All this was a sure proof – if we needed one – that the Maquis guerrillas were feared and were succeeding in their main intention of delaying the enemy. The troops we saw were both German infantry and Miliciens . . .

We had hardly arrived at a nice fold in the ground, bordered by bushes, when the noise of firing broke out on the road some kilometres to the rear of us, the other side of Bosmoreau. The noise of this ambush, though obviously some distance away, caused the whole convoy in front of us to stop. Officers and NCOs dismounted – we could now see every detail plainly – and began scanning the woods and hillsides with their binoculars. The troops themselves remained for the most part in their trucks, though light-machine-gun positions were immediately taken up near the road on the principle of 'all round protection'. Directly in front of us was a company of Miliciens nicely grouped together and looking chiefly in the wrong direction – a sitting target!

Suddenly an intense volume of small arms fire spat out from a spot parallel with our own position, about 100 yards to the left of us. It was the Maquis section going into action. There were obviously about six rifles (firing pretty rapidly for untrained soldiers) and two Brens emptying their magazines in rapid, prolonged bursts.

My two companions and myself opened fire immediately; one of us had a rifle, the other two had carbines. We fired as rapidly as possible into that mass of sprawling men, some of them tumbling from the trucks and others throwing themselves flat on the road. It was difficult to distinguish between dead and living and for one whole minute there was every sign of confusion and panic.

Then a curious thing happened. It seemed as if the whole division went into action against us. Small arms, heavy machine guns, mortars, small pieces of artillery, began plastering the woods on our side of the road over a space of at least 500 yards and although trees and bushes on our flanks and rear were churned up, nothing dropped near.

It was so typically German! They found it difficult to locate us, they thought we were more numerous than we were, so they shot at anything moving – even a branch in the wind. They were using a sledgehammer to crack a walnut – and missed the nut!

As soon as the Maquis section on our left ceased fire, which they did all together after a period of less than five minutes, as if under the orders of a good officer or NCO, we ourselves decamped. We went up that hillside as fast as we could on all fours in order to keep out of sight, and were soon in the woods. I looked back once. Small arms fire from the road was now being directed more in our direction and this was evidently covering fire according to a fixed battle drill, for two parties could already be seen 50 yards from the road coming up to encircle us and progressing by 'movement and fire' alternately. (It was very much like British battle drill for an attack, as laid down in the army pamphlet 'Fieldcraft and Battle Drill'.) Judging by the last glimpse I caught of the scene at the roadside, there must have been thirty to forty dead and wounded among the enemy. It is, of course, very difficult to estimate enemy casualties in such circumstances.

What is more important is the large amount of delay and trouble caused to so strong a body of troops. They continued to fire in our direction with all calibres long after we left that wood behind.[1]

Such loss of men and time and the emotional strain on the enemy indicates the sort of effort that forces inspired by SOE were able to mount in a thousand places at once behind the lines in France.

Amidst all the hyperactivity:

'On 7 or 8 June, on a hillside overlooking Guillestre, one of the chaps – I think it was Gilbert Galletti's brother-in-law – came in with a prisoner, wrists tied, and said this fellow lives about 20 kilometres away and we know he's joined the Milice. This was very shortly after de Gaulle had issued his execution order and that was why he was brought to Gilbert as local leader and myself and to the group living there.

I said to him, are you a member of the Milice?

He mumbled and said, yes he'd joined the Milice.

Had he joined the Milice of his own accord?

He nodded.

I asked him how old he was.

He said twenty.

I said, you know what this means?

I think he said no, or something.

I said it means execution.

That was all that was said. I took out my revolver and shot him in the back of the head.'

Silence.

Francis looked fixedly at the portrait of his father, unmoving, upright.

'I had to do that because I couldn't ask someone else to do it. We hadn't any chance of keeping anyone in prison at that time or that place. Later on we had quite a lot of prisoners and prison centres and people to look after them. With that little group we had absolutely nothing. We couldn't release him because that would tell the Milice immediately where we were. So there was nothing except execution. He was buried on the spot.'

Silence.

'De Gaulle's order probably gave the team a slight let out when it came to a sense of guilt. None of us approved of killing someone without trial. I suppose de Gaulle's broadcast might have been taken as replacing one; though in fact, everyone was being "tried". My French friends thought exactly as I did. It was a hateful situation but there really wasn't an alternative.

It was in total contradiction to my pacifism, my beliefs, but it had to be done. At what point one felt disgust, guilt, shame, I can't say – I've kept it from everyone. I only told Nan after we'd moved down here – in the last seven to eight years.

It's so exclusive. It's a totally isolated incident. Like the search of the car in Senas. These are incidents which every now and then, when you are talking or going through something, you trip over, so to speak. All right – every time it returns into consciousness I have the same soul-searching – could I have done otherwise . . . ? The answer is always no.

Though, I might have thought of it a thousand times. It was the worst because . . . it was virtually the only incident I never told anyone about. It sticks with me, not only because of the incident itself, but because in French law, for forty years, fundamentally I could have been taken to court and condemned. I had done something which was absolutely illegal and which attracted every penalty, if not the death penalty. Immediately after the end of the war obviously I wouldn't have been condemned. But for twenty to thirty years there have been retrospective trials – of Barbie for example – where the law was looking at wartime crimes in a non-war situation.

Did the family of the boy ever make any representation?

That runs through my mind all the time. I never heard the slightest murmur of family loss. He was from the region, not from Guillestre.'

Someone knew his name.

'Yes.'

There were other people in the group.

'We never talked about it. Because I'm quite sure they felt the same as I did. If I'd done things my way I might have upset the group. But because I was British . . . that was the degree of sophistication. I accepted de Gaulle's decision as a wise one. Although they weren't created until January 1943, the Milice did untold harm and their behaviour was much more savage than the Germans'. They weren't numerous but they were very highly trained, well-equipped and they were told to do everything they could to stop the Résistance. They were recruited everywhere. Let's leave it there.'

It would be established, post-war, that there were thirty-two Miliciens in the Hautes-Alpes and Basses-Alpes, two in Guillestre. For safety reasons they and their families were all lodged together at Montdauphin.

Soon after 8 June Francis received a signal stating that he was henceforth part of the FFI and appointed the Allied Liaison Officer for areas R1 and R2 (Lyon and Marseille) under Colonel Henri Zeller, the commander for the south-east, and so became a member of the vast and confusing underground military hierarchy. The order led to a new raft of responsibilities but there was no chance that he would immediately transfer the arms his groups had amassed and hand them over to the more 'orthodox' military system; that would have destroyed his whole organisation. In any case the arms had already been distributed and were nestling in the excited palms of his own cell members eager to put them to use. Some of the problems the new appointment brought with it, however, were neatly illustrated by mention of the name Barcelonnette, a precursor of the Vercors tragedy.

The principal town of the alpine Ubaye Valley, east of Gap, surrounded by mountain ranges and dominated to the north by the Tête de Siguret at 3032 metres, Barcelonnette's main military value lay in the fact that it held the key to the route over the Alps into Italy. Only five roads provided approaches, each one closed in winter, but their high passes and steep gorges were equally capable of closure through ambush and small mobile forces.

But the second reason for its importance at the beginning of June lay in the Byzantine world of French/Allied politics already hinted at.

General Eisenhower, it will be recalled, wanted the Résistance to keep German troops in the south pinned down and so incapable of reinforcing the Normandy defences or assisting any retreat eastwards back into Germany; all main routes north were to be cut and guerrilla activity intensified.

The French military had other ideas. Excluded from the planning of OVERLORD, and there being no apparent intention of integrating Secret Army forces into the invasion, they devised separate ideas for their own insurrections, especially in the south-east where everyone was convinced a second landing would take place. These plans in turn were kept from British and American commanders.

The principal idea was to establish several 'strong points' where mass airborne landings could be protected by well-armed resistance units and was called 'Plan Montagnard'. The Vercors plateau north-east of Lyon, towering over the Rhône Valley, lay at the heart of the original concept and in May 1944 Eugène Chavant (Clement), the civilian Résistance leader in the Vercors, with whom Francis had made contact the previous autumn, travelled to Algiers and obtained Gaullist support for establishing a strongpoint on the plateau and had been told to hold it for three weeks after D-Day, but not a day longer. The aim was to act as a magnet for German troops. Indeed, it worked in one respect – 20,000 German troops were tied down in the Vercors . . .

Barcelonnette was floated as a possible second strongpoint, and planning – to hold the Col de Larche approaches and therefore the principal route in and out of Italy – had been developed over a period of several months before 6 June. If the German garrison at Barcelonnette were to be neutralised, relief would have to come via the Larche Pass itself or down from Guillestre to the north, where they could be picked off.

Unfortunately, with higher-ranking FFI officers not in the area, Michel Bureau, commander of the Maquis in the Ubaye Valley, took his 5 June Action Message – 'Don't trust the toreador' – as a call for immediate implementation of the plan, especially its first phase – 'capture the German garrison at Barcelonnette'. With wholly inadequate resources, Barcelonnette declared itself a republic, free from outside rule, the tricolour was raised on the Town Hall and hostilities begun.

They were sustained in their excitement by the arrival of an inter-allied Mission, MICHEL, sent from MASSINGHAM, which included a Captain Alastair Hay (EDGAR) and others, all inspired by the conviction that the Allies would soon be disembarking on to French soil. The 'Plan Rouge' basically meant, gain control of the Ubaye Valley and establish a 'free zone' into which could be parachuted arms, equipment and reinforcements. And that is where the shortcomings of the planning kicked in – to what extent could the planners be sure of reinforcements and supplies being parachuted in from London, or more reasonably, from Algiers? The Ubaye Résistance had not received a single air drop arranged through SOE. Despite his ubiquitous contacts, Francis knew nothing of the plan.

Four days after the signal to start the national uprising, Colonel Henri Zeller (FAISCEAU) reached Barcelonnette. A career officer and later clandestine in his forties, freshly in charge militarily of the whole of the south-east , he had been in Lyon, Marseille and Aix-en-Provence in the previous days sorting out internecine clashes of personality among his leaders. There he was astounded to hear that Captain Hay had been reassuring the FFI officers that an Allied landing in the south was imminent. Zeller immediately sent word to Francis, his new liaison officer, to join him. They met for the first time at a crucial juncture in events – the local German garrison, housed in a resort hotel, had been overcome and a relief column from Gap had been stopped 40 kilometres west of the town. However, a more formidable force was reportedly on its way from Guillestre.

'I got the message to go to Barcelonnette the day after the execution of the Milicien. Gilbert took me – "I know the back way" – and that was when I first met Henri Zeller – dry, precise of speech beneath his benevolent moustache. With him was Captain Lécuyer (SAPIN), the officer in charge of the R2 region, a young Giraudist who said to me, no one supports de Gaulle, to which all I could say was – I don't think you'd better say that out loud around here. We met after the war and he had the grace to admit he was wrong. The local commanders and members of the MICHEL mission were there, too. I'll go over the "Missions" later. Plan Rouge was then explained to me.

Francis was astonished – in no way did it conform to any SOE instructions under which he was operating. In any case he was against full-scale engagements on principle – 'it's not what Résistance was designed for'.

'Barcelonnette as a strongpoint wasn't geographically suited and had never been armed as such. I asked them how many weapons they had and they replied 100 rifles and ten rounds per rifle. I said I didn't think they'd get very far with that. Knowing that I was in charge of SAP, I was then told to hand over all the weapons I had in the Hautes-Alpes! I said this isn't on – they've already been distributed to my groups. If you have a nice but very fierce dog and you give him a bone you don't put your hand out and take it away again. My people have been waiting for years for those weapons.

The paramount condition of carrying out the plan was that it would not last more than fifteen days, during which time there would be a landing on the coast. They obviously needed immediate assistance either by parachute drops or from me. But I had to throw cold water on their optimism by saying I was convinced they misunderstood the situation, that they couldn't possibly rely on a landing within fifteen days, nor on parachute operations at any time as there were innumerable factors which prevented aircraft from reaching them. Nor was I prepared to withdraw my materiel, which was being used against German lines of communication, in order to waste it by fighting a defensive pitched battle in a cul-de-sac like Ubaye. For that the young French officers regarded me as a "*dégonflard*" – a deflator – in other words a coward.

As their position was critical and the Germans were arriving from two sides, I agreed to send a small force to attack the Germans at the rear of their main advance, which was over the Col de Vars, but I warned them that my teams were not used to fighting open battles and could not prevent the town from falling. I advised them to try and modify their plan, though obviously once it had been put into motion, fear of reprisals and fear of losing the support of the civilian population, made their position extremely difficult.

I still hold a simple belief – our actions against the Germans would have been far more effective and much less costly if we had been a shadow enemy attacking in a small way in hundreds of different places and never showing the Germans where they could attack us. The very nature of the French military commanders, of their war training and their desire for "*Gloire*" and particularly their very understandable need to reinstate in the eyes of the world the greatness of the French army, made it impossible for them to conduct hit-and-run warfare. Unfortunately, the relief force which I sent arrived too late: they'd had to carry their materiel 60 kilometres over the mountains.

All this was happening at the same time as Koenig's absurd order arrived not to rush into action but withdraw, the assumption being that thousands of young men could be sent home safely! Eisenhower was in command and it was he who had made the original decision that all stops should be pulled out. I appreciate that in hindsight we have to accept that the reason for the muddle lay in Eisenhower and Koenig having concluded that the guerrilla attacks no longer served the purpose of deceiving the Germans about Normandy, but that was not made clear at the time. The unfortunate result was that the reputation of HQ was seriously reduced by the order.'

Zeller and Francis agreed that the whole Ubaye scene was a mess; time and inadequate arms were against any meaningful resistance and people were going to die. The only answer, sadly, was dispersal.

'SAPIN had a radio operator and he must have cabled Algiers saying that they were in desperate need of weapons. Under the circumstances I couldn't have asked for vast quantities of weapons because the Germans would have taken them – they were only half a day away.'

Captain Hay's implication that landings and reinforcements were imminent had been accepted as fact and not checked and certainly neither senior officer had been informed. This left the six-foot-plus Scot heart-broken. In fact a lieutenant-colonel, Hay had presented himself as a captain in order to underplay his authority – anything to get involved. From the outset he had thought he was being parachuted into a strongpoint to help *résistants* to attack. In his despair he felt himself personally responsible for events quite outside his control; it would lead to a suicidal, heroic death.

With the Ubaye Valley now completely cut off, the local leaders decided to try to hold a series of roadblocks with units of twenty men, leaving fifty or so guarding the immediate environs of Barcelonnette and to intensify their calls for assistance. While Francis's men struggled unsuccessfully over the jagged mountain paths, frantic messages to Algiers finally brought drops of over one hundred containers of arms and equipment on the night of 11 June – but too late for most of them to be located, retrieved and distributed. Untrained in such essential disciplines, volunteers took their places beside weary fighters who had not slept for two days; the madness and despair of courage. But it was all too late and, as Zeller left for his HQ in the Vercors and Francis at the same time rushed back to Guillestre to clear up essential business before joining him to take up his new post, painfully they could see enemy infantry descending over the mountains to attack.

Meanwhile, the young student Henri Rosencher, trained by the SOE in Algiers and in France since May as a medical adviser to the Résistance and also a member of the MICHEL mission, had joined his friend Captain Hay at a proposed roadblock over a narrow passage called the Pas de Grégoire 10 kilometres from Barcelonnette. There at dawn on 13 June, above the road, Hay installed his anti-tank Piat while Rosencher and others laid simple booby traps – grenades in jam jars delicately linked with light string for release at the slightest touch.

At two o'clock the explosions and the screams of the hurt started amidst the crossfire and retaliation 'It's all uproar, worse than thunder, deafening, one has to fight the panic!' Then Hay immobilised the first tank, only for the the gun turret to swing towards them but his second shot was a direct hit and the cannon fell silent. 'We jump up to celebrate our success then a machine gun burst slices the air – we hurl ourselves on the ground – I call out – Edgar you OK? No reply. Then I see blood spurting in fits from his neck; an artery is severed. I do what I can with my thumb and a hankie and after a quarter of an hour we manage to get him to transport, but dead. We're all overwhelmed by the fall of this giant. We return to the fighting until night when the order is given to disperse; the action is lost. With SAPIN we make for the hills and south to Colmars.'[2]

The Republic of Ubaye's dream lay shattered. One hundred and fifty of its defenders were killed in action and many more wounded and captured as German armour rumbled into the little medieval town.

> 'The FFI had taken forty-five German prisoners during the action and, very wisely in my opinion, released them before dispersing into the mountains. Many of the prisoners, however, preferred to follow the FFI rather than rejoin their units, but those who did must have told a tale of correct behaviour by the FFI and the reprisals taken against Barcelonnette and the surrounding villages were slight, a few farms burnt down and nine male hostages executed.'

On 7 July, Francis sent his '1st Report since the Allied Landing' to Algiers. It reflected the tensions arising out of frantic decision making, the levels and diverse locations of responsibility and the effect on those at the sharp edge of events unfolding.

After describing his own position and responsibilities as an SOE officer, especially towards his own network, he rails against the mixed-messages anarchy emanating from London and Algiers and the late notification of changes in policy. In these few paragraphs we begin to the hear the voice which will mature into cold fury in the Vercors:

> 'Finally. The High Command gave me six days after the messages had passed the job of Senior Liaison Officer to FAISCEAU. A job which could have led to something two months before the messages but which six days after was almost useless. The fact that I had no idea of FFI plans was immediately the cause of the fall of Barcelonnette as I could not bring my

reserves to bear. There has been the most complete lack of understanding on the part of directive which amounts to criminal negligence against which shot hostages, raped women and burnt villages can bear witness.

THERE IS ONLY ONE POSSIBLE SOLUTION TO THIS CHAOS WHICH HAS BEEN CREATED IN THE SOUTH-EAST BY YOUR DIRECTIVES:

1.Militarily.

FAISCEAU must know what zone you wish to have clear for an Allied advance through the Alps either from the sea or from the Italian Alps. By a miracle of organisation a lot has been saved, including a most wonderful morale, from this chaos. If we know where and when to throw our forces into the battle, a passage can be cleared for you. If we have to reorganise the whole area equally thoroughly nothing serious can be done in the time.

Liaison officers take a week over their journeys which are done on foot or on bicycle and they are often arrested. We must have at least a week's notice to prepare our blow. We cannot be kept waiting and we must know where to deliver it. A zone can be cleared in the Alps. Paratroops can be landed and protected at the spots I have mentioned except in Alpes-Maritimes, where in any case grounds are sufficiently far in the mountains and sufficiently deserted to give troops time to protect themselves.

2. By your support.

You must treat us as a serious military force and reply at once to all requests, e.g. bombing of CHABEUIL. Answers are so slow that tendency is growing to exaggerate in order to obtain half of what we ask. If the High Command do not agree to these plans they will also have on their conscience the unnecessary death of Allied troops and French civilians caused by unnecessary warfare on south-eastern French territory.

'Your choice of FAISCEAU as C in C was a stroke of genius. No man could have stood up under the brutal disillusion of your action messages and go on with such courage and excellent morale, organising a magnificent resistance. The mass of French people do not, thank God, know who let them down though they will soon begin to suspect it. Apart from him some of the officers of FFI are not capable of doing effectively their work and men to replace them are almost impossible to find.

Here again is a reason for underlining the important zones, so that best officers can be sent there, who will be capable of really uniting all effort of district.

'Situation. Region 1 being geographically better placed has saved more than Region 2 from chaos, but we can rally what is left of R2. Give us a job of work that is possible and we will do it.

Coupled with Italians we may be able to hold frontier Alp valleys, from VEYNES north to GRENOBLE, LYON and on the road to BESANÇON. We can certainly prepare a path and with the aid of parachutists in Basses-Alpes we will find you a way.

GIVE US A POSSIBLE JOB AND YOU WILL BE SURPRISED HOW WELL IT WILL BE DONE. BUT DON'T LET THE FRENCH DOWN AGAIN. This time it must be definitive and unchangeable.

My report coupled with my name and accompanied by a list of all unnecessary casualties should be published in red and hung in every office, so that the responsible person should know the result of his action.

CUTHBERT and FAISCEAU in their reports will outline precisely Military situation. I have discussed details with them and agree with their conclusions. I still believe, in spite of everything, that there will be a great and general uprising when a serious attack is made in the south east.'[3]

Most of the misgivings highlighted in the report were amply illustrated in the calamity of the Vercors.

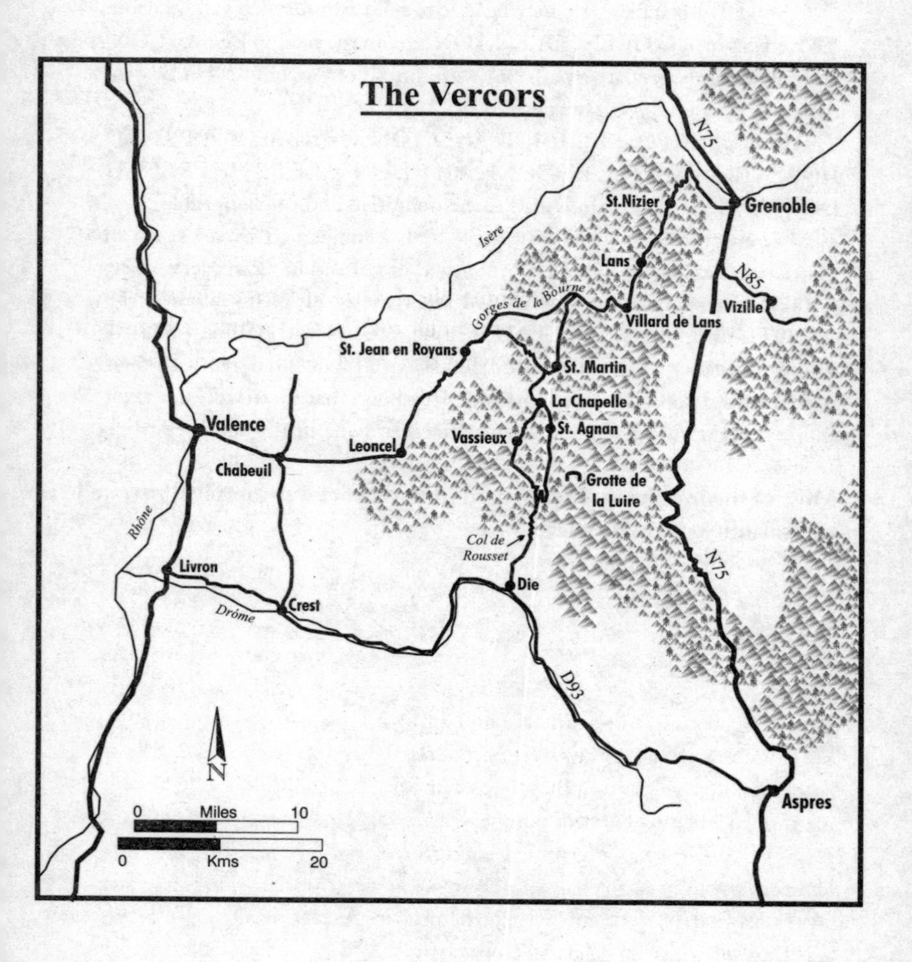
The Vercors
N75
St.Nizier
Grenoble
Isère
Lans
N85
Gorges de la Bourne
Vizille
Villard de Lans
St. Jean en Royans
St. Martin
La Chapelle
Valence
St. Agnan
Vassieux
Leoncel
Chabeuil
Grotte de la Luire
Rhône
Col de Rousset
N75
Livron
Die
Crest
Drôme
D93
N
Aspres
0
Miles
10
0
Kms
20

13

6 June 1944 (cont.). The Vercors

Several previous visits to the formidable Vercors plateau had led Francis to report, 'the Vercors has a very finely organised army . . . but their supplies, though plentiful, are not what they need; they need long distance and anti-tank weapons . . .' He knew the scene:

> 'The Résistance there comprised groups working outside the usual combination of Combat, Libération, etc, and the confusion over "Communist" stemmed from that. After the Germans invaded the south, the Communist Party took over the title of Francs-Tireurs et Partisans and the old FTP, which hadn't especially been on the far left before, just vanished, but it was said by anti-Communists that everyone in the FTP was Communist – totally incorrect. The FTP recruited in the mountains from the people there – including ex-mountain infantrymen and cavalry men – and although they were certainly anti-militarist and anti-Catholic, they were not tied to the Communist Party. They were part of the fusion created by Jean Moulin.
>
> In addition to the youth groups run by Durieu, which I've already mentioned, the real burst in numbers, as in many parts of France, was the result of STO, with determined young men seeking refuge in the hills, and they brought problems with them – the most pressing of which was, were they merely to be sheltered or be prepared for the struggle to come; was their presence to be passive or active? It was decided to arm them.'[1]

By the time Francis arrived there were four to five hundred men grouped in small camps, including volunteers as well as the STO 'defaulters'. Led by Eugène Chavant (Clement), the civilian side of the Résistance shared the same close ties to the Francs-Tireurs movement as the 'military' and it was from Clement, it will be recalled, that Francis had first learned of

'Plan Montagnard'. The original intention of the plan, which its founder Pierre Dalloz and his friends had presented to London (i.e. de Gaulle) in 1943 and 1944, only for it to end up ignored in a desk drawer until Clement made his belated trip to Algiers, declared: 'The Vercors card, if it's going to be played, must be as surprise against an enemy unsure and disorganised. It means not taking on an enemy in full possession of his means, but, by stepping in smartly, to aggravate his disorder. It means not locking oneself in the Vercors but moving out and attacking. It doesn't mean holding somewhere, but pushing out in every sense.'[2]

The Vercors was above all to be a reception area for airborne troops, who, linking with the local Résistance army, would be prepared to leave the plateau for the surrounding country; it was never to be regarded as an 'impregnable citadel' or hiding place but as a multi-purpose centre of activity. Indeed, it was ideally placed for such a purpose, surrounded as it was by four main lines of communication – to the south, the Drôme, already JOCKEY country, to the west, Valence and the Rhône Valley artery, to the north and north-west, the River Isère and to the east the Route Napoléon and the Route des Alpes d'Hiver, from Grenoble to Aix, Marseille and Nice, much of it covered by Francis's activity. Dalloz knew the Vercors and its access routes, and he had the imagination to see that in the fight against the occupation it could be of tremendous value if used properly.

On his return from Algiers in the spring of 1944, Clement brought back with him a chit from General Cochet, de Gaulle's voice in Algiers, which said simply, '*Bouclez le Vercors le jour J*', 'Call out the Vercors on D-Day', but without specifying whether he meant D-Day in Normandy or D-Day on the south coast and the strongpoint needed only to be held for three weeks maximum. So, immediately after 6 June, when news of the Normandy landings broke on the radio, the Vercors, like Barcelonnette, declared itself free, but again, without the guaranteed military support, set itself up for tragedy.

Twenty-four hours after D-Day, and well before Zeller and Francis's arrival, Colonel Descour (BAYARD), Commander of the R1 region (Lyon), on reaching the Vercors with his General Staff and his pianist, Captain Robert 'Bob' Benes, immediately (though not as naively as it sounds because dropping zones had already been prepared in the area of Vassieux and La Chapelle-en-Vercors) petitioned Algiers for support:

REMIND YOU URGENCY TO PARACHUTE MEN AND ARMS REGION VERCORS STOP COULD RECEIVE AT LEAST ONE REGIMENT OF PARA TROOPS STOP

MOBILISATION CARRIED OUT AT VERCORS BUT ARMAMENT AT PRESENT INSUFFICIENT STOP CANNOT RESIST IF ATTACKED STOP LACK LIGHT AND HEAVY ARMAMENT FOR 2000 AT VERCORS STOP IT IS URGENT TO ARM AND EQUIP THEM STOP 'TAILLE-CRAYON' 'COUPE-PAPIER' AND 'PAPIER GOMME' (THE THREE MAIN DROPPING ZONES) READY TO RECEIVE DAY AND NIGHT

No reply, so another urgent message was sent:

TWO THOUSAND VOLUNTEERS TO BE ARMED AT VERCORS STOP INITIAL ENTHUSIASM FADING OWING TO LACK OF ARMS STOP DESPATCH OF MEN ARMS FUEL TOBACCO EXTREMELY URGENT STOP HEAVY ATTACK POSSIBLE STOP IMPOSSIBLE TO RESIST EFFECTIVELY UNDER PRESENT CONDITIONS STOP DEFEAT WILL ENTAIL MERCILESS RETALIATION STOP WOULD BE DISASTROUS FOR RESISTANCE IN THIS REGION END

On 11 June, precisely at the moment Barcelonnette began its quick slide towards defeat, another appeal went out to both Algiers and London:

FOR VERCORS REPEAT URGENT DEMAND FOR LIGHT ARMAMENT FOR 18 COMPANIES AND HEAVY ARMAMENT FOR 6 COMPANIES STOP MOBILIZATION WAS ORDERED FOLLOWING FORMAL ASSURANCE OF ARMS DELIVERY STOP IF PROMISE NOT FULFILLED IMMEDIATELY SITUATION VERCORS WILL BECOME DRAMATIC END

Finally, a reply came from Colonel Constans, de Gaulle's representative at SPOC (Special Projects Operation Centre) in Algiers:

ONLY OBSTACLE AT PRESENT ARE ATMOSPHERIC CONDITIONS STOP WILL DO OUR BEST TAKING INTO ACCOUNT LIMITED AIR TRANSPORT FACILITIES

But such anodyne apologetics dimmed into insignificance beside the stupefying lunacy of Koenig's order from London which was already playing havoc in Barcelonnette and elsewhere:

SEND THE MEN HOME BECAUSE MOBILISED PREMATURELY

Colonel Huet (HERVIEUX), in overall command of the Vercors, had put his written orders into effect and ordered a general mobilisation. His fury was almost indescribable:

THERE IS NO QUESTION OF CLEARING OFF AFTER HAVING COMPROMISED THE WHOLE POPULATION AND NOT OFFERED A SINGLE SHRED OF RESISTANCE WHATSOEVER!

In the rapture of remobilisation and to galvanise the general population, an immense tricolour flag had been hung on a peak overlooking Grenoble near Saint-Nizier, but the gesture would be paid for a hundredfold.

Francis arrived at a point where increased German retaliation was causing definite unease. A feeling had grown among the Maquisards that the Germans, fighting to hold the Normandy beachheads and fearful of a landing on the Riviera, could not spare sufficient troops to launch any serious offensive against them. But the Germans concentrated four hundred troops at the Tour-sans-Venin and on 13 June attacked Saint-Nizier. They were opposed by an equal number of callow Maquisards and after twelve hours' fighting withdrew with heavy losses. However, the Maquisards had used up all their ammunition and were still not used to holding a position; they were hungry, thirsty and exhausted. So when, two days later, in the early dawn, the SS attacked again but this time after an artillery bombardment and aircraft support from Chabeuil, the commandeered aerodrome some 20 kilometres from the plateau, they could only offer token resistance. Additional support for the Germans came from the Milice wearing tricolour armbands like the *résistants*, which sowed utter confusion among the Maquisards. This time the Nazis reached Saint-Nizier, set it ablaze, almost completely destroying it, and moved on to Villard-de-Lans without bothering to occupy it, forcing the Résistance down into the southern part of the plateau. Tellingly, the Germans had opened up a way of penetrating deep into the heart of the plateau from the east via the Gorges de la Bourne, the narrow, spectacularly twisting transverse valley dividing the northern and southern sections of the Vercors. The south was the main reception area and home to the independent republic.

Even today one feels the reality of that division – the northern part is for skiing, the southern, with its main 'towns' of La Chapelle-en-Vercors and Vassieux, for remembering; roadside plaques, museums to the memory of the fallen, execution sites still call out in pain unexpectedly at turns in the road . . .

'One was acutely aware of the awkwardness between Allied and French thinking; they were combat-dominated, we were not. We were agents not soldiers and we had to emphasise that in all our relations. Henri Zeller treated me as a friend, as did Clement, and although I was promoted to lieutenant-colonel at the end of June it was more to give me equivalence with the colonels I had to deal with daily than anything else; everybody knew that I preferred to be considered civilian rather than military.

Socialists, Communists, civilians, were all anti-military – they believed the army had let them down in 1940 – which meant there was always a hidden danger of division between the groups on the plateau. If and when it did flare up, people like Zeller and myself were always keen to calm down any conflict; there were bigger enemies.

Every day I met Clement and the civilians at St Martin and then I'd go and talk to the soldiers – that was my routine but not fixed. I joined the civilians for their breakfast cup of coffee outside and we talked a lot about the best use to be put of our means of communication, both civilian and military, the great thing being to keep harmony between them. Zeller and I lived in a little farmhouse opposite the "radio house" at La Britière, near St Agnan, which sheltered the combined talents of Benes (BCRA), Pecquet (Military Missions), Albert and Antoine (SOE London and Algiers) and everything I did was communicated to him and to Clement.

Then, for a couple of hours, usually alone, I moved from one Maquis group to another helping with training, going to where the need was sharpest. The Chasseurs Alpins taught the weapons they knew – I usually trained with the new ones. We had a few Piats – anti-tank guns – now and that meant careful tuition. They had discs on the charger and when fired they shot back at you; self-protection was vital! At about 30 yards it was extremely effective and easier than a bazooka which shot backwards. The training meant going up on to the sawtoothed ridges running north to south in the eastern Vercors and the groups hidden there could only be reached by walking and climbing. But mercifully there was water whereas on the western side, with its deep forests, there was none. To get water one had to cross the single "main" road in the southern half to the other side and during the German massacre that could and did prove hazardous.

Despite the increasing proximity of the Germans we could fire guns – the Vercors was now a free republic with its own laws, currency and flag! It was foolish but very understandable given the passionate need to erase the shame of 1940 and it was all part of that – a very important part of it.'

A flavour of this passion comes from an account of those heady days written by Commandant Lemoine of the HQ of the FFI in the Vercors:

'From 9 June the Vercors declared itself free, withdrawing from any control by Vichy. Civil power is guaranteed by CLEMENT, President of the Committee for Liberation, and he set up his headquarters at Saint-Martin and assumed the role of Préfet with the perfect agreement of the Military authorities. M. Yves Farge, designated by de Gaulle as a Commissaire of the Republic, on the occasion of a visit to the Vercors, exercised for the first time in public his new functions by regularising the relation between the two powers.

Grave problems presented themselves daily and had to be solved immediately. Separated from all central administrative control, the Vercors had to become self-sufficient. Security and the Police (for the arrest of suspects) re-set up, the creation of a Justice Tribunal too, communications with the world outside, establishing and maintaining a Postal service, organising transport in common on the plateau, the requisitioning of vehicles and buildings, procuring charcoal and petrol for vehicles, guaranteeing the feeding of the population and commercial exchanges of all kinds (dairy products for market gardening), assuring the salaries of post-office employees, teachers, road-workers, tax-collectors, etc . . . and regular pay and allowances . . .

Thanks to the good-will, patriotic enthusiasm of everybody and the energy of those in control, it all worked as one wished in the tiny Republic. One has to have lived through those days to truly understand how great a jump into newness it was for a whole region reclaiming its freedom for itself!

"Here begins the Land of the Free."![3]

'Most days too I left the plateau to visit the cells of my circuit fighting in the south Drôme, in the Isère, in the Vaucluse and so on to check things were working as we were receiving a great deal of materiel. To get on and off the plateau we used ambulances a great deal – you laid down on a stretcher and they put a sheet over you. The run from the Vercors to Lagarde Apt, north of Marseille, was one of our longest – that was where the very effective pick-up and parachute drops took place. But Avignon, Marseille – wherever – one would aim to be back in St Martin by the evening. Decisions had to be made about who blocked off what, what railway lines and roads to attack in a constant effort to put further brakes on any SS preoccupation with the Vercors. In the south my daily need, after the arrests, was to check on personnel – were they still in place – vital.'

The German airfield at Chabeuil, although only 20 kilometres from the Vercors, on a flat plain and therefore clearly visible, was heavily defended and difficult to attack except perhaps from the air. Hence the persistent calls to Algiers and London for it to be bombed. Already, months before, Francis and Roger Poyol had seen gliders ready with parachutes attached to their tails hidden beneath trees; such craft would be totally ineffective in front-line battles but ideal against Résistance pockets on the plateau . . .

From mid-June the Germans realised that sabotage activity was being directed from the strongpoints so they attacked deeply in the Ardèche and caused severe dislocation. They then attacked the Ain and made the FFI withdraw into the hills. But for them the real threat to the Rhône Valley communications with the north remained the Vercors and its geographical advantages made attack by infantry alone almost impossible. The solution would lie in air attack.

But despite the Maquis having carefully carpeted the forests of Corrençon and de Lente with mines, having conducted outside sabotage and nervelessly rescued from prison in Lyon fifty-three Senegalese sharpshooters and their NCOs who then sided with the Résistance – Dalloz-imagined work at its best – it was German units that gradually took and kept the initiative. By 19 June they had laid seige to Villard de Lans and by the 22nd they controlled the plateau de Combovin in the west, completing the first part of a pincer movement. As in the reaction to Saint-Nizier, aircraft from Chabeuil used their control of the air mercilessly.

Chabeuil had to be the primary target for Algiers.

A spectacular drop of 420 containers by the Americans on Sunday 25 June during a memorial service conducted by Colonel Huet – a bizarre augury of the infamous drop to take place on 14 July – raised hopes that things were changing, that paratroops would follow; but they did not. Ominously, the Germans took the drop as evidence that the Vercors was well provided with weaponry and munitions.

The reasons for Algiers' silence probably had more to do with the general war situation in the north, about which those in the south knew little, rather than callous indifference, but the effect was the same. It was not until 29 July that British and Canadian tanks in the north broke through the German lines near St Lô and Caen was taken after heavy fighting. The south would have to wait.

Although the second half of June saw a temporary lull in German attacks on the Vercors, it was clear to everybody that they were regrouping in the towns where they were billeted, and merely waiting for reinforcements before mounting an all-out attack.

Zeller, Descour and Francis plied Algiers and London with signals. The messages sent by Francis have been described by the French war historian François Rude as 'the most important which came from the Vercors'.[4]

SUPREME HEADQUARTERS HAS LED THE CHIEFS OF FFI INTO THINKING THAT LANDING IN SOUTH-EAST WOULD FOLLOW WITHIN FORTNIGHT OF ACTION [in Normandy] STOP GENERAL IMPRESSION GAINED FROM MESSAGES IS THAT THEY WERE FORCED INTO PREMATURE ACTION STOP DELIVERANCE ONLY POSSIBLE IF LARGE SUPPLIES OF MATERIEL SENT IN FAILING WHICH ENTIRE RESISTANCE ORGANIZATION IN SOUTH-EAST WILL COLLAPSE . . .[5]

. . . NEEDED PIATS HEAVY AND LIGHT MACHINE-GUNS RIFLES GAMMON GRENADES NOT STEN GUNS STOP AT LEAST TWENTY PER CENT OF AMMUNITION SUPPLIES DESTROYED UP TO NOW STOP NEEDED TEN MILLION ROUNDS AMMUNITION IMMEDIATELY STOP IF POSSIBLE A COMPANY OF PARATROOPS

By now news was coming in that bombers and fighters were being assembled at Chabeuil:

RENEW REQUEST FOR URGENT AND REPEATED BOMBING OF AIRFIELD CHABEUIL STOP FIFTY TO SIXTY LUFTWAFFE PLANES: PERMANENTLY ASSEMBLED ON AIRFIELD STOP WE LEARN OF ASSEMBLY NEXT MONDAY OF 120 TROOP TRANSPORT LORRIES AT VALENCE BUT BECAUSE ASSEMBLY IN TOWN CENTRE PLEASE AVOID BOMBING

Daily, in the spirit of Dalloz, Francis tried to carry out diversionary operations with his groups, especially in the Western Isère, and Colonel Descour gave similar orders to FFI units in the area with combined success:

DEPARTEMENT ISÈRE REPORTS FREQUENT INTERRUPTION RAILWAY TRAFFIC GRENOBLE–CHAMBERY GRENOBLE–VALANCE GRENOBLE–VEYNES GRENOBLE–LYONS STOP ALL TELEPHONE AND TELEGRAPH COMMUNICATIONS CUT

For which they were warmly congratulated by General Cochet again. Another message went out:

> YOU MUST BOMB IMMEDIATELY AERODROME CHABEUIL STOP IT IS ABSOLUTELY CERTAIN THERE ARE 100 AIRCRAFT THERE FROM SALON AND AVIGNON WITH MUCH MATERIEL STOP VERCORS IS MENACED FROM THERE STOP THIS IS ABSOLUTELY ESSENTIAL STOP VERY LARGE QUANTITY OF BOMBS HAS NOT YET BEEN PLACED IN HOLDS STOP HAVE SENT COPY [of this signal] TO LONDON

Daily, demands were made for the bombing of Chabeuil. Unknown to the leaders on the Vercors, General Cochet had gone to his superiors but the American General Ira C. Marshall, commanding the Allied Air Forces based in Naples and Sardinia (with some five thousand aircraft), and the British Air Marshal Sir John Slessor, in command of the RAF Mediterranean, maintained that tactical bombing of German airfields was part of the strategy of ANVIL and must be left to their judgement.

> 'What made us so angry was that three weeks *after* the defeat in the Vercors the N7 road in the Rhône Valley was bombed like hell, twisted metal everywhere. They could easily have put three little airfields out of action. We'll come to our final telegram and what I really thought and felt. But then in Algiers there was an element highly nervous about the armed Résistance. All the men they sent to the Vercors were too few and arrived too late.'

In moments of quiet there was still an awareness of the obscenity of what was being sought; bombing kills. Just as his close friend Harry Rée had witnessed the extent of 'collateral' damage during the failed bombing of a French factory in Sochaux,[6] so, on 27 May, Francis had been in Avignon when the Americans had bombed the railway passenger station where no damage whatsoever was wreaked on the yards:

> 'On that particular day I stood under the bombs outside the station and watched them come down – it was unbelievable, really useless, ignorant, damaging bombing. I wanted to shriek out loud – how many of us are you going to kill before it's over!!! Imagine a crowded Victoria Station . . . in railway stations, bus stations from Marseille to Chambéry, there must

have been 10,000 dead! They simply didn't know a German troop train carrying tanks would never go through a passenger station!! Or anywhere near it . . .

If any Allied aircraft made a mistake, as far as the French were concerned it was the fault of the Americans; anything good was down to the RAF. American bombing was generally discredited because they bombed from a great height whereas RAF bombing was low level and at specific targets; the bombing on 27 May was from 10,000 feet.

I talked to a pilot later who said he'd learnt his direction finding by road signs and he didn't know. He'd had very little training and had been a civil aviation pilot before the war.

Afterwards the Americans said that 27 May was the first day of preparing the south for the landings and was based on the possibility of "enemy retaliation". The bombings, like those in the north and west, were "build-ups". To excuse these Allied bombings phoney maps were released – they said they were so ashamed that they had no other option but to invent the excuse.'

'All the men they sent to the Vercors were too few and arrived too late.' The statement requires elaboration. At the end of June, Algiers began dispatching four types of special forces to the mainland – Jedburgh teams, American Operational Groups (OGs), SAS troops and Inter-Allied Missions. Each Jedburgh team consisted of an Englishman, an American and a Frenchman, i.e. two officers and a sergeant wireless operator, all trained in guerrilla tactics, leadership and demolition work. Uniformed, their job was to provide a general staff for the local Résistance wherever they landed, to coordinate the local efforts in the best interests of Allied strategy and, wherever possible, to arrange further arms supplies. Like almost all the other SOE agents going late into the field, the Jedburghs had to build on work already done for them by other agents or by local Résistance leaders they met on arrival and often that produced tension. The American OGs were uniformed groups of fifteen or more and decidedly military in intent, well-trained, though not of the desired regimental size places like the Vercors were calling for. The role played by men of the SAS (British Special Air Service), of whom nearly two thousand were directly involved post 6 June all over France, has been well celebrated, which leaves the Inter-Allied Missions.

As the name implies, members of the Missions were not of the same nationality and generally this was not a problem; what was a problem was the detail of their briefing and their often skimpy awareness of the exact situation into which they were being dropped. Francis, in his role as Senior Allied Liaison Officer, was responsible for allocating them work; often they had no notion of this, nor who he was, nor he who they were. Sometimes, however, their orders were clear, i.e. for specific work on the Italian border, but more often than not it was a question of thinking fast. Francis received about five Jedburghs in the south-east and fifteen Missions, and some of them had been teams originally intended for Greece and transferred to France as the civil war there developed. He was told nothing: 'they just arrived'.

An example of the chaos often produced by these unscheduled arrivals, with personal consequences, arose with the appearance of EUCALYPTUS.

The EUCALYPTUS Allied Mission dropped on to the plateau, together with a fifteen-strong OG, on 28/29 June. The mission was to attach itself to the HQ of Colonel Huet, overall military commander of the Vercors, and its brief, not communicated to Francis prior to arrival, was to help arm the now 2500 less active Maquisards with Stens, rifles and grenades – thus ignoring all previous requests to Algiers and revealing little awareness of training that had been going on furiously throughout June. Their orders included a warning 'that the Vercors is not given a high priority at the present time' and 'that it is your duty to advise the local leaders to undertake small operations aimed principally to interfere with the enemy communications . . . avoid open fighting with the enemy'.[7] Ignorance was about to meet incredulity head-on.

The mission was led by Major Desmond Longe, an ex-bank clerk, and he had with him his friend Captain John Houseman, formerly an estate agent, both aged thirty and neither of whom spoke French. However, they were supported by a bilingual American, 2nd Lieutenant Pecquet (PARAY), the W/T link with London, and 2nd Lieutenant Croix, a Frenchman, the W/T link with Algiers. Two others joined them on 14 July. Pecquet's Top Secret report details the tensions on arrival as well as the resulting story, which would end in a Court of Inquiry in London involving Longe, Houseman and Francis.[8]

What went wrong from the start was that they had not been told there was a senior liaison officer, Francis, and when he introduced himself as such and said it was his job to direct them to where they would be most useful, they bristled, feeling that both Francis and a Major Martin (regarded by the French as 'a little young man') resented their arrival.

'What Pequet said to me when we met again was – you had your orders to direct us, we knew nothing of them and we were hot and irritated. But my sympathy for him came later, after Longe and Houseman had run away and Pecquet insisted on staying with Huet.'

EUCALYPTUS was gradually accepted by the French and worked under Colonel Huet. Francis packed Martin back off to Algiers with messages because the 'little man' had got engaged just before arriving in France and missed his fiancée. Major Longe, according to London's wishes, had put Pecquet in charge of the W/T links with Algiers and London and his relationship with Francis became friendly. Good work was done on the plateau.

Pecquet, as aware as everybody of the imminent German onslaught, felt that the 'fair amount of radio equipment' should be properly and safely stored yet be easy to access. He turned for help to Gustave Boissière, a gifted speleologist working for Colonel Huet, who knew the Vercors caves intimately. Pecquet's account then began to etch in the fateful divisions to come:

> From 14 July on we were bombed and strafed without respite. Colonel Huet, foreseeing a dispersal of the Vercors forces, made preparations. He created a commando unit picked out of his HQ personnel and included Major Longe and Captain Houseman and M. Boissière, the latter to be very useful as a guide. As the 'équipe radio' with the necessary equipment . . . obviously could not follow the moves of a group involved in guerrilla warfare . . . my plan, approved by all, was to remain at our hidden cave and transmit from there; contact with the commando force to be by liaison agents. The French Command believed that in the event of defeat the enemy occupation would not last longer than three days . . . based on the experience of the 'liquidation' of other Maquis.

Amidst the hell of the German air landings and attacks on Maquis, civilians and buildings alike, which will be detailed later, and while the radio equipment was transferred, Pecquet attended a conference at Huet's HQ together with Colonel Zeller, Francis, Major Longe and Huet's senior staff:

'Colonel JOSEPH (Zeller), having besides the Vercors other responsibilities, Huet insisted he should go. Major Roger and Pauline would follow Joseph. They would have to leave the Vercors before 0900 hours on the 22nd in the Die area as after 0900, according to Huet, the exit passage would be blocked.'

While Major Longe and Captain Houseman set off with the commando unit ostensibly to somehow let the outside world know of their position, Pecquet's team left to inspect his cave only to find it a virtual rabbit hole, damp and useless. Alternatives proving fruitless, they stayed put and in heavy rain made contact with London. The next day, surprisingly, they met Colonel Huet at St Martin; contact with Major Longe had been lost and there was fighting on all fronts. Huet sent the following signal via Pecquet to London:

> HAVE HELD OUT FOR 56 HRS AGAINST 3 GERMAN DIVISIONS. HAVE NOT UNTIL NOW LOST AN INCH OF GROUND. TROOPS FIGHTING COURAGEOUSLY BUT DESPERATELY FOR THEY ARE PHYSICALLY EXHAUSTED AND HAVE ALMOST NO AMMUNITION. DESPITE OUR REPEATED REQUESTS WE ARE ALONE AND HAVE RECEIVED NO HELP OR AID SINCE THE BEGINNING OF THE BATTLE. THINGS CAN GET DESPERATE ANY MINUTE BRINGING HIDEOUS CALAMITIES ONTO THE PLATEAU. WE HAVE DONE OUR DUTY BUT WILL BE FULL OF SADNESS AT THE BREADTH OF RESPONSIBILITIES TAKEN BY THOSE WHO DELIBERATELY AND FROM AFAR HAVE BOUND US TO SUCH AN EXPERIENCE. HERVIEUX.

Barely two hours later they were told to get into the woods as the enemy now had control of the heights. 'Saw the American OG moving up the slope behind the HQ. Last I saw of them. In spite of all our efforts we were unable to locate them.' Constantly on the move, 'the three days we had set as the limit for our reunion with the Major had elapsed by many days', but on 6 August they managed to get to the cave again and found Boissière's vest under a rock and at a nearby farm 'I was handed a note signed Desmond, dated 30 July':

> We dare not wait any longer for you and not knowing what has happened to you, we have decided on the following move to the Prophet's* farm near Villard de Lans for about three or four days. If we cannot get W/T contact with London there we intend going on east to SWISS. If we get contact with base we will ask for orders. I leave it entirely up to you to decide what to do, either follow our route which is easier or go south-west to SPAIN.

* Boissière's field name was Weather Prophet.

We have failed to make contact with anyone useful and it is no use any of us staying in this area. We are all well but had many near misses getting to our r.v. with you where we waited three to four days.

Good luck to you all and all thanks for your great efforts which I shall duly report to LONDON – I hope!

DESMOND, JOHN, WEATHER PROPHET.

Remember the woods between CORRENÇON and VALCHEVRIÈRES are mined.

A report reached us in August that the Major with Capt Houseman had contacted another Maquis en route for SWITZERLAND. Of the group with which the Major originally was part, most members, perhaps all, according to Boissière, were dead. Miss X, the nineteen-year-old secretary already mentioned – her body was found in the St LAURENT region (west of La Chapelle). Her legs had been pulled up behind her back. She was opened from top to bottom and had her guts round her neck.

According to all reports and to Lt-Col Huet, a great number of the Vercors men lost their lives trying to slip out of the woods and mountains. This is also confirmed by the mass graves discovered at St NIZIER, by the bodies fished out of the ISÈRE river. Those who were unable to 'stick it out' in the woods met with disaster. We left the Vercors on August 17th or 18th. Grenoble was liberated on August 22nd.

Later in Grenoble I met Roger, now Lt-Col. He asked me what I had told the French regarding Major Longe's and Capt Houseman's departure for SWITZERLAND. I replied I had always said LONGE and HOUSEMAN had gone east in order to re-establish contact with the outside, report on the Vercors in particular and on the Maquis in general. Lt-Col Roger said this was the right explanation to give.

Met Lt-Col Roger upon his return from London. He informed me that a Court of Inquiry was to be held regarding LONGE and HOUSEMAN's going to SWITZERLAND, that should I have difficulties with LONGE and HOUSEMAN, he would back me up. This I believed, in case they should blame me for failing to make contact with them.

Lt-Col Roger also informed me that the French were going to write a report re LONGE and HOUSEMAN. This was news to me as I was on intimate terms with Col DESCOUR and Lt-Col HUET and they had never made comments to me on Major LONGE or Capt HOUSEMAN.

I saw M. BOISSIÈRE three times in September. Gave me the story of events that led to Major LONGE's and Capt HOUSEMAN's departure of the Vercors. BOISSIÈRE also wrote a report, the first part of which I brought over to Gt Britain . . .

I have tried to give facts. May I add that the Equipe Radio had a terrible time whilst in the woods, but that to leave the VERCORS can be considered a more dangerous feat.

Signed 1ST Lt ANDRÉ E. Pecquet USA

Captain Houseman's enthusiastic diary of the Mission's activity and the events leading up to the Inquiry, often strangely dated, testified to hard work, was keen on the generosity of the French and reveals total recall of all meals consumed. But where the central issue of the Inquiry – were they guilty of 'running away'? – is concerned, the evidence is shadowy.

At 7am an HQ group came to collect Desmond, me and Bois (Boissière). Before leaving, Desmond arranged a rendezvous with André Pecquet four days later at his cave, also communications to be sent via bôite-au-lettre [sic] in the farm up the track.
Plenty of rain, no water anywhere and very inadequate rations for 20 men and a girl, with aircraft constantly searching the woods. A descent back down into St Martin found it empty. Squeezing moss for 2 to 3 hours produced 3/4 pint of muddy liquid. No sign of Cmdt H or Pecquet.
26 July. Realising the futility of sitting where we were, getting nowhere and gradually growing weaker besides the fact that no-one had contacted us, which was the primary object, we – Desmond, Bois (who said he'd like to come) and I decided to cross the valley and try and make contact with André and possibly Comdt H. We said goodbye to the rest, took a few rations and left.

We were to learn later that the remainder of the party were surprised by a German patrol. The men, after castration, were beaten to death with rifle butts and the girl (Lea Blain from Chatte) disembowelled and left to die with her intestines wound round her neck. I saw the photographs later – they were unrecognisable.

They cross German lines, finally find water but the effect on Bossière – 'he was at least 45' – gave real cause for alarm; he began to lose his sense of direction . . . Two days later they found the cave – no message from Pecquet – 'perhaps he had no means and our only contact with London was lost. Desmond left a note for André saying we would stay in the vicinity for three days, in case he returned after we'd left.' They took some spare kit and tobacco and abandoned the woods, desperate for water.

Boissière was left on 1 August to make his way home to Villard de Lans; deprivation and 'his almost fanatical fear of the Germans, with imaginary machine guns round every corner, had crumpled him into a weak, unreliable (though always charming) old man'. They struck north and made for Switzerland, which they achieved by 13 August. Their amazing stamina, fortitude and the leadership skills of Desmond Longe make epic reading and are beyond question but need not be detailed here. Imprisoned by the Swiss, they ultimately got a message to London.

> We were increasingly anxious to return to France and to rejoin one of the Maquis groups nearby. We kept up a stream of applications and eventually, after the three-week period (of detention) received our clearance to go. On arrival at Berne we heard that permission had been cancelled but, thanks to a fast taxi driver, managed to reach the frontier at Martinique with five minutes to spare. Not until that moment did we discover that the southern invasion had overtaken the area and that we were now behind our own lines.

And Francis's riposte?

> 'First point – at no stage was I told there would be various kinds of Missions, or with specific aims, and it was difficult for me to distinguish between Jedburghs and a Mission. All I knew was that I'd been told to represent the Allies and as far as I could I did that. As with Pecquet they were therefore arguing with me because I didn't know in this case they'd been sent specifically to deal with Colonel Huet and the Vercors and not me at all.
>
> Second point. M. Boissière was vital to the Vercors – he knew every inch of it – Huet needed him. But Longe and Houseman said, "You've got to show us the way out!" when they should have stayed, all of them. They left without telling Huet. They said they were hiding in the forest and they couldn't find him. If you can't find your friend down the road, you go further down the road. Huet was there and he was findable. Their brief was to help Huet as much as possible, whatever happened. They were SOE, they were FFI and that justified the line I took on it all. They should have been better prepared to help – they were helpers. Captain Pecquet stayed behind because it was obvious to him he didn't think anyone should

leave. Pecquet was a very fine Franco-American and he stayed behind and worked with Huet right up to the Liberation. Then we started with him saying, "We hated your guts – you made a mess of our Misson"; he also admitted my attitude had been right. Later I thanked him and said, "You saved the reputation of parachuted officers. You are someone to whom we all owe a debt of thanks." As to the others . . .

Third point – the Inquiry. When I met Boissière after the Liberation I asked "what about the Mission?" and he said with a deep sigh, "they buggered off to Switzerland". Then, when I got back to London, Harry Rée was working in the empty HQ and I rang him up and he said, "What about the Military Mission?", and I said, "They ran away to Switzerland and left a stink behind. They should be bloody shot."

His secretary in the office heard this, told Houseman, Longe demanded an Inquiry and one was set up, chaired by General Gubbins. I told them my story and they said you'll have to apologise. I said I'm not going to apologise. When you say someone ought to be shot that's a joke – an opinion not a sentence – you're not condemning him to death.

It was a nasty incident. It didn't cause me any sleepless nights.'

The Court of Inquiry, concluded in a single morning, found 'that the conduct of these officers was in accordance with the traditions of the British Army, and that their activities were entirely justified'. Gubbins recommended Longe for an MC in recognition of 'courage and tenacity in very arduous circumstances'.

14

7 July 1944. The Vercors

Amid the cluttered world of Missions, OGs and flown-in help, the period around 7 July witnessed two highly significant incidents. A ferocious ambush on the edges of the plateau by the fifteen men of the OG – one hundred Germans were killed in ten minutes – led the enemy into believing that the Americans were of battalion strength, a misconception that soon gave birth to hideous reprisals.

The second event was the arrival of 'PAQUEBOT', a Mission led by French air force Captain Tournissa (PAQUEBOT) together with four others, one of whom, an American, Lieutenant Francis Billon, broke his thigh on landing. Ironically, Tournissa's job was to build a landing strip at Vassieux capable of taking delivery of heavy armaments, field guns and mortars, that couldn't be dropped by parachute . . .

But PAQUEBOT also included the already legendary Countess Krystyna Skarbek, Christine Granville, or PAULINE, aged twenty-nine. Francis described her: 'A half gale was raging, and she had been blown four miles off course. She'd hit the ground with such force that the butt of her revolver was smashed and her coccyx badly bruised. Yet apparently she was on her feet in a second. When we met, four days later, I saw a beautiful, slender, dark-haired young woman. Even in those rough conditions I was impressed by her features and bearing. Her face was sensitive and alert . . .'

Major Xan Fielding, himself a newly arrived agent, later wrote:

> They were an imposing pair. Algiers HQ had given me no description of Roger, so I was not prepared for his great height and apparent youth. I had pictured him as a swarthy, middle-aged man . . . Instead I was faced with a smiling young giant whose coltish appearance was exaggerated by

> sloping shoulders and an easy resilient poise. To begin with, these features obscured the contradictory qualities of leadership and modesty. For him Résistance was tantamount to a new Religion, which he had been preaching and practising with remarkable success for some eighteen months.
>
> Christine was similarly dedicated and appeared to be more obviously so, only, perhaps, because I already knew something of her exploits in the past. She had been employed on the most hazardous missions in other parts of Europe and this reputation of hers led me to expect in her the heroic attributes which I fancied I immediately divined beneath her nervous gestures and breathless manner of speech. Not that she in any way resembled the classical conception of a female spy, even though she had the glamorous figure that is conventionally associated with one; this she preferred to camouflage in an austere blouse and skirt which, with her short, carelessly combed dark hair and the complete absence of make-up on her delicately featured face, gave her the appearance of an athletic art student.[1]

On his return to London in November 1943, and after the catastrophe of Alice's arrest at Montélimar, Francis had continued to press for a female agent to help him – 'they could go to places and do things which a young man of military age would only manage via pretty serious danger. Anyway, they couldn't find one or they had too many places to send them to, I don't know, but the next thing I did know was Christine being sent.' Twenty days later he reported to Brooks Richards in Algiers, – 'Christine is magnificent, what couldn't I have done if she had been here three months ago!'

Born of aristocratic landowning stock that had only survived through a prudent marriage link with a rich Jewish banking family, Christine admitted in a rare personal account of herself: 'I must have been something of a tomboy; my father had to move me from one convent to another because of my pranks. Once during Mass when the other girls dared me I held my candle to the priest's cassock and suddenly he was on fire. I was very sorry, and helped to beat the flames out. The priest was kind about it and laughed, but the Mother Superior was not amused and my father had to find another convent school for me quickly . . .'[2]

From her philandering father she had inherited good looks, a love of nature and animals, fine horsemanship, an independent spirit and a deep pride of race and love for her country. Married for a second time at eighteen to Jerzy Gizychi, she'd lived a full, eccentric, aristocratic lifestyle through the Depression but the rise of fascism woke her up. As the fierceness of her patriotism grew she joined the Polish Resistance, linked up with Brigadier Colin Gubbins and began to work for British Intelligence, smuggling out information via Hungary and Yugoslavia. She then joined SOE.

Like that of her lover – Andrew Kowersky-Kennedy, a lame patriot of towering physical and organisational abilities – her stamina was extraordinary, matched only by a flashing intelligence and determination. No barrier to resistance was acknowledged by either. 'Anything that threatened her liberty or that of anyone else became a personal issue.'[3]

Men adored her. Although married, 'in that golden adventurous age only the now was important. Past and future had no substance, and the emotions of these young men and women, unencumbered by the weighty baggage of the past, were stripped down to the bone.'[4]

Vera Atkins, a shrewd judge at Maurice Buckmaster's side in SOE HQ and a monitor of all comings and goings in Orchard Court, found her 'very brave, very attractive but a loner and a law unto herself. After the war she was quite unable to adapt to a boring day-to-day routine. She lived for action and adventure. Don't diminish her by whitewashing her faults. She was no plaster saint. She was a vital, healthy, beautiful animal with a great appetite for love and laughter and she had tremendous guts.'[5]

Sir Owen O'Malley, formerly the British Minister in Budapest, said of her, 'She was the bravest person I ever knew, the only woman who had a positive nostalgia for danger. She could do anything with dynamite except eat it.'[6]

Within seven to eight weeks Francis and Christine had made contact with JOCKEY's fifty or sixty centres:

> 'She had met all the people I had found in two years. Her personality was an enormous help. She made friends everywhere. In spite of the conditions under which we lived, she managed to enjoy herself and in the most difficult situations she would sometimes be shaking with laughter. Christine was a completely independent human being, answerable to nobody. I found a little bungalow for her at St Julien-en-Vercors. It was known as "*la maison de Miss Pauline*" and remained so until recently.
>
> Our job was to lend a hand with every kind of problem. Then, as things began to accelerate, there was little time for explanations but Christine

didn't need them; she got on with the job in hand and was absolutely reliable and trustworthy. I believe the two things that mattered most to her were the fate of her Jewish mother and Poland. By the time we met she had seen and endured so much.

She did not believe in political solutions and had little patience with the Polish Government in Exile. She housed an ironic respect for the British government and a deep dislike for any form of pomposity or hypocrisy. For her there were only "good" and "bad" people.

Like all those who are suspicious of rationalisation, Christine was highly intuitive. She was a romantic and often her emotions dominated her reason.

But it was because of this she had antennae which men have not. For the first time I believe, in provincial France Christine found perfection. There is something very special in the extent to which French cultural education had penetrated the provinces. Once I sat down with the stationmaster of some tiny place and we talked for five hours about Proust, though I was dying of fatigue and he had left school when he was thirteen.

In the Hautes-Alpes Christine had one very special friend – Paul Héraud. Christine recognised the purity and perfection of his personality. She could work and live with people like Paul, and she needed his level of grace.'

Christine returned the compliment within weeks of meeting Francis. In a report to Brooks Richards in Algiers she wrote:

I am very happy with my work. Roger (Cammaerts) is a magnificent person. The unity in the whole of the South of France depends on him. They treat him as the only 'neutral' person and take all his advice having known him and his work for the past eighteen months, when there was nothing and nobody at all to be with them and to help them. You must support him and back up his prestige as much as you can. Tell all our Missions that contacts got through him are guaranteed. Every Frenchman I have met during the three weeks, and I have met many hundreds, trusts Roger entirely. We need as many Jedburghs and Missions as possible, and for God's sake do not wait until the war is over. Send at least one Jedburgh and one Mission to each department, and instruct them all to listen to Roger's orders or advice.[7]

Christine's original brief had been to mobilise her Polish compatriots in France, tens of thousands of whom were working in German forced labour camps or had been pressed into units of the German army. Subsequently where Francis's and her work meshed was on the vital French–Italian border where many Poles were involved. Being a first-class climber, high mountains never fazed her and, under Gilbert Galletti's guidance, contact with the Poles became possible and before that with the Italians.

Historically in the Hautes-Alpes, long since in the gift of Paul Héraud, the four day war and the subsequent Italian military occupation of the area had resulted in the sad conflict between the Italians and the French across the border, a conflict which was, according to an Italian historian, 'an unpopular one, imposed on a nation with whom we had privileged ties, a similar culture, mutual traditions. When we read the names of soldiers on war memorials either side of the frontier, we find the same names belonging to identical family stocks. It was military and political demands that transformed the mountains into barriers, not the mindset of those living there. Furthermore from the moment war was declared, no one rejoiced in the houses of Piedmont.'[8]

Then, from the first week of September 1943, when Marshal Badoglio replaced the imprisoned Mussolini and signed an Armistice with Britain and the USA, some returning Italian soldiers and prisoners released by the British, including officers and NCOs, defied the threat to their families from the Germans and Fascists and took to the hills to avoid deportation. Their first actions were to raid the abandoned barracks for arms and ammunition, form themselves into small groups and scatter. They were the *partigiani*, and it was Paul Héraud's aim to construct an 'entente' between them and the Maquis. This was achieved in May 1944.

But, first, the martyrdom of the Vercors.

*

Despite frantic and incessant signals to Algiers and London, it was not until 14 July that a large-scale response finally arrived.

> 'The proud Republic of the Vercors was to hold its celebration of Bastille Day at Die, not the wisest thing to do, but Die was after all the county town of the *département* and Christine and I went down with Yves Farge and a host of senior officers and there was a march past.
>
> Then in the middle of the joy the wickedness of the mass daylight drop on the Vercors took place – seventy-two American flying fortresses dropping masses of stuff, the white parachutes clear as hell against the

sky. It was lunacy. You drop at night! As fast as we could we got back up on to the plateau . . .'

Joseph La Picirella, a prominent *résistant*, noted in his diary:

At 9.30 a.m. we heard the drone of the engines which got louder and louder. Our planes had arrived! There were about a hundred of them flying in groups of twelve and the fighters circling round the bombers. The noise filled the whole of the plateau and must have been heard in the plain of Valence. The fortresses flew over the landing strip while fixing their positions and then they flew off in the direction of Valence and returned to us flying low. Then the parachuting began. From 72 flying fortresses poured a stream of 15 to 20 containers each. It was a splendid spectacle!

Henri Rosencher, last seen in Barcelonnette, caught the excitement, too:

The sky was filled with a hundred Allied planes glittering in the sunlight sowing hundreds of parachutes which burst open in the blue sky like the corolla of white flowers, descending joyously and carrying around 1200 containers. It was a magnificent fete! The planes dipped their wings in salute, the sky full of them! It was more beautiful than a fireworks show! It was an imposing spectacle, enchanting and elating! Among the Maquisards the enthusiasm was indescribable.[9]

The festivities lasted half an hour, then:

While people were helping to load the containers on to the lorries, two fighters suddenly appeared. Everyone thought they were English planes, but as they dived towards the landing strip, the dreaded swastika was plainly visible. They dived to about eight metres on the open plain where everyone was standing and opened fire at point-blank range. This was only the beginning of the horror – bombs began to rain down on the landing strip and on the village.

. . . German bombers were coming from Chabeuil, the aerodrome ten minutes away. From ten o'clock to five it was uninterrupted mayhem purely meant to stop the Maquisards from collecting the containers.[10]

By eleven our communications were cut and we were completely isolated on the plateau. Having sprayed us lavishly with bombs, the enemy planes then inundated the plateau with dozens of grenades calculated to rough up the terrain so badly that it was unusable . . . Vassieux was on fire, PAQUEBOT (Captain Tournissa) was organising the western defences of Vassieux . . . in the meantime we kept making dashes out to try and grab the white parachutes which made such vivid targets.

There was no let up in the bombing. Fighters and bombers flew over us in waves. As soon as one lot left, the next took over . . . The enemy spared nobody. The population, livestock, houses, the roads, even the harvest, all were ruthlessly destroyed. Death and fire took over. The first objective of the enemy pilots was Vassieux. By 3.30 p.m. the church was a mass of smoking ruins, and the incendiary bombs were still falling fast.

Towards five o'clock the enemy concentrated on another target. While an ambulance was transporting the wounded to the hospital at St Martin-en-Vercors, the Germans started to bomb La Chapelle-en-Vercors . . .[11]

The hospital at St Martin-en-Vercors was at full stretch. The injured had flocked there since the end of June following the bombardments of St Nazaire-en-Royans and Pont-en-Royans. Every day those injured by shell-splinters, women, children, even a baby at the breast arrived. Now, to these, had to be added the victims of the bombardment of La Chapelle, Vassieux and the landing strip.[12]

*

'The night of the 14th, Christine and I spent together in a burning hotel at St Agnan. It was the first time we'd made love. We were absolutely certain that we were going to die the next day; it was all over, this was the end – the hotel was on fire, bombs were falling, the troops were gathering on the side of the mountain . . . we simply went into each other's arms.

In the morning we were standing at the window and a fighter with a bomb slung beneath it made for us. We could see the pilot's face. I said – if he releases it now we've had it – and on the word "now" he fired. The bomb skidded across the roof and buried itself in the ground behind the hotel without exploding. Christine gripped my hand and laughed – "They don't want us to die!"'

In the days that followed, again the signals became more and more desperate but despite the 'token gesture' of 14 July no more meaningful support arrived. The bombings simply gave notice that General Pflaum, commanding the German 157 Reserve Division with responsibility for dealing with resistance, would soon unleash his 14,000 troops against the 4000 defenders, who still, with only a few mortars and bazookas despite the drops, could only hope to but delay the action. Colonel Huet had already mobilised his final reserves yet the only manpower support flown in by the Allies had been twenty-five men and one woman. The SS, on the other hand, drew on five hundred men from Strasbourg especially for 21 July.

On 20 July, on the eve of the horror to come the next day, Francis, with Christine standing by, sent this signal in the name of Colonel Zeller:

> FIERCE BATTLE FOR CAPTURE OF VERCORS IMMINENT STOP WITHOUT YOUR HELP RESULT UNCERTAIN STOP URGENTLY REQUEST REINFORCEMENTS OF ONE PARACHUTE BATALLION AND MORTARS STOP REQUEST ALSO IMMEDIATE BOMBING OF ST NIZIER AND CHABEUIL STOP COME TO OUR AID BY EVERY MEANS[13]

At nine o'clock on 21 July the rapidly increasing drone of aircraft again filled the plateau – help at last! The new airstrip at Vassieux, where work had carried on throughout the previous carnage, was ready to receive . . . but once more it was the familiar swastikas streaking in from Chabeuil – first fighters strafed the ground, then heavier aircraft dropped 200-kilogram bombs . . . and finally came the coup de grâce – planes, towing gliders:

> 'These were the special gliders we'd seen hidden at Chabeuil. As they were released they literally dived perpendicular to the ground and had little parachutes which put out as they landed. It literally took two to three seconds from us seeing them to them touching the ground and fifteen to twenty SS jumping from each glider. It was enormously effective because we didn't have time to fire at them and the ground was still covered with the materiel which had been dropped on the 14th – but never having been able to be properly collected; some of it had been rescued at night – but seventy-two aircraft's worth!'

An SOS was sent:

> MASSIVE ATTACK BY AIRBORNE TROOPS LANDED AREA VASSIEUX FROM ABOUT TWENTY AIRCRAFT EACH TOWING ONE GLIDER STOP STRONG INFANTRY AND TANK UNITS PROCEED TOWARDS DIE HAVE PASSED SAILLANS STOP OTHER

ENEMY UNITS ARRIVING ON ROUTE NATIONALE 75 STOP WE HOPE TO BE ABLE TO MAINTAIN RADIO LINK ADIEU

Against these highly-trained commandos, the lightly-armed Maquisards, who had somehow managed to hold the cliff-tops on the previous days, had little answer and were now about to be overrun, as was the whole plateau. They had wanted to fight away from the hamlets and farms so that civilians would not be involved, but such tactics made no difference. The invaders made no distinction between civilian and Maquis, age or sex. There was no escape; the east to Grenoble was heavy with troops, the south already manned, and the entire Isère Valley stretching along the north-western slopes was guarded by one man every 50 metres. The Germans were there to end once and for all the 'problem' of the Vercors and their atrocities in doing so must be chronicled.

Francis's last signal for Colonel Zeller reflected the fierce morality running deep in his personality, the fury of the boy 'who hated it when things went wrong', yet who rarely lost his temper, all still held in check by a very British poise and sense of duty towards others:

LA CHAPELLE VASSIEUX ST MARTIN BOMBED BY GERMAN AIRFORCE STOP ENEMY TROOPS PARACHUTED AT VASSIEUX STOP WE PROMISED TO HOLD OUT FOR THREE WEEKS STOP TIME PASSED SINCE TAKING UP ACTION STATIONS SIX WEEKS STOP DEMAND REVICTUALLING MEN STORES AMMUNITION STOP MORALE OF OUR PEOPLE EXCELLENT BUT THEY WILL TURN AGAINST YOU IF YOU DO NOT TAKE ACTION IMMEDIATELY STOP THOSE IN LONDON AND ALGIERS UNDERSTAND NOTHING ABOUT THE SITUATION IN WHICH WE FIND OURSELVES AND ARE CONSIDERED AS CRIMINALS AND COWARDS STOP YES REPEAT CRIMINALS AND COWARDS

Commandant Pierre Tanant of Colonel Huet's General Staff, whose patient account of the Vercors tragedy he dedicated to 'the seven hundred known and unknown heroes, civil and military, who fell on the henceforth sacred soil of the Vercors', contains pages which put faces to the appalling figures. Many of them are catalogued in a report of moving simplicity compiled by the local priest, M. l'Abbé Gagnol, proving that at Vassieux the Wehrmacht perpetrated their worst wrongs.

One is tempted to quote the full litany of old and young who were so brutally and summarily murdered in the days following 21 July but they are still remembered and mourned.

Of one child, Commandant Tanant wrote:

> The following Thursday, 27 July, M. Pierre Revol, farmer, asks the Abbé Gagnol to go with him to the Château where he had hidden some clothing. While he did so the Abbé walked around the hamlet, then M. Revol joined him in front of Mlle Blanc's house. While they were talking it seemed to the curé he could hear a voice coming from the ruins and he mentioned this to his companion.
>
> 'I doubt it,' replied the other, 'everybody's been dead in there for eight days.'
>
> 'Help me, help me,' moaned a small voice.
>
> The Abbé leaned in at the window to try and see from where the voice was coming.
>
> 'M. le curé, help, hurry, get me out of here!'
>
> It was the grandchild of M. Firmin Blanc, the little Arlette, twelve years years old, one of the first communicants of 4 June.
>
> 'Of course, little one, we're going to get you out.'
>
> 'M. le curé, get me something to drink!'
>
> 'You haven't had anything since last Friday?'
>
> 'No.'
>
> 'Have you seen anybody?'
>
> 'Only M. André Martin (disabled in the other war) who couldn't move me. I saw my auntie Martine who tried to get me out and she put a rope round me, then to my leg but because she's got a bad arm she couldn't and I haven't seen her after.'
>
> (Mlle Martine Blanc has since disappeared without trace.)
>
> 'And then I saw some Germans and I asked them for water; they just looked at me, didn't give me anything, they couldn't care less.'
>
> Arlette had her left leg trapped between two corpses, themselves wedged beneath stones and joists. Then she pointed out the dead bodies among whom she lay.
>
> 'That's my grandma – my Auntie Suzy here and Auntie Adele. Under them is my sister Jacquie [seven years old] who was crying for a whole day because the fire was eating her feet. There's maman who only died on Tuesday who was always asking me to go and get her water but I couldn't. Over there, under the ruined bits, is my brother Maurice [eighteen months]. I don't know where my grandpa is or my Auntie Jeanne.'

After several hours which seemed interminable due to the stench which rose from the bodies and the presence of Germans billeted only 500 metres away, and when we had moved all the decomposing corpses, Arlette could finally be freed. Laid in a wheelbarrow she was taken a distance of four kilometres across fields and through woods to the house of M. Achard, not far from St Agnan.

There she was changed, washed, nursed and put to bed. Her first words were:

'You must write to papa. He lives at 24, rue Joseph Bouchayer, in Grenoble.'

The poor man had obviously believed he was sending his family to safety in the country.

Up until Sunday 30th everything seemed normal. Arlette had only this mad desire to see her father and to get better. At midday she ate well, then she slept. Then towards three o'clock she woke up and complained of stomach pain. Then a few seconds after:

'My chest hurts! My face hurts! Oh! It's horrible!'

And the agony started, a terrible pain which lasted until eleven o'clock on Monday 31st.

'I didn't think you had to suffer so much to die! I'm going to die and my papa isn't here . . . where are they going to bury me?!'

The poor little one who suffered so much in dying and who had already suffered so much in front of the Germans trapped beneath the bodies of her family . . .

. . . was buried in the corner of M. Achard's garden. A small cross and a few flowers mark her grave: 'Here rests Arlette Blanc, died 31 July 1944, at twelve years of age. Pray for her.'

Arrested by a patrol while trying to revive some of the victims of Vassieux, the Abbé was ordered to stay in St Agnan and it was only on 6 August, after the last of the Germans had left, that he could rejoin his parish. His account ends: 'Of the 150 houses that make up Vassieux, 140 are completely destroyed, demolished by the bombs and incendiaries. The church is nothing more than a charred shell. All livestock has completely disappeared, a good part of it burnt alive in the stables. Putrefying corpses lie everywhere, their nauseating smell spreading far and wide. Not a living soul.'[14]

*

Francis, with Albert, Casimir and Christine, was completely at the disposal of Colonel Zeller and spent hours every day prior to the 21st at the

Headquarters between St Agnan and St Julien-en-Vercors coding and firing off urgent signals to Algiers and London, while maintaining contact with his own *réseaux* and attending meetings under Colonel Huet.

Those meetings culminated on the 21st when a decision whether to fight to the last man, make a breakout with the combined forces going via one spot, or to disperse, had to be made. The regular soldiers favoured the breakout but when the map was looked at it became clearly impossible to get four thousand men together and force a way out. So dispersal was accepted. In drenching rain the order was given on the 23rd.

'Dispersal as far as we were concerned was quite precise; it meant melting into the woods in the Vercors – which were huge – and perfectly possible, but a few officers of groups round the perimeter of the Vercors thought that it meant trying to edge out. As a result there were an awful lot of arrests and massacres of people trying to leave the plateau. The civilian resistance people came largely from Valence and the breakout of that kind to the north was virtually impossible – you had the ravine to cross.

We sent some pretty fierce messages and after the Vercors, something I'm ashamed of now, I said there ought to be a list of all those who died on the Vercors, in red ink, posted on the walls of the offices of those who had failed to make the proper decisions. Many in France regarded the abandonment of the Vercors as treason. It wasn't treason but it was pretty serious incompetence and probably basically due to the stupidity of the Vercors being under London control. The north of France was controlled by General Koenig, in London, and the south was supposed to be commanded by General Cochet in Algiers. The exception to that was the Vercors which was under Koenig in London – totally ludicrous because the Vercors straddles two southern *départements* – the Isère and the Drôme – and you couldn't have a military command commanding everything except for a tiny fraction of one of them!'

'It has been argued that the decision to disperse was taken too late – that Colonel Huet should, by all the rules of guerrilla warfare, have ordered it five days before. But he was a dutiful soldier, caught between two necessities, attempting to put a stop not merely to the massacre of those for whom he was militarily responsible but also sickeningly aware that the enemy's complete disrespect for human life endangered everybody. The new reality of 'total war' involved everybody; all were now potential victims.

'In early darkness on the 22nd, with the battle still raging, Francis and Colonel Zeller, their collective network responsibilities too large to risk capture or death, together with Christine, Albert, Casimir and a few Maquisards, found transport to the Col Rousset, the one route out of the Vercors:

'Trying to make no noise whatsoever, we stumbled down through the undergrowth which was not easy because it was very steep and 1000 metres down and we had very heavy gear, radios and all our own personal equipment with us. Finally we reached the valley and then we had about six kilometres to the road and the Drôme river. We were at a point just west of Die. We crossed fields very slowly because we were aware German troop movements were using that axis. We never saw them and we reached the river and forded it up to our knees, climbed to the railway, crossed it and the N93 was another 100 metres away. It wasn't a large arterial road, just wide enough for two lanes of traffic, and it wound through the valley with very steep sides; every step you took with great care and darted across it one at a time. We then took a little side road which led towards St Nazaire-le-Désert and in that whole 10-kilometre walk we didn't meet a single person before we happened on the local Resistance committee who were also making for St Nazaire. I knew where I was going – I was travelling the whole time and the roads that would carry a bicycle or truck I was very familiar with; you had a pretty clear map in your head of those areas where you were active.

At St Nazaire they were able to give us a snack and there was a *commerçant* who had a small producer-gas delivery vehicle we could all get into. He took us down from what were substantial foothills to the south Drôme, to the junction of the N93 and the road to Sisteron, and then via the main road to Gap where a baker in a little village, Monnetier-l'Allemand, who was part of our team, took us up to Seyne-les-Alpes where I'd suggested to Colonel Zeller we should set up our HQ. We had covered seventy miles in twenty-four hours of almost non-stop walking. I still don't know how the hell we did it.

Finally, I should say this – and it's important. Coming down towards Die we'd met the ambulance with the badly wounded making its way back up to the Vercors. They'd tried to transfer their worst cases to the hospital in Die but a totally hysterical matron had waved them away – "the Germans are coming, you'd better go back!" – and that was what they were doing. Unfortunately that was their tragic mistake because eventually they used

> the Grotte de la Luire as a hospital which was bound to have been discovered sooner or later because it was quite a famous cave; virtually everyone there was killed on 27 July. If they'd gone south, where we were going, they'd have been all right. But they went the other way.'

At night during the massacres on the south plateau and the systematic dynamiting of houses and villages (including the radio house at La Britière), the military hospital at St Martin had been transferred to La Grotte de la Luire – a large scar some 20 metres wide, 30 high and over 300 deep in a chalk cliff face – surrounded by thick woods and invisible from the 'main' road 600 metres away.

The badly injured, after some use of vehicles, had then been carried on stretchers with huge difficulty up hidden paths to the cave. Inside, sharp stones which might have ripped the stretchers had had to be cleared before the patients could be laid down, side by side and as far as possible from the entry, where at least they were sheltered from the elements. The wounded included four Germans or Poles. Finally, a large Red Cross flag was draped against an outside wall.

But in the continuing havoc and chaos around them the doctors knew it would only be a matter of time before they were found. Therefore it was decided to move all those who could walk, helped by nurses, further away into the surrounding forest or other caves. That left twenty-one badly injured patients, three doctors, nine nurses, a priest and an almoner. One of the nurses, Sylviane Rey, was a friend of Francis and Christine.

On Thursday 27 July, a plane flew over the grotto several times, leaving behind a deathly silence. Commandant Tanant once again:

> At 4.30 p.m., twenty green silhouettes appear at the mouth of the cave and bullets ricochet against the wall of the cliff. The German prisoners scream, 'Don't shoot! Don't shoot!' in German and are motioned to one side. The staff are ordered out, hands in the air, and lined up against the wall while anything of worth is plundered from the interior. Those capable of walking are ordered to get up – eleven of them – while the others are closely guarded. One after another, the staff and the walking wounded are made to march towards the hamlet of Rousset. On the way they are ill treated and told they are going to be shot.
>
> At Rousset they are locked in a foul hole. A nurse who had received permission to stay with the bed-ridden wounded, suddenly arrived, traumatised, in the middle of the night . . .

. . . Apparently after the little column had left for Rousset, the Germans had thrown themselves on those incapable of moving, dragging them 200 metres, taking a sinister pleasure in jolting them, reopening their wounds before indolently shooting them. That done the bodies had been rolled down a hillock until they came to rest in a pile, one on top of another.

Towards midday on 28th the staff, nurses and two wounded from Vassieux were loaded into a coach to be transferred to Grenoble. Then, moments later, the remaining wounded were assembled in a field and shot. Lieutenant Francis Billon, the American who had parachuted in with the Mission PAQUEBOT and been badly injured on landing, is taken away and shot separately, the Germans having let it be understood that they would spare him as he was a regular soldier and uniformed.

Once in Grenoble, two of the doctors and the priest were shot, the third managing to escape. Six of the nurses in the grotto were deported to Ravensbrück; few return.

Sylviane Rey, having escorted her wounded men to a place of safety, finally managed to make her way back to Crest.

Henri Rosencher, too, escaped the tragedy. He had to continue his work as an organiser of medical supplies to other Maquis but his story would lead to arrest and, inevitably as a Jew, to Dachau.

There was nothing we could do. People did go up from the Drôme and witnessed the masses of bodies left in the open to rot; the smell was absolutely overwhelming. The Germans having made no differentiation between civilian and Maquis, it was my first vision of 'total war' and it meant the killing of civilians and that is what will now happen in war up to and including Iraq. Even in 1944, there was no difference between Flanders Field and the Vercors, Oradour, Coventry or Dresden.

It didn't affect me physically, no. It was what I would have expected. It wasn't in any sense a surprise. Even the massacre of the Jews. It justified my reason to participate.

15

Seyne-les-Alpes

Zeller's last signal from the Vercors via Francis had read:

HAVE LEFT VERCORS VIOLENTLY ATTACKED BY GREATLY SUPERIOR FORCES OF ABOUT TWO DIVISIONS SUPPORTED BY AIRCRAFT AND ARTILLERY STOP FOLLOWING THE ATTACK LANDING OF GLIDERS AND CAPTURE OF DIE SITUATION EXTREMELY DANGEROUS STOP MANY OFFICERS HAVE DISAPPEARED BELIEVED KILLED STOP AM TRYING TO JOIN PERPENDICULAIRE[1] WHOSE WHEREABOUTS I DO NOT KNOW STOP TROOPS AND COMMANDERS CURSE FAILURE TO PROVIDE AIR SUPPORT STOP HOPE FOR EARLY LANDING IN THE SOUTH STOP SEND ME NEWS.

The reply from Colonel Constans in Algiers read:

FULLY UNDERSTAND YOUR SADNESS AND YOUR FEELING OF ISOLATION STOP THE AIRCRAFT EARMARKED FOR DROPPING TO YOU MEN HEAVY ARMS AND AMMUNITION HAVE BEEN READY FOR THE LAST SIX DAYS STOP THIS MATERIEL AND MEN WILL NOW BE DROPPED INTO AREAS OF DRÔME AND HAUTES-ALPES STOP AM CONFIDENT THAT VERCORS TROOPS DESPITE DISPERSAL WILL HAVE SUCCESS AND REVENGE THROUGH ACTION AS GUERRILLAS

The irony is breathtaking.

But Colonel Zeller's barb 'failure to provide' in his last signal merits closer attention. At the post-war Inquiry into the Vercors tragedy, de Gaulle's Minister of Air insisted that he had not received any official notification of the Vercors messages from the Comité d'Action en France until the morning of 26 July. This body had been set up by de Gaulle in Algiers, under Jacques Soustelle, to organise direct assistance for the

Armée Secrète (Secret Army), and all other units and groups of militant *résistants* under whatever control. It was in close contact with SOE HQ and therefore would have known the situation. The Minister further claimed that although he had made all necessary preparations, the operation even having been code-named 'Patrie', the air units were never assembled because the urgency of the signals was never passed on.

Blame and counter-blame has pursued the name Vercors ever since 1945, but many believe that politics had a distinct part to play in the tragedy. The Minister, Fernand Grenier, was a Communist and he accused de Gaulle of failing to take action in order to discredit him and the Communists in general. When news of the tragedy reached Algiers on 27 July, Grenier signalled de Gaulle, 'I cannot be associated with a criminal policy which consists of having forces at your disposal and not using them when our brothers in France appeal for help.' Grenier was, as a result, dropped from the cabinet and Soustelle promoted to Minister of Colonies. Soustelle's subsequent right-wing activities deepened and culminated in a central role during the Algerian War. Was the battle weaponry for whoever would take over the reconstructed Republic after the war – Gaullists or the left – already being polished?

Guerrilla activity was by now acute over all south-east France and among the principal reasons Francis had suggested Seyne-les-Alpes to Colonel Zeller for his new HQ had been the fact that he knew the area well, he knew the best parachute grounds and the availability of 'absolutely admirable teams'. A notable exception was Zeller's No. 2, nicknamed 'le Sanglier' – the Wild Boar – because he hid himself some eight kilometres away from Seyne and never emerged from the undergrowth, regarding Seyne as a very dangerous place.

Zeller and Francis had to decide which command areas needed attention. The Hautes-Alpes was well looked after but in the Basses-Alpes there had been arrests. The area included important JOCKEY cells like Forcalquier, Manosque, Valencome and Mezel and Louis Malarte in the Vaucluse was a priceless asset.

Their biggest problem remained the part they should play in relation to the probable Allied landing on the Riviera. They knew they could not neutralise the coastal defences entirely or go any way towards sabotaging gun and defence installations because of the arrests. But what was equally obvious was that the coastal defences were nowhere near strong enough to resist penetration by a determined Allied force and Francis had already set his men to prepare to act as guides for advancing troops. What they were sure of was that, in spite of all the difficulties of organisation in the FFI, they could clear the roads and block the Germans in their garrison towns so that an immediate Allied advance to Grenoble along the Route Napoléon was possible.

'As I've said before we reckoned that the maximum time necessary to get an armed force to Grenoble was seven days. There was nothing new in this scheme, *but we could not get any hint that would help us to muster our forces and allow us to ration our materiel, particularly ammunition, for the landing date*.'

Wireless contact having proved useless in obtaining an answer to the problem, Colonel Zeller, who had been promoted to general by London, decided he should go himself, to, in his words, 'see if I can straighten them out while you work with the Sanglier and try and get as much order into the situation as possible'.

While travelling south on 26 July towards Apt to be picked up by Lysander, General Zeller had time to reflect and came to realise that the Vercors had not represented a true picture of the occupation.

> My black mood evaporated; no train had run since 15 June on the two Alpine lines, Grenoble to Aix-en-Provence, and Briançon to Livron. No isolated German courier could travel the highways, no enemy roadblocks, no control existed outside the garrison towns. No traces of military works or mine fields. The Germans are prisoners in their garrisons, from which they only emerge in force for supplies or on a reprisal expedition – and these columns are attacked, one out of every two times, by an uncatchable enemy.
>
> After two months of this situation, the German soldier is bewildered, demoralised, fooled – we know him, we steal his mail. He looks with fear on these mountains, these forests, these crags, these narrow valleys from which at any moment a thunderbolt can crash.
>
> He awaits the arrival of the Allied soldiers, like a deliverance.
>
> If one excepts the high Alpine valleys where fighting is still going on, as well as the highways along the Rhône valley and around Grenoble, the centre of the massif is ours.[2]

These facts plus a full, detailed and passionate assertion of the readiness of the FFI to assist any invasion, impressed de Gaulle, who showed Zeller a copy of the top-secret ANVIL/DRAGOON Operations Plan which envisaged, 'in a few days' establishing a beachhead on the Riviera, taking Toulon and Marseille then striking northwards up the Rhône Valley. Zeller noted that Grenoble's estimated capture was placed at D+90. Furious, he asserted that in those ninety days the FFI would be massacred! Yet if the Allies could hold a bridgehead thirty miles inland they could be in Grenoble in forty-eight hours!

Flown to Naples, Zeller repeated his views to General Patch who, in turn, was impressed and the result was that General Truscott, whose VI Corps would bear the brunt of establishing a beachhead, organised a fast-moving unit of motorised armour ready to make such a move, commanded by Brigadier General Fred W. Butler, a man Francis would end up wishing to murder.

Because General Zeller had seen the invasion plans he was henceforth a security risk and after service in Corsica only allowed to return to mainland France after the Liberation.

In Francis's words, 'a wonderful man'.

With General Zeller incommunicado and no one any the wiser as to when or where the invasion would take place, preparations nevertheless continued. It was hard going because Seyne was tucked away on steep roads and 35–40 kilometres from Gap, itself fairly high up.

Whereas previously Francis had been peripatetic, now leaders from the Vaucluse, the Isère, the Drôme, etc, invariably came to Seyne and the attacks on lines of communication, to which they were all dedicated, continued to be more successful than anyone could have hoped. Mindful that a three-week battle might be about to happen, one set of rules governed the whole network – don't waste – don't sit on stuff – move it around, spread it and hide it well. When Francis did travel south from Seyne it was precisely to check those points and ensure that materiel would be available to defend the Route Napoléon and the airborne troops' landing grounds if necessary. In addition, he urged the disruption of trucks with food supplies, i.e. not just the military but the sources supplying the military and therefore attackable; if possible capture food.

Apart from the coastal defences the only German troops that remained mobile in the area and who presented any danger to invading forces were the two divisions that had been engaged against the Vercors. The sole route where the Germans could move with any kind of freedom was the Rhône Valley and there Francis made quite certain that the FFI could handle any attack on the Route Napoléon which might come reactively from the Rhône area. But the main danger remained the German troops in northern Italy who might attack over the Alpine passes and take the Allied troops advancing on Grenoble on their right flank. It was believed that the Germans had, if necessary, seven divisions in Italy for such an operation. To prevent this, the Military Missions coming in had been given the frontier passes as their main targets to work on.

On 1 August a Mission, 'TOPLINK', under Major L. G. M. J. Hamilton, was dropped with such instructions and to coordinate the activities of the FFI and the *partigiani*, but as in many cases the Missions, eager and dedicated as they were, were dropped too late. If they had arrived on 15 May they would have solved all local FFI problems as their presence alone united the various Résistance elements. But much work was already being done and none more imaginatively than by Christine and her contacts.

After the escape from the Vercors and a full twenty-four hours' sleep, Christine left for the Italian border on the back of Gilbert Tavernier's motorbike, he being the Head of the Winter Sports Centre at Briançon. Her link with Gilbert Galletti in the Queyras, the magnificently forested area up to the Alpine passes, was one of mutual admiration and had already enabled her to establish contact with a leader of the partisans, Marcellin, at Sestrière, eight kilometres over the Col de Montgenèvre on the Italian side. With Gilbert Galletti she was setting up links between groups, scattered among the crags and slopes, who were already receiving a great deal of supplies and were well into their job of harassing any German convoys that ventured along the winding and vulnerable Alpine roads. They also constantly reconnoitred the high ridges of the Alps.

> 'Despite her passion for her homeland, as the end of the war crept up there was the virtual certainty that she wouldn't be allowed to go back and that, I felt, was fundamental to her day-to-day living, at the root of her almost *violent* independence and her willingness to be involved in everything, totally.
>
> On one occasion she and two or three friends were on the frontier when a German patrol saw them and chased them with dogs. Christine hid in a bush where a dog found her, and she just stroked its head a dozen times and when the patrol moved on, having lost their dog, she took it back to Gilbert who kept it for years until it died. That came as no surprise to many of us who knew her because a dog, like any human being, would

simply be drawn to her like a magnet. There are people like that who draw your eyes; she was an intensely compelling personality.

All our work in that area bore fruit after the Liberation in that many there went on to give their time helping the resistance in Italy.'

Before three further American OGs – now doubled to thirty men each – and five other Jedburgh teams were parachuted into JOCKEY country – often needing to be 'placed' – British Missions had landed agents relevant to our story. One, on 6 August under Major Purvis, 'CONFESSIONAL', contained Captain John Roper, and with Major Hamilton's Mission they cooperated in the defence of the Italian frontier in the Hautes-Alpes under Paul Héraud; they assisted technically in blowing up the bridge at Savines between Briançon and Gap, and at Prelles on receipt of their final Action Messages before going on to take part in the fighting around Briançon. On 21 August John Roper, insisted on and received the surrender of the fort at Montdauphin.

'I'd met John on the rugby pitch – he was at Harrow when I was at Mill Hill – then we'd met again at Cambridge. He went into the Foreign Office and I went to Belfast. I hadn't seen him since 1937. He landed in a field south of Seyne and said, – "Francis, what the hell're you doing here!" So much for my reputation in Algiers.'

A second Mission under Major Havard Gunn, a charismatic and kilted Seaforth Highlander, dropped on 8 August, and with him came, among others, Commandant Christian Sorenson who would be arrested with Francis together with Major Xan Fielding, who landed on 9 August, as Liaison Officers to the FFI under Francis.

Then, almost immediately, with the invasion imminent, the region suffered its greatest loss.

On 8 August, east of Gap, a secret meeting took place in the woods beween La Bâtie-Neuve and La Rochette, attended by all the Résistance leaders in the Hautes-Alpes plus Serge Barret, the Secretary-General of the Préfecture, American and French Mission members, Christine and Francis. The purpose of the meeting was to hear Paul Héraud present his proposed military plans for the liberation of the *département*. They were unanimously approved. In the ensuing respectful silence, Francis said simply, 'You have a leader ideally qualified to carry through these operations. Have total confidence in him.' The same evening Commandant Pelletier of the Mission 'CONFESSIONAL' said to M. Jacques Guérin of Savournon and head of the SAP Service, 'Your chief is a complete man; I have never met anyone like him.'

'Everywhere he is present' was another description freely used of this remarkable man. He was the thinker, the chief, the organiser, the passionate leader who would give his last meal and bed to the lowliest, audacious yet 'despite that prudent because he always had an acute sense of possibilities'. His energy was as phenomenal as his commitment, geography presented no problem to him and he nurtured contact with the Italian resistance with the same degree of determination as he did with his own. He was a unifier, an amalgamator of groups whose political tendencies were often dangerously diverse yet who, under his spell, came to concentrate on the one thing that mattered – ejecting the invader from the soil of France. The lucidity of his thought was matched by an equal clarity with words: 'The path that General de Gaulle has opened up is so wide that all Frenchmen, whatever their opinions, can march down it together and they must, hand in hand, because the tasks of tomorrow as much as those of today, demand the cooperation of every Frenchman who wills the health of his country. The *résistants* will know, in peacetime, how to preserve between them "that union born in conflict, that union that will give them victory".'[3]

A few days before 8 August meeting, Paul Héraud said to a friend, 'the end is coming, but not everybody will see it'. Presentiment or not, the truth was bitter: he, among many others, did not live to see victory.

On the 8th he'd let it be known that he was going to the Drôme the following day but during the night he changed his mind – perhaps because of news of the arrest of Serge Barret who had been at the meeting the previous evening (yet who he must have known would be swiftly released through the intervention of the Gendarmerie). Whatever the reason, he decided to go instead to Savournon to talk to Guérin.

The next day, having sent a message to Gilbert Galletti, – to stockpile all his explosives ready for the coming liberation of Briançon – he left Gap at noon on the back of Gendarme Meyère's motorbike. To avoid roadblocks on the Route Nationale they took the smaller Gap–Neffes road which rejoined the Tallard road below Logis Neuf and, half an hour later, there they came face to face with a German convoy.

What happened next was partly witnessed by a French driver 'requisitioned' by the Germans to drive a lorry in the convoy.

The Germans ordered the two to stop and demanded their papers, finding it incomprehensible that a gendarme should be transporting a civilian. Héraud, as they were about to search him, suddenly burst away and leapt into a copse bordering the road to Rousine. Taken by surprise, the Germans fired round after round in his direction but they didn't chase him; turning back to the gendarme one of them shot him dead at point blank range. It looked as if Héraud had escaped.

But, unseen from the road, face down in the copse, with the bullets slicing the bushes around him, Héraud was frantically tearing up important papers he dared not leave on his person, Later, if necessary, he'd make some sense of them again but for the moment he squeezed the scraps into a ball, hard in his hand.

Gradually the firing became desultory and then stopped. Silence. But Héraud ignored what was happening on the road. Whatever the cost he had to get to Savournon and see Guérin. On his belly, he reached the edge of the copse hiding him. Ahead a field, further on, high vines and an orchard lining the road. On his right, 200 metres away, an undulation sheltering a small building which he had to reach; beyond that he would be well covered.

Just before three o'clock he stood up and raced diagonally across the field but shots rang out and he fell, his body riddled, at the point where the safety of the undulation began. With a last reflex he must have thrown the ball of notes away as far as he was able; they are picked up by a local that same evening.

The face of the dead man was youthful, unshaven, his complexion bronzed and his long hair matted.

Both corpses, under orders from the Germans, were buried, denied any ceremony whatsoever, after identification.[4]

Gilbert Galletti carried out his orders to the letter. Twelve days later, amid the initial success of Paul Héraud's plans, on 20 August, Gap was liberated.

Despite his death, Paul Héraud's instinctive military and organisational genius had left his thirty groups in the Hautes-Alpes secure and ready for action, but Francis still had to deal with problems arising out of the FFI command structure in areas R1 and R2. After the Vercors, resistance in R1 (Lyon), he reported, 'had managed to assume sufficient unity to assure effective action. Colonel Descour (BAYARD) provided the necessary skilled military directive and the work of

Yves Farge, Commissaire de la République, a very able, energetic and diplomatic politician, had undisputed authority deriving directly from General de Gaulle.'

R2 (Marseille), however, presented a very different picture. From mid-July to mid-August, Francis was almost entirely occupied with the same tiresome internal affairs Colonel Zeller had been trying to resolve prior to Barcelonnette. The local military chief, Levalles, had given Captain Jacques Lécuyer (Sapin) carte blanche from 6 June to work out the disastrous 'Plan Rouge' from a base at Barcelonnette (see p.140). After its fall he turned against Lécuyer and, without interviewing him or letting his military chief, Colonel Zeller, know, Levalles denounced Lécuyer, called him a traitor and told all the Maquisards to go back to the towns.

The confusion and uncertainty in all ranks of the FFI multiplied when Levalles was arrested. Maxence (JUVENAL), the political and civilian FFI chief, then assumed complete military command. He was an inveterate foe of the right-wing Lécuyer and showed no inclination to try and reach any compromise. A severe split in policy resulted.

Maxence and many MUR (Mouvements Unifiés de la Résistance) and FTP leaders, mostly left-wing, claimed that the big towns, Marseille and Avignon, should be heavily armed, without, as usual, having any constructive proposals to make as to how this should be done or what the townspeople would usefully do with the arms. On the other hand, the resistance in the country was achieving concrete results, though it too was divided through lack of leadership and conflicting directives. Algiers appeared to have the matter in hand and was about to send over new FFI commanders when the arrest and swift release of Louis Burdet (CIRCONFERENCE), the Regional Military Delegate, de Gaulle's Representative of the French Provisional Government, further exacerbated the situation. Although a delightful man, a London hotelier who Francis got to know well after the war, his freeing left everyone suspicious. Had he talked? Whatever the truth, he was finished and the region was leaderless.

What was certain was that Lécuyer controlled important mountain forces in the Alpes-Maritimes as well as east of the Basses-Alpes. The Durance Valley was left without a leader but Francis was near enough to this area to be able to give a directive to local leaders. The west of R2 was very largely under Pierre Michel (ARCHEDUKE) who was responsible for vital parachute operations in the Marseille region and especially the double landings above Apt – Spitfire and Lagarde Apt, one for dropping and one for landing – and, after Burdet, he became the new leader in all but name.

Why a resolution to these problems mattered hugely was because, although still not made known to those working in the south-east, the areas covered by R2, especially the Var, were vital to Allied planning; the landings of Operation ANVIL were going to be along its coastline.

As any advance inland would involve the Basses-Alpes and the Vaucluse, the lack of leadership troubled the Seventh Army planners of the amphibious landing force of some 50,000 men. General Alexander Patch, commanding, had already on 4 July made clear what he wanted from the FFI in their support of the advancing troops – 'a list of railway lines and roads, the cutting or controlling of which would obstruct German efforts to bring its southern occupation forces to focus on Marseille, Toulon and the beachhead'. This meant safeguarding the major routes from the Massif Central, Lyon, the Atlantic coast and Bordeaux, the Route Napoléon – from Grenoble to Nice – so named because the Emperor had followed it after his escape from Elba – and from Italy and the Franco-Italian passes.

Many of these routes involved JOCKEY areas and many of General Patch's strategic needs had already been set in motion by the Résistance but the absence of clear leadership and the problems of inter-communication between the various groups remained unresolved.

The lack of coordination centred on a lack of trust between Robert Rossi, (LEVALLOIS), an air force captain, the pro-Communist regional FFI chief, and the right-wing Captain Lécuyer. Then, in mid-July, tragedy scuppered well-meaning efforts to straighten out the situation.

Through betrayals the Gestapo managed to identify a number of Marseille Résistance leaders. They then learnt that the Basses-Alpes Liberation Committee planned to meet at Oraison on 16 July. The local Milice broke in on the gathering and arrested eight members. The next day Rossi was arrested with several others. Twenty-six in number, the prisoners were taken to a secluded spot some 24 kilometres north of Toulon and seven from the tiny hamlet of Signes: 'There on 18 July, in a natural hollow encircled by grubby shrubs and rocky outcroppings, all of them were shot and buried in shallow graves. The lonely grove, seldom visited, has been identified since as a melancholy memorial: the *Charnier de Signes* – the Sepulchre of Signes.'[5]

Thus, with Burdet released but powerless and Rossi dead, R2 lacked both a delegate and a military commander.

On 4 August Francis had met with Lécuyer and other local leaders to try to re-establish a logical command structure. 'But the discussions, stormy and prolonged, paralleled in micro-form the divisions of French society, right against left, politicians versus soldiers, and among the latter, divergent views of strategy and tactics . . . members of the Departmental Liberation Committee believed that, just as in normal times, the military should be subordinate to political control, many regular officers like Lécuyer viewed the committees as representing the same quarrelling political factions that had enfeebled the Third Republic.'

Much, then, rested on the new leaders from Algiers, still yet to arrive.

During the secret meeting in the woods near La Bâtie-Neuve, Paul Héraud had suggested to Christine that she should concentrate on the Poles at the frontier, an 'order' she took little time in translating into action. Stories had continued to abound about her and her unhurried nerve, for example:

> On one occasion she was trapped on a road with a German patrol in front of her. She was in full view so that any attempt at evasion or turning aside would have aroused their suspicions. She realised she had in her pocket one of the silk maps with which people who went into the field were often equipped by SOE – a map printed on very fine silk which could be easily carried or even crushed without coming to any harm. On an impulse, Christine whipped the map from her pocket, and tied it round her throat like a scarf where it looked perfectly normal and attracted no attention from the Germans.[6]

Francis had asked Paul Héraud to provide somewhere on the border that the Mission agents could fashion into a 'Headquarters' for their activities and as a fall-back position. Gilbert Galletti took on the task and found a site at Bramousse, above Guillestre and halfway to the frontier passes. Francis's clear advice to agents and leaders never changed – 'Before doing anything, make contact with Galletti!' Following the accord Paul Héraud had made with the *partigiani*, Christine used Bramousse constantly in her efforts to contact the Italians, not always at the cleverest moments: 'Just as the Germans had wreaked heavy damage on the French Resistance after the Normandy landings, so in Italy, as the Allies forged past Rome, the German forces in northern Italy needed to safeguard the passes – especially those of Tende, Larche and Mongenèvre – to make certain no flank attack moved against them across the French–Italian frontier.' Failing to meet her contacts, Christine tried to return to Bramousse which involved fifteen days of wandering through the ensuing 'battlefield'. At Bramousse everyone feared for her life to such an extent that Major Hamilton decided to go looking for her, but with no success. When she did finally turn up she only paused long enough to demand that parachuted arms should be sent to the partisans in their new valley. Then, once again, she was off.

Constant in her endeavours had been the need to employ her Polish to maximum effect and she decided to attempt to subvert the garrison in the fort held by the Germans at the Col de Larche, a 2000-foot pass dominating the surrounding terrain and the military route to Digne, having discovered that the fort was manned mainly by Poles from western Poland. It was a task made for her and she decided to climb to them.

According to her guide who drove her to the spot chosen to take her up through the dense larch forests shrouding the precipitous mountainside, her climb was a triumph of mind over matter. Though climbing steadily she would often slip through the deep carpet of sharp larch needles. When she returned her legs were bloody and swollen.

The climb took her a day and a half. Once in the lee of the fort she managed to attract the attention of her Polish contact there and then, with a loudhailer, she spoke to the Poles in their own language.[7]

Francis greatly admired the *inevitability* of Christine's behaviour: 'They asked her what they could do and she said, "Well, for a start you could take the breech blocks from the heavy guns, throw them away and render them useless. And when you come over bring as many mortars and machine guns as you can." Which they did – they were amenable to her charm, but, more important, they did it with immense enthusiasm! Don't forget they'd all been "recruited" on the strength of threats to their families and children. She was an avenging angel.'

Thus, on 13 August, she succeeded in 'demobbing' the sixty-three Poles in the German garrison at de Larche and leading them into the Résistance, an action which left the Maquis free to blow up the main road.

On the same day she learnt that Francis had been arrested.

Two days earlier and three days before the long awaited Allied landings on the south coast, Francis had received word that Algiers had finally sent over the new senior officers to fill the debilitating gaps at the head of R2. They were the impressive Colonel Widmer as the Regional Military Delegate, Commandant Amiot as the Military Director for the Vaucluse and Basses-Alpes and Colonel Constans as FFI Commander with an extended regional command. Again, in their wisdom, Algiers had woken up to a need, albeit, as Francis reported, 'too late to change the situation to any extent'.

As Senior Allied Liaison Officer, Francis felt he had to meet them and fill in details on the ground. For the experience, he took with him two newly arrived agents – Xan Fielding (CATHEDRALE) and a French officer, Commandant Sorenson (CHASUBLE), 'a suave, silent man with greying hair, neat dark features and a tired, urbane manner', but who limped having injured his leg on landing. The Red Cross car was driven by Claude Renoir, grandson of the painter Auguste Renoir, and nephew of Jean Renoir, the film-maker. They made for the parachute grounds at Lagarde Apt.

'Our drive,' wrote Fielding, 'was so uneventful and enjoyable that I had to keep on reminding myself that I was not on holiday but on active service – a fact which escaped me at each of the delightful villages, where, while "Roger" conferred with each of the local leaders, I drank a glass of wine outside the café under the plane trees.'[8]

The discussions with Constans and Widmer centred primarily on the role of Captain Jacques Lécuyer, who was left in charge of the eastern section of the region, Algiers not wanting any leftish plots against him to succeed. No mention at all was made of the date of the coming invasion, but the need to appoint Paul Héraud's successor was critical. Three possible candidates were considered – Paul's deputy, Etienne Moreaud, Colonel Daviron, the departmental ORA chief, and Captain Bertrand of the Gendarmerie. Francis favoured Bertrand because Moreaud possessed no military background and Daviron, while a career officer, had demonstrated little initiative. Finally, Constans chose Moreaud over Bertrand.

Before they left for the return trip to Seyne the next day, Francis was handed a large sum of money which was then divided between the three men – after months of extreme care, a bad mistake.

As they were about to enter Digne air raid sirens sounded and soldiers in German uniforms appeared, shouting and waving down road users. They were the 'Mongols' – units of Armenians, Georgians, Bashkirs and Tartars – belonging to the 'Oriental Legion against Communism' of the Wehrmacht. Illiterate and violent, none of them knew French or German. Although Francis felt secure with his 'genuine' forged papers as an official of the

Highways Department and Xan Fielding's as a manager of the Compagnie de l'Électricité at Nîmes, and with Commandant Sorenson travelling as a civilian, one 'Monsieur Chasuble', he was acutely aware of the unpredictability of the 'Mongols'. Claude Renoir was told to turn into a side street and drop his passengers away from the soldiers; they'd make their way by foot and meet him on the Seyne road the other side of town.

When the all-clear sounded, the three mingled with the crowds emerging from the shelters and casually joined the car waiting at the rendezvous. A narrow escape.

Almost immediately they saw a roadblock ahead manned by still more 'Mongols'. Their papers were 'read' and, as they were motioned on their way, a German car drew up behind them no doubt to order the dismantling of the roadblock

'Hold on,' warned Francis, 'Gestapo.'

A young civilian, obviously in charge, directed a stream of questions at Renoir, appeared satisfied, but suddenly insisted on checking Sorenson's and Francis's papers. Finding them in order he turned to Xan Fielding. Although French was Xan's mother tongue, it was rusty. He was told to hand over his (Algiers-prepared) papers, including the money from Lagarde Apt. The civilian asked why he was travelling to Gap.

'To see my parents.'

'Where is your home?'

'At Nîmes.'

'What is your job?'

'Employee at the Electricity Works.'

The civilian waved two documents.

'Why is this identity card out of date? And this one has no stamp?'

Xan, worried his faulty French might be more suspicious than the state of the documents, merely shrugged his shoulders. Asked to identify his travelling companions he said he had no idea who they were, he'd just been given a lift. At that point he was pushed back into the SD car and the young man turned again to Francis and Sorenson and ordered them to empty their pockets. Their wallets and identity papers were re-examined while Fielding was wordlessly pulled from the car; something was terribly wrong.

'You say these two men are total strangers to you?' repeated the young man.

'Never seen them before in my life,' replied Fielding.

'Can you gentlemen explain how it is that the money each of you is individually carrying belongs to the same series?'

Silence.

Claude Renoir was allowed to drive on, his genuine Red Cross papers saving him. While he sped back to Seyne with news of the calamity the three others were bundled into the SD car and driven to the central prison in Digne, 'a dreary barracks of a place,' according to Francis.

After being made to stand for some time facing a wall in the courtyard with their hands above their heads, they were pushed into a basement cell, furnished with a half-filled bucket of excrement and urine, and four dirty bunks in two tiers, one of which was occupied by a recumbent figure, obviously a plant. The three did not speak to each other until it was safe to do so; exhausted, they slept.

For twenty-four hours they were denied food or water before being transferred to the official Gestapo headquarters at the Villa Marie-Louise on the riverside at Digne. The very small building was notorious as the place where *résistants* were taken to be tortured.

Individually, they were interrogated again. Francis judged the young man, addressed always as 'Herr Max', not to be a native French speaker, perhaps Alsatian and not particularly bright, his questions 'stupid' and obviously generally badly informed.

'As I watched them with admiration,' Xan Fielding recalled, 'I could not help wondering if they were genuinely less frightened than I was, and if not, how they were able to conceal their feelings with such a brilliant display of self-assurance.'[9] Xan Fielding was the only one to be treated roughly – punched in the face and kidneys by SD thugs. Much to their relief, the three were reunited but they had no chance of escape before they were returned to the main prison. They had all pretended they were on a black market deal – but they were not believed.

> They thought we were resistance people but there was no way they could check that. Since October 1943 we'd seen that armed resistance could cut the Germans off from all contact with their main HQ and after 6 June they did just that and any contact, except by large convoys, became impossible. It was now 13 August, their communications had been virtually nonexistent for a couple of months. They were isolated. Of course we were in danger, in any case we were a nuisance. Having questioned but not tortured us, it had obviously been decided it was better to execute us, get rid of us. We would be shot as spies. That was determined.

16

Early on the morning of 13 August, Christine, returning from the Italian border to Seyne, found a grim scene at M. Turrel's house. Dr Jouve and other members of the team were discussing the chances of raiding the prison at Digne but she knew force was not the answer. Besides, there was so little time or transport available to organise it thoroughly; groups were highly active or poised for the landings. Reluctantly, Dr Jouve agreed.

Already Albert had signalled Algiers to stand by. M. Turrel was convinced that once the Germans discovered they had caught the keenly sought 'Roger', he would be moved to Lyon, or murdered out of hand.

Taking the initiative, Christine cycled the 40 kilometres to Digne to recce the situation. Before she left Dr Jouve gave her the name of a possible double agent. It was a dangerous offer: the man was a captain in the Gendarmerie.

Christine's manifold gifts did not include mastery of bicycles: she feared them as others fear horses. Yet, in the next thirty-six hours, refusing Claude Renoir's offer to drive her there, she nevertheless rode to Digne and back and walked throughout one entire night After she had left, John Roper arrived from Briançon, equally distraught at the news yet knowing, like the others, that all he could do was to sit and wait.

The first check Christine made was to find out if Francis and the others had already been moved away. Wearing a dark scarf, tied peasant-fashion round her face – a cover she'd used on countless occasions on the frontier – she slipped in through the gates and joined the milling crowd seeking news of relatives held inside. As she circled the 'dreary barracks of a place' she hummed loudly the tune of 'Frankie and Johnny', a song she and Francis both liked and had often sung together to keep their spirits up when climbing or driving. For some time there was no response, then, suddenly, someone was singing, or rather bellowing the words; it was Francis.

> 'Hearing her singing . . . was simply an awareness of presence. Yes, her presence if you like could mean there was a possibility of being saved but it was . . . merely a chance. You see, I'd had the experience with Cecily Lefort when, after her arrest, I tried to do everything I could and it was just impossible – to stop her being deported to Ravensbrück. I was very aware of the strong feelings involved – that if you could possibly help the person you would, but enormous obstacles still . . . as far as I was concerned, hearing Christine was simply her saying "I love you".'

Christine's next step was to find out if she could visit Francis; no one was interested and no help was offered. The Germans did not allow visits. Despite the risk, Dr Jouve's double agent seemed her only chance. Having traced his office, she demanded an audience.

Because Captain Albert Schenck, an Alsatian, spoke fluent German, he acted as a liaison officer between the Préfecture and the Gestapo; therefore he knew everyone. Although for obvious reasons the scenes that follow cannot be retold in absolute detail, their gist has passed into SOE legend.

Christine attacked from the start. She knew the tactic – *impress the French, never implore*. She admitted the Gestapo had arrested three very important Allied agents. One of them was her husband, while she herself, a British agent, was a niece of Field Marshal Montgomery. Schenck must know the Allies had landed and that very soon they would be at Digne where things would go very badly for anyone involved in the death of her husband and his friends and he could be absolutely sure that if the soldiers didn't shoot him, the *résistants* would take great pleasure in arranging his death – if only to avenge the murder of so many of their comrades.

Schenck knew that there were rumours of the Allied landings. He decided to call her bluff. He himself could do nothing but there was a man, a Belgian, one Max Waem, who was 'officially' the interpreter for the Gestapo. He *could* help but to make his intervention worthwhile would cost two million francs. Unflinching, Christine told him to fix a meeting with M. Waem and she'd see what she could do, knowing that a major part of the £10,000 would make its way into Albert Schenck's wallet. Coolly, she told him that if he reneged on the deal she would shoot him personally; no one interfered with her leaving.

Back at Seyne, Albert reported Algiers' concern and Brooks Richards urgently wanted to know how he could help. The answer was simple – they needed two million francs, the price for Francis's life, and immediately a dropping zone was organised.

By 4 p.m. the following day Christine was in Frau Schenk's flat waiting for Max Waem, masking her impatience, knowing that time could be running out fast for the three men. Waem arrived, small, with aquiline features, in Gestapo uniform. For three hours Christine attacked with the same devastating bluff she'd used on Schenk – the Allies would arrive at any moment, she was in constant contact with the British forces – and as proof she threw some broken and useless W/T crystals on to the table between them: the Germans could not communicate with each other, the Allies could.

Waem stayed silent. Christine repeated the same threats she'd used to turn Schenk – if anything should happen to her husband, or his friends, the consequences would be swift and fatal. He surely knew that his reputation, like that of the Capitaine, guaranteed no reprieve.

Waem finally spoke. If he got them out, how would she protect him?

In the name of the British authorities Christine gave her word that if he did get the three out of prison everything would be done to protect him from death. As soon as the Allies reached Digne she would make sure he was protected in every way; what he would have done would save him.

Waem nodded his agreement.

At best she knew, after hours of argument, she had only won a reprieve for Francis and the money had to arrive before Waem changed his mind. Again, unhindered, she marched out.

On the night of 15 August – the day of the Allied landings on the south coast – the money was dropped to Seyne, the fastest SOE response on record.

What specific deal was struck between Schenk and Waem before the money was handed over remains confused. The accounts left by those involved vary quite considerably, but, again, the main moments are clear.

Christine must have trusted the arrangements because she would only have handed the money over if she were sure the three men were still alive. Most accounts agree that she reminded them of the gun in her bag. Given the ragged state of German communications already mentioned, whether news of the Riviera landings having taken place was a factor that sharpened their resolve will never be known. Success hung on the degree of Waem's terror.

*

In their cell the three men were surprised to be served a decent meal of vegetable soup and brown bread; it felt ominous. Use of their cyanide pills was not contemplated even though they were convinced they were 'going to the wall'. This was translated into certainty when the cell was unlocked and Max Waem stood there, revolver at the ready. He ordered them out.

'He now wore over his civilian trousers a Wehrmacht tunic,' wrote Xan Fielding, 'which invested him with the same air of formality and ceremonial gravity as the black cap on the head of a judge.'[1]

Francis was the last to file out and, to his silent amazement, Waem complimented him on his wife: 'what a wonderful woman you have'.

Waem was saluted by guards as they headed for the prison gates. 'But,' runs Xan Fielding's account, 'outside the prison gates, instead of turning left towards the football pitch which apparently the firing squads normally used, he led us in the opposite direction, walking with Roger by his side while Chasuble and I followed a few paces behind. A thin drizzle, darkening sky – three against one – our last chance of escape? – all seemed to be happening outside myself.

'After a few hundred yards we drew level with a waiting car and were ordered – "Quick, get in, all three of you!!" He got in beside the driver and we were away.'[2]

They sailed through a roadblock, thanks to Waem's uniform, only to stop later at an isolated building round the first bend in the road. A single figure stood there, outlined against the white wall – Christine. She squeezed into the front seat.

Presently, on the edge of a steep embankment, the car stopped Waem leapt out and motioned Fielding to follow. 'We slither down to the river bed and bury his uniform jacket. We get back in, the car drives towards the mountains and Christine turns and smiles; we realise we are free!'[3]

One last word from Xan Fielding. 'As an individual Christine would not have hesitated to barter her own life for the lives of three others; as an agent, however, she was obliged to assess the value of those lives against hers and if it were proved to be worth more, it was her duty to keep it.

'In the assessment she made, it was Roger's life that weighed the scales in favour of the decision she took; for in comparison Chasuble's and mine were of small account. Had Roger not been arrested with us, Christine would have been perfectly justified in taking no action if action meant jeopardising herself. Indirectly, then, I owe my life to him as much as I do directly to her.'[4]

'Did we say anything to each other? I don't remember any conversations. Just holding her hand. It was part of the relationship.

John Roper was in love with Christine and John and I were old friends. So that in every sense I wouldn't exhibit my love for Christine in front of him. We were three people together who understood each other and that was it. And the others were hardly in the picture.

That quotation about Christine's motives . . . yes, I think it's reasonable to say that, but I haven't read the book.

It was like that night of possible death in the Vercors, it was simply something that was happening, there was absolutely nothing you could do to avoid it. Everything was stacked against you. What do I think she felt for me?'

A long pause.

'I think she was very much in love with me. And I felt as much for her as she did for me. And this was before she saved my life which she did partly because she was in love with me but not entirely. We'll come to the way she was treated after the war and the wider repercussions and my role in it, but I know it was and is possible to be *totally* in love with two people at one and the same time. I know it's possible, I've been there.'

'Thinking back about very strong feelings, deep emotions, yesterday . . . was a bit unusual.'

Days later, Albert Schenck was executed by the Résistance and the fate of the ransom money left ironically unclear. However, in July 1945, Francis was contacted by the Foreign Office when Mme Schenck, apparently unaware that her husband had been a double agent, yet pleading that her flat had been used to secure the release of the British agents, sought a certificate from the British authorities to legitimise notes she was trying to cash in post-war banks while being unable to explain how she'd come by the money. She failed, but Francis and Christine helped her to return to Alsace with her family.

Christine's promise to Waem was honoured. He was handed over to the British Parachute Brigade and then sent by the British Field Security

Police to Bari in southern Italy. He even offered to take part in action in the Far East but after the war he was repatriated to Belgium.

Utter jubilation greeted their arrival at Seyne twice over – they were free and the landings in the south had taken place and American troops now controlled a great semi-circular beachhead, 50 miles east and west of St Tropez, extending 50 miles into the interior. What had happened on 15 August?

Hampered somewhat by inclement weather, by dawn of the 15th more than seven thousand paratroopers from the First Airborne Task Force and the British Second Independent Parachute Brigade had taken Le Muy, just south of Draguignan, the Prefectoral seat of the Var *département*. The Germans, having concentrated their defences round Toulon and Marseille and access to the Rhône Valley, had left the smaller towns with garrisons of a thousand men more or less trapped there by the Maquis. On the eve of the landings a major radar installation at Fayence had already been entirely destroyed, and many OGs and agents, flown in with the advance forces, joined the Maquis in uprooting anti-glider stakes – known as Rommel's asparagus – planted in the fields. As a result there was a loss of barely 4 per cent of the Task Force which had come in with 220 vehicles, 213 artillery pieces and 1000 tons of equipment. But the quick fall of Draguignan meant that, by 17 August, General Patch had landed unopposed at St Tropez with 100,000 men and 10,000 vehicles at his disposal. The full drive east, west and north could begin.

One of Francis's favourite human beings, Havard Gunn (BAMBOOS), with whom Christine had trained in Algiers, was in Valberg, some 80 kilometres north of Draguignan, working with Captain Lécuyer, now the FFI chief for the Alpes-Maritimes, when they received Alert Messages of the imminent landings. He insisted they should make contact with the landing forces as soon as possible to inform them of the situation in the north and east. Unaware of what Christine was doing in Digne, he hoped also to reach some American troops and persuade them to help rescue Francis.

Resplendent in his regimental kilt, together with Lécuyer and two FFI scouts, Gunn drove south in a tiny Peugeot on 16 August and reached General Frederick, the commander of the First Airborne Task Force, which was soon to be relieved by the Infantry. 'Why are you hanging around,' demanded the major. 'I've just driven 50 miles and not met a single German. The Route Napoléon is clear. If you don't believe me, I'll turn round and drive in front of your fellows all the way back.' Intrigued, General Frederick ordered a detachment of armoured jeeps to accompany the two officers up to the Route Napoléon It was indeed clear.

While Captain Lécuyer left for Nice, Gunn drove on up to Castellane, newly liberated, and then south to Callas. Quickly passed from level to level, he dined with General Dahlquist, was then directed to General Truscott who finally conferred with General Patch. He was believed. General Patch could now plan for the Rhône Valley push, knowing his right flank – the Route Napoléon – was clean. The west bank of the Rhône would be the responsibility of the French First Army under General de Lattre de Tassigny. The Résistance's scorn for the need to hang around for ninety days was wholly vindicated. To 'secure' the Route Napoléon, General Butler's Task Force, consisting of some 3000 troops and 1000 vehicles, was ordered to push north to Grenoble. Within a matter of days, Sisteron and Digne were liberated.

Major Gunn, having learnt that Francis had been freed, returned happily to Captain Lécuyer's command post at Thorenc, bringing with him six trucks loaded with captured German arms and other supplies offered by the Americans for resistance groups along the Route Napoléon. He and Captain Lécuyer then set off to cooperate with the Allied forces as they drove eastwards towards the Italian border.

One other factor, besides proud Maquis assurance, helped to convince General Patch that the route was clear and in fact governed a great deal of his subsequent decision making.

On 17 August, coders and decipherers working on the captured German Enigma machine at Bletchley Park in England, had intercepted a signal from German High Command ordering all forces in southern France to begin a withdrawal *except those defending Marseille and Toulon*. The message marked ULTRA – the top secret classification – meant no officer below General Patch was privy to it and, once delivered, it was instantly destroyed. Its existence remained secret until 1975.

Three salient features of Hitler's order were:

1. Withdrawal of all forces from southern France, with 11th Panzer Division as rearguard of Nineteenth Army in Rhône Valley.
2. Defence of Franco-Italian border by LXII Corps, with 148th Division (Cannes area) and 157th Division (Grenoble area) protecting eastern flank of Nineteenth Army.
3. Protection of port cities of Marseille and Toulon 'to the last man'.[5]

With the LXII Corps already captured, with General de Lattre de Tassigny intent on reviving the glory of the French army via Marseille and Toulon, and with General Dahlquist's division able to move up and support General Butler's Task Force if necessary, liberation through pursuit could now begin in earnest.

Back in Digne only days after his release, Francis, together with Xan Fielding, joined in the liberation celebrations with more than a touch of wryness; lucky to be alive, there was the distinct possibility that their war could be over. As agents, their function had been to help prepare and arm those Frenchmen who wanted to liberate their country, which they were now doing with commitment, ferocity and intelligence. SOE agents were not soldiers, they were *enablers* and Francis, with all his experience, knew that, under such circumstances, a senior military rank in the Secret Army was no job or place for a foreigner.

Together they searched for the SOE representative, Captain Banbury, who had travelled with the Butler Task Force, but he was in Seyne. There, meeting by chance, he was able to bring Francis up to date, explaining the aims of the Task Force and General Patch's strategy. General Butler was at Sisteron and Francis decided to report to him there immediately with Christine. 'When we knew that the landings had taken place, that Patch had created the Butler unit and sent it up through the Alps; we knew things were all right! This was our victory! This is what we foresaw in October 1943! And it was absolutely bloody marvellous!'

This point was also the parting of the ways for the three men who had shared the death-cell in Digne. Xan Fielding left for Greece and Commandant Sorenson took up a senior position in intelligence in Paris.

His confidence in the Résistance justifiably sky-high, Francis descended from Seyne to Sisteron to pay his respects and offer his assistance. Although after the war General Butler would praise the Résistance, there was a grudging tone to his words: 'It is only fair to state that without the Maquis our mission would have been far more difficult.' However, in his fine book *Hidden Ally*, which deals with the French Resistance, Special Operations and the landings in southern France in 1944 from an American angle, the American historian Arthur Layton Funk quotes the following from the historian of the 117th Cavalry:

> We were beginning to meet more and more Maquis. The groups we were meeting were better trained, better disciplined and more heavily armed.

> Their assistance is invaluable, *as they mop up the rough country between the roads up which we advance*. Their enthusiasm and sincere desire to be of assistance is most gratifying. Unfortunately the commanding officer of the Task Force lacks confidence in them, with the result that they are not being employed as well as they might be. The information which they give to us as to enemy movements ahead has, up to this time, proved accurate in composition and timely to within six hours.[6]

One more important fact has to be fed into the confrontation about to take place. Colonel Constans (Saint Sauveur), who Francis and the others had travelled to see prior to their arrest, now, as FFI head in the region, contacted General Butler to work out ways in which the FFI could be deployed alongside the Task Force. Butler felt comfortable with him: 'Officers of the old French army were coming in now,' he wrote, 'and the assistance of these trained officers was invaluable.' Constans is the single French officer referred to by name – but only by his field name – in Butler's memoirs. They worked out liaison plans which would prove fruitful but, on Butler's side, it was obviously military man speaking to military man that called forth respect. On the same day, 20 August, Francis and Christine, in makeshift uniforms, presented themselves to General Butler: 'I said to him he might have been told of me and if there was any way I could be of help – at which point he told me to bugger off, he didn't want anything to do with private armies, bandits, and turned back to his maps.'

The two are literally thrown out.

> 'Granted, Christine and I were a pretty scruffy looking couple – all kinds of insignia, pips on one shoulder and none on the other – but that hardly excused his conduct. He might have been fanatically anti-British. Perhaps he simply didn't like the look of our faces. The advance had been so quick, presumably there had been little chance of alerting troops as to Résistance behaviour. I've touched on this before – it's not individuals who are necessarily wrong but what is is the State Department's complete lack of basic understanding of the complexities and responsibilities involved in "occupation". Yes, they should at least know who is on their side and you don't have to be dismissive of something you don't understand. But the unchanging legacy of such an attitude will be Vietnam and Iraq.
>
> When we came out we were pretty cross and had to be calmed down

by one of his intelligence aides who apologised for Butler's behaviour. I wasn't far from a major insubordination!'

From an American point of view, Arthur Funk's comment is relevant:

> The historian can only deplore Butler's short-sightedness in ignoring the one Allied officer who knew more about terrain and the people in it than anyone else. Granted that Constans, Widmer and others had competence as liaison officers with the Resistance, but none of them had lived in France, like Cammaerts, for most of the previous eighteen months. None had travelled so widely or knew more French patriots. Clearly Butler preferred to deal with the French military officers, but he could have done this without losing the counsel and support offered by one of the SOE's most capable agents.

At Butler's HQ Christine and Francis learnt of the imminent move to liberate Gap and, helped by a Task Force officer, they were able to reach the town before the advance troops began their attack, only, like the Americans, to discover that by 6.30 that evening the Germans had already surrendered, Serge Barret having persuaded them that it was all over. While the population went wild, German troops were herded into a cinema and guarded by Boy Scouts as FFI groups, from all directions, descended into the municipal square to join in the celebrations. At some point, above the town, Francis and Christine had got out of their jeep and rolled down the steep hillside, unbridled, like a couple of ten-year-olds.

When the tanks arrived the next day expecting a battle, there was little for them to do but head a parade. But as the *résistants* marched with them, tears poured down the faces of every man and woman; Paul Héraud, the one person who should have been there – to whom the liberation truly belonged – was absent.

'Yes, I wept. We all wept. You know what I felt about him.'

A long silence.

'We named my only son after him. Paul.'

A half-excuse for General Butler's behaviour possibly rested on the fact that Gap itself still lay in the danger zone. Intelligence reports that Francis could have relayed to him, and Constans most certainly did, anticipated a German counter-attack over the Col Bayard just above Gap and on the road to Grenoble. At the same time General Butler and his main Task Force had been ordered westwards towards the Rhône to join the main push and he was concerned his forward troops would be insufficient to face a full-scale counter-attack. He was to take up his next HQ in Aspres, ready to move down the Drôme, but called in on Gap, delighted at the sight of so many German prisoners. He promised help over sending the prisoners to the rear and made reinforcements available to Captain Piddington, his Troop Commander, for the defence of the Col. In the event when the Germans did attack at 10 a.m. the next day, they had turned and fled by 10.15. The three hundred men were pursued and captured and added to the pool of prisoners.

But Francis, Christine and Captain Piddington had already solved the problem posed by the thousand or so prisoners, several hundred of whom were Poles – turn them.

In the large, improvised camp in a meadow near Tallard, Christine, given a megaphone, slight, passionate, addressed them in Polish and Russian:

> 'She asked them – were they willing to fight with us? We could give them some rifles but they had to take their uniforms off because under the Geneva Convention you weren't allowed to fight in a foreign uniform – we have no others to offer you, so you'll have to go forward *torse-nu* [naked to the waist]; and they tore them off, exultant! The Col de Larche all over again.
>
> Captain Piddington said you'd better go and see Butler because we can't really do this without his permission, and that was reasonable enough. So we went again to his HQ to try and get his authorisation but he wouldn't see us and just sent out word saying, "You've been buggering my prisoners about – if you don't get out of here I'll have you put in prison yourselves!"
>
> Again, we were both very very angry. No, I never saw the man again.'

A sympathetic Intelligence Officer once more apologised and suggested that they should go down and report to General Patch in Draguignan.

What they were about to be asked to do by General Patch, together with the attempt to recruit the Poles at Gap, would bring to an end all of Francis and Christine's efforts as SOE agents to rally the Résistance east of the Rhône. They were about to exchange their private battlefields for the long journey into nostalgia.

17

If any proof were needed of the collapse and surrender of the German forces before the Allied push up the lower Rhône Valley it was there, metres high by the roadside, military armour of every kind burnt, overturned, abandoned, defiles of equally broken prisoners in their hundreds straggling past the twisted symbols of their former arrogance and control, shepherded to the sides of the N7 to keep access for the victors free. Francis and Christine touched on this khaki route at Montélimar before cutting across country to Draguignan.

The bridges over the Rhône and its tributaries – the Roubion, the Drôme and the Isère – had been targets for incessant bombing in the fortnight up to D-Day, especially bridges over the Drôme between Crest and the confluence with the Rhône at Loriol and Livron; long JOCKEY country. On 13 August the Americans had bombed the railway bridge at Crest, missing the bridge – which in any case had been rendered useless by the Résistance two months earlier – but inflicting huge damage on the civilian population: 550 killed, 713 wounded, together with the destruction of 1221 buildings.[1] On 16 August they had been back to bomb the two bridges at Livron, one a road bridge, the other carrying the railway: this time they had been more accurate and they had left the highway bridge to the Résistance.[2] The destruction of its massive southern stone arch, leaving a gap of 35 metres, has passed into legend in the Drôme: 'They did a wonderful job because they made a hole wider by one metre than any equipment carried by the Germans could span, so they couldn't cross the river. Caterpillar tracks could manage the shingle but not wheeled vehicles. And that was what blocked the German retreat and set the scene for the battle of Montélimar.'

The battle of Montélimar – which saw the withdrawal of the Germans on 28 August – had always been about control of the N7, but although they had lost over 2000 vehicles and 300 pieces of artillery, they were by no means defeated. In spite of huge assemblage of fire power by the Americans, the Germans managed to keep the Allied forces at bay long enough to get General Blaskowitz's Army Group, which still counted 130,000 men, including the almost intact 11th Panzer Division, across the Drôme river and northwards towards Lyon. The retreating troops stretched over 160 kilometres.

Often, in the pursuit of the German retreat, delays occurred and, with no blame, pointed up differences in approach. The FFI used guerrilla tactics – rapid attack with small arms and grenades and a hasty retreat. The Americans preferred to bring in artillery, set up observation posts and call up the batteries, a tactic that lost time and any element of surprise. Nevertheless, the progress of the two forces, which had united at the liberation of Avignon on 25 August, was remorseless.

Francis and Christine were cordially received by General Patch who indicated that his main anxiety was the protection of his left flank on the west bank of the Rhône Valley and, appreciating their status and know-how, asked them to act as his liaison team with the Résistance forces in the Gard, Ardèche and Rhône right up to Lyon. It seemed an unnecessary caution for it was an area already assigned to the French First Army and they could easily establish their own liaison Missions. But, willingly, they returned to their jeep and made for Avignon.

> 'Of the two or three columns we met we simply asked the people guarding the prisoners where they were going and had there been any threats from German forces moving that way. None. What in fact the Germans had done was to move westwards and link up with the forces going up the west side of the Massif Central and on the way committing atrocities like Oradour-sur-Glane.[3] At any largish town we'd stop and ask the new authorities if there were any information on troop movements, they'd say "no", so we'd get back in the jeep and make for the next one. Between Avignon and St Etienne we stopped, say, half a dozen times and always got the same answer. So on we'd drive and those were long summer days . . .
>
> St Etienne was liberated before we got there but we by-passed it on our way to Lyon. Nobody checked on us.'

After the battle of Meximieux, north-east of Lyon, Lyon itself was abandoned by the Germans and the sadistic power base of Klaus Barbie liberated on 3 September. Apart from isolated, demented Milice snipers still firing from windows and rooftops at the giddy celebrations, in quieter moments the memory of Jean Moulin still caught at the throat.

> 'There were parties but it wasn't feasting. The war was still going on. The tragedy of Poland was driving Christine mad with impotence and impatience. But, generally, it was a huge sense of relief everywhere; it meant people just walking in the streets and being able to do the *normal* things they'd been denied before. There was a certain irritation, too, at American excesses – loading surrendered German prisoners with oranges – fruit that had hardly been seen locally for four years – or them destroying things they no longer needed, but which others could have made much use of, like a depot of undergarments burning 50 tons of wool – something the local population could neither understand nor forgive; a total lack of appreciation of real needs. There was a terrible consistency in this kind of incomprehension.
>
> I am not anti-American, but it seemed at that time I was always having to explain them to the French. I was intensely irritated, but, as I've said, they had been so little prepared and one must not forget the change they brought about by coming into the war or the bravery they showed and sacrifices they made in the North.'

Lyon was the limit of Francis and Christine's remit. They arrived in the seething town a day after its liberation and stayed for forty-eight hours. One special friend looked up was Sylviane Rey who had miraculously escaped from the massacre of the Grotte de la Luire. She vividly remembered Christine: 'I teased her about the number plate of the jeep in which they were driving around – it was MI5. We had luncheon together, chatting like parakeets, then we walked to the Place Morland where she suddenly discovered a run in her stocking. She was upset, as nylons in those days were as rare as snowballs in summer. Luckily I was in a position to provide her with a new pair. She was delighted. She was very feminine and fastidious about her appearance.'[4]

After Grenoble the pair reported to the Bristol Hotel in Paris where they were told the quickest way back to the UK was via the formidable SOE agent Richard Heslop (XAVIER)'s HQ, north-east of Lyon, but even for that they would have to wait. In the next ten days Francis drove a Mercedes from Paris to the south-east and back three or four times to distribute SOE moneys to widows and families of those who had worked specifically for

SOE units and who were at first excluded from French help. They had contributed in ways which had stopped them from taking part in other kinds of resistance action and people were critical of them for having apparently 'refused' to conceal weapons or radios or whatever. It all needed straightening out locally and this Francis could and did do.

Once money had been allocated to SOE during its existence, it will be recalled, it was never audited and therefore had to be used; like SOE's very existence its finances were secret:

> 'On my first visit to the treasurer of SOE, he simply hauled out two million francs that had been put aside for the JOCKEY circuit and said, distribute it to orphans and widows most in need but be careful no one knows about it. I was very careful because nothing would have offended de Gaulle's plans for social control more than finding out that foreigners were providing much needed services!
>
> Another problem, little understood, was that the French organisations like Libération, etc, and the FFI gave ranks to all their chaps. I didn't, it wasn't my job to do that. All the people I'd recruited had later been told you belong to the FFI now but they were "unregistered", on no one's books, and that needed me to say to local people "don't worry, they belonged to the FFI".

> 'But it was time to play! In Paris we met up with Jacques Langlois. The Langlois family hasn't featured too much in our story but they were all excellent. Jacques, Michel and Suzanne were, like Jacques Latour and Pierre Agapov, residues of the CARTE organisation, with whom I was happy to work without having to worry about them having been infected by the ridiculous Girard. They were paid 2000 francs a month (£20) with no expenses. They travelled and received the kind of hospitality I did and never asked me for money. Suzanne married Pierre Raynaud (ALAIN) but later, sadly, committed suicide. God – if I'd had the chance to talk to her she'd have stayed miles away from the man.
>
> Jacques had a friend who was a horse trainer and we met him at what was the first race meeting after the Liberation at Auteuil. The friend said I would like to say thank you in a real way. I've trained a horse which is running and it's going to win at 40–1. You can't ignore a tip like that! I had 100 francs, put it all on the nose, it won and suddenly I had 4000 francs. So I said to my friends – let's go and have a night out and celebrate on my winnings! Nancy Fraser-Campbell loaned me her kilt, we had

a wonderful meal, then off we went to a nightclub where I danced on the table and we all staggered back God knows when, the whole caboodle having cost about 5000 francs! Lovely.'

Francis's original trip to Grenoble was partly due to a need to check what had happened to the Vercors and the Allied Missions and it was on meeting again with Lieutenant-Colonel François Huet, newly in command of the FFI in the Isère and the Drôme, that he learnt of the 'escape' of Longe and Houseman (see pp.158–165). The deeply conservative, devoutly Catholic soldier informed him they'd 'fucked off' and taken Gustave Boissière with them, he who had been so invaluable to Huet. André Pecquet, the bi-lingual American, had stayed with him as his radio operator and was now his liaison officer with the Americans. Not one to blush in the telling of any tale, on this occasion Huet blushed. The reason?

Even in those early days of the Liberation, de Gaulle was doing all he could to minimise the role anyone else had played in the freeing of France; that included the Allies and, of course, SOE F Section – i.e. the British. Huet blushed because the behaviour of Longe and Houseman, which was outside normal military practice, justified de Gaulle's attitude in his eyes, yet he also knew of the real contribution SOE agents within his compass had made and he was facing one of the best of them at that very moment.

> 'We as foreigners had a very sensitive role and one that many agents failed to observe and definite mistakes were subsequently made, e.g. they gave orders and they shouldn't have done, and in so doing justified de Gaulle's irritation and anger. Pierre Raynaud in the south Drôme took a military command which, as an SOE officer, he should never have done. Yes, he was very young but it was Maurice Buckmaster's mistake in recruiting him in the first place because there was an agreement with de Gaulle's committee not to recruit French citizens.
>
> My relationships with Zeller and Descour had been much more in the nature of fellow officers who were doing a job together, whereas with Huet it was more a case of, I will do what I can to help. He wasn't warm with anyone at that time; it wasn't prejudice, it was just his nature. That was what made the blushing so special.'

After the horror of the Vercors, Huet's job had been to look after and use those elements of the armed Résistance who had correctly stayed on the plateau rather than attempt to escape. He thus still commanded two to three thousand men. The whole of France was not yet liberated and probably 50 per cent of his men, as elsewhere, wanted to join a French army bent on pursuing and clearing the Germans from France. The remaining 50 per cent were urgently needed at home, on farms, in rebuilding, in local politics, etc. Leaders guiding the FFI had to make sure no disasters had been overlooked and then to help the men in their decisions – army or home.

Because the pace of change was hectic. With Paris liberated and his Provisional Government installed, de Gaulle lost no time in liquidating the FFI and bringing irregular units under fresh army control. Regions R1 and R2 – JOCKEY country – became once more traditional military districts and so, for many of the Maquis, as for Francis and Christine, 3 September marked the point where the armed struggle and personal sacrifice for the Liberation of the south-east of France came to a successful and joyous end. The heroic days were over.

Two achievements remained utterly clear in Francis's mind whenever the immediate post-war situation in south-east France is considered. The first was a certain justifiable pride in the part JOCKEY had played in clearing the Route Napoléon and the closing off of German access via the Alpine frontier passes. General Eisenhower and General de Gaulle paid tribute to this south-east activity in shortening the war by some months and both governments have as a result rewarded Francis and others with high honours.

In January 1945. André Malraux hailed the clearing of the road as a major repayment that the Résistance had made to the Allies, 'which amply made up for the admirable help that English (he means "British") parachute operations had brought us for so long. We must not forget that the Allies did help us; that we were armed by them; that without them we would have had nothing. At the present moment, in this respect, France can be grateful, but Résistance owes no debt.'[5]

Secondly, that achievement was matched by Francis's admiration for the seamless civil takeover after the Liberation. Within forty-eight hours of the last German fleeing a town or area, Gaullist administrators were in place – food and fuel were available, the Préfectures ran – the stunning legacy of Jean Moulin.

The powerful agents of the transformation were the Commissaires de la République and side by side with them mention must be made of a good friend – Eugène Chavant (Clement), the 'Préfet' of the Republic of the Vercors:

'He was a small, four-square man with natural authority; people didn't question him. In the communities and organisations which ran and eventually restored the Vercors he was a hugely respected, smiling presence, energetic and always knowing where to go to get things done. He had no problems with Central Government because of his friendship with Yves Farge, who was going to be a Minister in the new government. He established the Pionniers (Pioneers) of the Vercors and was determined they should raise the resources to restore as much as they could out of the ruins and the terrible losses. I don't know how the money was made available, nationally or internationally, but it must have been considerable and more than probably due to Yves Farge. There was an awful lot of self-help and, just as they had looked after and fed six thousand troops for nearly two months, so they were able to get things back on their feet with smaller numbers. Dwellings and replacing livestock would take time, yes, but there were the untouched markets and the local and neighbouring peasantry as helpful as they had been from the start.

Three years later I went back to the Vercors and three-quarters of the work had already been done. Not only was there a fresh smell in the air, they were living ordinary lives again.

Résistance leaders were not of a type. Eugène Chavant, Paul Héraud were *unusual* – interestingly, neither ever used the titles of any of the organisations of the Résistance they belonged to in their area. But there were other outstanding leaders and, for the reasons we've covered, not necessarily Gaullist.

De Gaulle showed his individual flair in often giving authority to people he must have disliked; he used them to realise his own vision. Most of the Commissaires I knew or knew of came from the other end of the religious and political spectrum from de Gaulle. For example, Raymond Aubrac and his incomparable wife Lucie, who became the Commissaire in Marseille. His parents died in Auschwitz; he was both Jewish and a Communist and was personally picked out by Jean Moulin. No, de Gaulle's objective was to show the Americans how wrong they were about him and to put the French Republic back on its feet – that was what mattered.

Yet the emergence of Paul Héraud and Eugène Chavant belongs to the realm of mystery. Why did it happen? How did one man in Gap achieve an unquestionable authority which was never challenged by anyone?

I'm often asked, would he have gone on after the war to involve himself further? I believe that as soon as it was possible, which would have been very quickly after the freeing of the Hautes-Alpes, he would have gone back to his studio and his craft. He would have gone back to his young mountaineers to lead that life which he enjoyed enormously and knew how to achieve. He was a very fine looking man who must have been very attractive to women but as far as I know women meant nothing in his life, nor men. Friendship was something he knew all about and I'm quite sure he knew the effect he was having on me – a young twenty-seven-year-old. He knew that and that was why he gave me his full trust and confidence; he knew that was instinctively the right thing to do. As he did with others.

'With François Huet I was still officially a British officer; with Yves Farge I was a friend. Yves was an example of a certain kind of human being who was in some ways post-First World War. He had a passionate need to listen to good music, look at beautiful things, as did his wife who was called by friends "Fargette". They were a delightful couple who enjoyed the kind of things my father had taught me to enjoy. He didn't want to become professionally involved in politics but like a lot of people in leading positions he was pushed into it by an awareness that he had knowledge and control that others didn't possess and he could help them by it. Through my pacifism I felt a close fraternity with Yves although he was probably six to seven years older than I was.'

Yves Farge's career touched the Résistance at most of its important stages of development. A journalist, after the Armistice he worked on the first newspapers, then contributed to the founding of the Francs-Tireurs movement where he caught the eye of Jean Moulin who charged him with helping to militarily organise the Vercors. He was a member of the first cadre of the Secret Army and, after the arrests of General Delestraint and Jean Moulin, he chaired the Committee of Action against Deportation (CAD); within the framework of STO that meant making and distributing false food and work cards and collecting funds for the Maquis.

In April 1944 he became a Commissaire for the Rhône-Alpes area where he was responsible for eight *départements*. On 21 August, twelve days before the liberation of Lyon, he succeeded in persuading the German general in charge of Montluc to hand over the keys to his garrison thus saving, in extremis, eight hundred hostages from the firing squad. Finally, for one year, after the liberation of Lyon, he was made

Police Chief of the Republic before returning to his calling as a writer and journalist.

'The Commissaires were the top level of the immediate post-war reorganisation and although their offices didn't last more than a year what I admired so much was the speed at which problems which could have been chaotic were solved – e.g. distribution of food. People had been hungry for five years and having been liberated food had to be distributed quickly and fairly – that was one of Yves's jobs, priority No. 1. Next, the distribution of fuel especially for food transport and oil and coal – all these had to be dealt with otherwise there were going to be areas of starvation. This succeeded because his best work had been in the six months before the Liberation and was far more dangerous than fighting with weapons. In the country as a combatant you could hide, be cared for, but to organise local activity, detached from the military side, you had to operate in the town where the fatal tip-off to the enemy was but a whisper away; that's where the people you needed worked and lived. To make things sure you had to employ employees already in local government and who might be suspected of collaboration. That was one of the most delicate and dangerous jobs the Commissaires had to perform – weed out the existing structure while the wheels had to continue to turn. The committees that were set up prior to the Liberation were of the Résistance and therefore *illegal* and only supported by people like us. Because you had to have committees and they had to meet, that couldn't happen in a village; furthermore, you couldn't pretend to be democratic if you didn't include people. It was dangerous and there were a lot of urban arrests because of numbers. The Gendarmerie helped because they were powerful locally and could warn of possible arrests.

It worked because the Commissaires were the right kind of blokes, themselves *résistants*, sons of Moulin, who knew the place, were amazingly competent and did things well. Everywhere the Résistance had two wings – one was fighting, the other was putting into immediate position people who knew how to run railways, post offices, the Gendarmerie and so on. I know it happened because I travelled back and forth across France time and time again and never had any problems at all. The black market was there but violent looting I never heard of, even in places like Marseille and Toulon.

Yves, like his fellow Commissaires would start by estimating the value of other outsiders – the Freemasons and Communists who were already organised and tightly run. Class came into it. Some of the Communist organisations were limited to workers in trade unions and didn't reach out beyond their group. At this period most of them were rural and their strength had been somewhat weakened by the Hitler–Stalin pact, but most of those remaining said, "We just shut our eyes and started resisting in spite of it." The rural Communists I spoke to about collective farming, for example, just roared with laughter – share it with him down the road? Bugger off!'

In 1946 Yves Farge was sent as a government delegate to attend the atomic experiment on the Bikini Atoll and in the same year was appointed Minister of Supply. Killed in a car accident in Tbilisi, Georgia, on 31 March 1953, he lies buried in Nice.

*

On 21 September, Francis and Christine flew from the Jura to London towards inevitable, different destinies. They made their reports to Baker Street and the War Office and then gently parted. They met every time she was in London but they had never lied to each other and Christine strained every fibre of her being to renew contact with Andrew Kennedy and the great love of her life – Poland – now the helpless ground of ghetto and massacre but, in the second case, without success.

Francis refound Nan and his two daughters and together they set about trying to breach the silence of the past two years. Nan and Christine met once, a contact Francis felt to be 'brief but necessary'.

*

Despite many horrendous failures – notably the complete control by the Germans of the Dutch Section for eighteen months – what had SOE achieved, and especially in France, with the original F and RF sections? Always bearing in mind SOE's unfair reputation for amateurishness, resulting in thin logistical support, the answer has to be a great deal. Compared with Bomber Command, they had represented genuine economy of effort – e.g. the total poundage of explosives used in the hundreds of acts of industrial sabotage in France – about 3000lb – was considerably less than the load of a single light Mosquito bomber in 1944. SOE had come under MEW, Ministry of Economic Warfare, a body Bomber Harris hated. Yet the targets of Bomber Command and the SOE had quite often been identical – oil, communications, aircraft factories, airfields, submarines, morale – even if Bomber Command had frequently lost more personnel in one night than SOE had in the entire war. In France, SOE had never involved itself in mass destruction and only very rarely in assassination, though there was total delight when Darlan was executed in Algiers. Militant Maquis groups regularly assassinated individual German uniformed officers and men, despite the inevitable reprisals, but that was part of their revolutionary strategy and far less effective than SOE's sabotage coups, 'mosquito bites', that accumulatively unsettled the enemy and undermined morale. One group from SOE RF had been consistently brilliant in this regard – ARMADA – 'a fireman, a chauffeur, a garage hand and a student, who between them put out of action one of France's principal armament works, killed off a dozen tiresome Gestapo officials, and brought canal traffic between the Ruhr and the Mediterranean to a standstill at a critical period of the war when both for industrial and naval purposes the Germans particularly needed it'.[6]

In the Normandy and Riviera landings systematic outbursts of sabotage had undoubtedly been of direct tactical help to the invasions, putting rail and telecommunications out of action on D-Day or just after. Forcing delay was a hugely silent and resonant strategic success. All this ran parallel with acts of individual courage, skill and nerve.

General Eisenhower wrote to Sir Colin Gubbins on 31 May 1945:

> Before the combined staff of Special Force Headquarters disperses I wish to express my appreciation of its high achievements.
>
> Since I assumed the Supreme Command in January 1944, until the present day, its work has been marked by patient and far-sighted planning, flexible adaptation to the operational requirements of Supreme Headquarters, and efficient executive action during operations. *In no previous war, and in no other theatre during this war, have resistance forces been so closely harnessed to the main military effort.* (My italics.)
>
> While no final assessment of the operational value of resistance action has yet been completed, I consider that the disruption of enemy rail communications, the harassing of German road moves and the continual strain placed on the German war economy and internal security services throughout occupied Europe by the organised forces of resistance, played a very considerable part in our complete and final victory . . .
>
> Particular credit must be due to those responsible for communications with occupied territory. I am also aware of the care with which each individual country was studied and organised, and of the excellent work carried out in training, documenting, briefing and dispatching agents. The supply to agents and resistance groups in the field, moreover, could only have

> reached such proportions during the summer of 1944 through outstanding efficiency on the part of the supply and air liaison staffs. Finally I must express my great admiration for the brave and often spectacular exploits of the agents and special groups under control of Special Force Headquarters.[7]

Maitland Wilson, the other supreme allied commander operating across France, unofficially estimated that the existence of the resistance forces reduced the fighting efficiency of the Wehrmacht in southern France to 40 per cent at the moment of the Riviera landings.

Yet despite overwhelming popular support for British help across large areas of France, a situation to which Francis constantly testified, early post-war French historians were often reluctant to credit SOE with any significant role in the overall Résistance success.

> 'It was a reflection of the political situation of the New France officially trying to avoid any idea of non-France being important in the liberation of France; absurd and just understandable.
>
> I have talked over the nature of SOE for nearly sixty years now with all sorts of responsible French people and I've never met one who understood what SOE was. The French thought SOE was a part of IS – the Intelligence Service – and linked to the Foreign Office and therefore with the centuries-old history of sore relations between the two countries. But we weren't. Far from it. We were a paramilitary body with our own means of intelligence, and RF Section couldn't have operated without our help.
>
> The spread of the news of the collapse of the PROSPER circuit was hugely attractive to the people who wanted to play down the role of British help, and still is to a lot of French historians; the role of the gay young Oxford or Cambridge graduate languidly living a life that was a real thing yet in terms of security tragically stupid at the same time. The Peter Churchills and the PROSPER folk were typical of people who saw themselves as sons of the Count of Monte Cristo – living a fantasy.
>
> Thankfully, what has emerged is the serious local historian and the discarding of mythology so that people like Jean Garcin in the Basses-Alpes were people who were telling the story correctly and, because the nature of the organisation was such, he didn't attempt to move outside his *département* – that was quite enough for him and there's one book at least like that for every *département* in France. *Le Temps du Refus*, from the

Queyras region on the Italian border, is really valuable in its need to record the details of what happened in a relatively small area and also in its dedication to lists of people in groups – so that no one will be ignored or forgotten; I find that very, very moving.

Change in the reporting of history has taken a long time because of the rebirth of France and the need to protect its reputation and hide Vichy's anti-Semitism and so on; enormous issues were involved. Modern historians were children when it was all happening – hence the pressure on the oldies who are still alive to "get it all down". We now have the situation where the first generations were bored but their children are interested in what grandpa did!'

18

The long silence between Francis and Nan had now to be faced but it soon emerged that it had been one-sided. Nan had known all along what Francis was involved in in France and on a couple of occasions had been fed gruesome possibilities of his fate – none of which she could even hint at to him. Vera Atkins had kept her informed monthly with cryptic reassurances – 'He's OK' – though not of the arrest at Digne. Having moved back to Lincolnshire for a short period – the soundless landing of one or two V2s convincing her that the children's safety came first – Nan had half let slip this knowledge when she'd burst gaily into the kitchen waving a telegram and crying, 'Look, they've made me a Lady!', on learning that Francis had been promoted to lieutenant-colonel. She loved Kipling's 'the Colonel's lady and Judy O'Grady / Are sisters under their skins'.

But what eased their struggle somewhat was Nan's lifelong unwillingness to look back, or dwell on the past; whether this was a form of hiding or an in-built commitment to the moment and the future it is difficult to say; perhaps it was both. She had had a lonely war which in turn had nurtured a skilful self-sufficiency that impressed all who would in time get to know her.

Nevertheless, it is difficult to imagine the willing continuation of their silence that these two intelligent people were yet again imposing on themselves.

> 'I had often sat trying to imagine her preparing herself for bed after the children, alone. She would never appear anywhere at any time without being properly groomed. Even when I turned up at the flat after it all she wouldn't greet me until she was ready. I've often tried to get people to understand what women at home went through – I'm doing it now. It has been my constant song since the Liberation – what women put up with

and they did, and what men couldn't possibly have been able to do without them – whether it was people like Nan at home or the people who looked after me in their homes in France. She had many medical skills, too, which she had studied herself; I don't think they were any consolation to her until much later. Hers was an utterly empty life except for the babies.

No, I don't think there was hiding between us. Nan wanting to look forward was only part of the answer; the other was what had happened had been huge, something we hadn't shared. The real latent tension at this stage was that her war had been a horror, an enclosing, but for me there had been no reduction in my life, only an expansion, especially in the closeness and affection I'd experienced with my wartime friends. There was no quick way to order the exchange of knowledge with each other or the rebirth of love and the acceptance of unknown relations and lovers. Therefore, there was a lack of balance in our relationship which had to be worked on.

Jay here, even now knows little of what went on because it was never mentioned. The friendship and love of people I worked with – *that* we talked about because the family met them when they visited – like the Malartes who became very much part of our new world; but the Vercors, no. In our own ways we never stopped being pacifists. We took part in the war and then we knew that the idiot ugliness of great parts of it were profoundly repulsive and we didn't want to talk about them.

At least now that desperate silence could more or less be shared. Essentially, though, we didn't have to change our relationship; I had to change because now I had two girls and that was quite new and different. I had missed out on their first words, first play, first kisses and grabbed fingers.'

But the war wasn't over and it could and did still interfere.

Partial relief from the tension came almost immediately in the autumn of 1944 when Francis was invited by Maurice Buckmaster to join one of several JUDEX missions sent to former SOE circuits in France. Ostensibly a stores and intelligence inquiry, in reality it was an excuse for speech-making and the chance to meet again and thank old friends for their help. Wine flowed.

Buckmaster had always been an admirer of Francis and this testimony speaks for itself:

Roger was probably the most loved figure in the Isère. His friends were numerous and varied. I have been privileged to meet very many of them, and have marvelled at Roger's ease of transition, from a sophisticated Avignon salon to a forester's hut in the Drôme, from a Marseille millionaire's office to the grocer's shop in Seyne. The transition was far less disturbing than it sounds, for each one of these patriots was resolved to throw himself body and soul into the task of liberating his country. Roger provided some of the means of doing so.

All, moreover, were united in their admiration for the man. Not a man among them would not have fought to save Roger; not a woman who would not have hidden him from pursuit at the risk of her life: not a child who would not have undergone any form of torture rather than betray '*l'ami anglais*'.

His work was exhausting and continuous. Roger was on duty twenty-four hours out of twenty-four. Each day brought new problems. Pressed though he was, he had to exercise infinite patience with the farmer who wanted time for reflection, or with the railway worker who expressed the view that the next day or next week would be soon enough and led the way to the bistro where pastis awaited the party. Roger never showed any sign of impatience or irritability, and, in consequence, arrived at results more quickly. He was as much at ease in the mayor's parlour as in the cellar of a Var vineyard owner, or a cabin in the high mountains. But he had also another side to his character which he never showed to his French colleagues, the side which directed his actions as representative of the Allied Staff. This only appeared in his reports and messages to London.

He is our star turn. He is so well known to the authorities here that I need not go into details as to his work. Suffice it to say that he organised and ran with the utmost efficiency the whole of the south-east of France for eighteen months.[1]

During the trip Francis fell ill with a high fever and was rushed to an American Military Hospital in Marseille: 'When it calmed down the American Medical Colonel said they had sent samples of my blood all over the place to try and establish if I had any known ailment – result nothing. Then the doctor said, you must've been leading an irregular life! I said I had. Sleep and diet had indeed been irregular.'

On returning to London, via a still rejoicing Paris, he was next asked to go to the Far East which he refused to do on the grounds that he had nothing special to contribute – he knew nothing of the culture and even less of the needs of orthodox warfare. Yet again 'stupid orders' he could not obey.

> 'The problem with the likes of me was that we were overpromoted and severely lacking in military skills and they didn't know what to do with us. Then the folly of SAARF (Special Allied Airborne Reconnaissance Force) surfaced.
>
> Someone in SHAEF – (Supreme Headquarters Allied Expeditionary Force) realised that there were resources, us, no longer being used. Of major concern at that time was how the diehard Nazis, like dogs glowering as they are being killed, would take to failure, especially in POW and concentration camps, plus the obvious problems of displaced persons everywhere. So they took us chaps who had been trained for independent work and sent us out to deal with any potential crisis. What in fact we were were groups of independent-minded, undisciplined fellows who realised during the weeks it took to "retrain" us on Wentworth golf course that it would all be too late.'

Although as early as 1943 Allied planners had suggested that the POW contact teams that were then attached to the various Allied armies might be expanded to include airborne teams that would parachute into the vicinity of POW camps and thus help pre-empt many possible disasters, nothing was done until February 1945. Then, with the downfall of Germany closer, the safety and early evacuation of the camps became a top priority and in March 1945, as the Allies forced the Rhine, SAARF was created.

Most of the personnel were SOE or OSS agents – French, British, American, Belgian and Polish – including several women who had served with distinction as SOE agents but were not allowed to be used in an airborne role.

'We hung around for weeks. Nan came and visited and met Auguste, Antoine, Henri Bochenek and others, and that was good. We were SHAEF troops but we had no guidance or direction. I was the Senior Officer but knew nothing of what we might do or how we might do it.'

The basic operational unit was a three-man team (although some women served on some teams) – two officers and an enlisted radio operator, usually of the same nationality. As the collapse of Germany proceeded more rapidly than anticipated, SAARF was restructured. The sixty teams that had completed their training were retained in an airborne role while the remaining teams, including Francis's, were redesignated air-transportable, a force of roughly one hundred jeeps to spread across northern Europe.

> 'In fact we were sent out around the time when the Armistice was about to be signed. Hitler had committed suicide. We managed a few things – our basic activity being to ensure that there were no last-minute massacres in the camps. And so we went to Belsen.'

If for Francis the viciousness of what was perpetrated on the Vercors was 'inevitable' given the nature of war, what he and others witnessed who were among the first through the gates of the Dachaus, the Belsens, the Sobibors, in the spring of 1945 was 'unbelievable', the scale and ingenuity of the sadism beyond war. Words are in most hands totally inadequate, the images beyond the unreal so that one cannot be sure how to interpret them, but 'Behind the barbed wire and the electric fence,' wrote Martha Gellhorn in *The Face of War*, 'the skeletons sat in the sun and searched themselves for lice. They have no age and no faces; they all look alike and like nothing you will ever see if you are lucky'. She detailed the experiments and other obscenities: 'if you want to rest from one horror you go and see another'; the crematorium and its gas chamber, the 'jail' which held the *Nacht und Nebel* prisoners who were held in unlit solitary confinement for years until they were removed by the SS on a final death transport into Night and Mist – none of them ever being heard of again. 'It is not known how many people died in this camp (Dachau) in the last three years. Last February and March two thousand were killed in the gas chamber, because, though they were too weak to work, they did not have the grace to die; so it was arranged for them.' . . . 'I have not talked about how it was the day the American Army arrived, though the prisoners told me. In their joy to be free, and longing to see their friends who had come at last, many prisoners rushed to the fence and died electrocuted. There were those who died cheering, because that effort of happiness was more than their bodies could endure. There were those who died because now they had food and they ate before they could be stopped, and it killed them' . . . 'I do not know how to explain it, but aside from the terrible anger you feel, you are ashamed. You are ashamed for mankind.'[2]

Francis, thoughtful and very articulate, was by nature a man who 'liked to remember the good things and forget the bad'. He rarely avoided any direct question, confident as he was in his ability to provide an answer. Therefore, when his words came after a longish pause they surprised by their halting, painful tone, their simplicity warding off any desire to impress. He could be trying to make contact with Nan in the middle of their silence.

> 'Sickness is the word that comes to mind most quickly . . . We didn't learn anything we didn't know . . . The changes of control of the camps were . . . invariably slow. The senior German officers had gone off in cars leaving lesser ranks to . . . tidy up bits and pieces or destroy records or whatever.'

Silence.

> 'When I went to Belsen those sort of . . . residual Germans were leaving . . . A real shock I had was three miles outside Belsen, a small village and I stopped to ask the way. The man spoke little English and my . . . German was very bad. And he said why are you going there? I said "concentration camp" and he said, "Oh, I didn't know". Now I'd been smelling Belsen for ten miles before I arrived at his village!!'

Silence.

> 'I don't know what the numbers were but there were still some . . . some thousands because a lot of them were very sick and unable to move. The Royal Army Medical Corps were doing what they could. Belsen was in the British Sector.'

Silence.

> 'Our brief was to ensure by any means we could conceive of that there were no last-minute massacres. Almost always it was too late and therefore pointless. That was the trouble of being SHAEF troops We weren't sent into any danger. We went in and found that things were already in hand or we couldn't do anything to stop anything that was happening as that had already been done.'

Silence.

> 'Later I stopped in Hamburg to visit Harry Rée's uncle and that was the first . . . crushed city that I saw. Those were the images for those of us

> who passed through Germany at that time . . . It was the *smell* that hit as . . . strongly as anything . . . The smell of rotting . . . people and buildings . . . opaque . . . it was still very strong when we got to Berlin and a sense of shame crept up on you.'

The identical sense of shame lay with them when it came to visiting the concentration camp at Ravensbrück – the name that struck terror into any woman caught active in the war against Nazism. Chosen by Himmler and built on his estate near a large lake north of Berlin as the site for the only major concentration camp for women, its population by the end of 1939 was already 2290. Most of the women taken there were brought, not for anything they had done, but to punish the men and the families they had been taken from, in order to deter resisters to Nazi occupation. The same inhuman routine as in other concentration camps became the norm – daily death by starvation, beating, torture, hanging, shooting, and 'medical experimentation' and in November 1944 the gas chamber. At the end of March 1945 the SS decided to transfer their archives and workshop machines to a safer place. On 27 and 28 April, all women still able to walk were marched away. The camp was liberated by the Russian army two days later and the survivors of the Death March saved in the following hours by a Russian scout unit.

Of the 132,000 women and children incarcerated in Ravensbrück an estimated 92,000 died, among them SOE colleagues Violette Szabo, Denise Bloch, Lilian Rolfe and Francis's courier Cecily Lefort who, witnesses told Vera Atkins, had received a letter from her husband seeking a divorce just before she was gassed.

> 'Auguste had joined SAARF with me as he was still a British as well as a French officer, a captain in both armies. We would have stayed together in any case, he again as the vital radio operator, but that paled beside his need to find his wife and daughter. Through a friend we were introduced to a Russian officer to whom we explained the situation. He was very nervous and twitchy about it but said he understood our problems but it would have to be done quickly and quietly. We drove in his jeep into the Russian Zone and went straight to the camp. He was saluted.
>
> He gave the official in charge Mme Floiras's name and they fetched her as she hadn't yet been moved out; she was alive. She came in and Auguste could touch his wife – she was real. I don't know what was said because I felt I had to look away. It was very moving. We asked about

Paulette and she explained she was at a work centre where she'd been better off by not being in the camp most of the time. We were with her an hour and a half. We couldn't take them away – there was a programme of evacuation – that was the Russians' job . . . and we weren't supposed to be in the place anyway. Mme Floiras would be lucky and be transported back to Marseille, others would just have to walk out of the gates into life . . . Germany at that stage was like the invasion of France – country roads cluttered with people, bewildered, not knowing whether they were coming or going, displaced – at least there weren't Stukas strafing them.

Auguste's wife in fact suffered greatly from her experiences. She never fully recovered and died some years later. Auguste remarried so as not to be a burden on his family. Paulette, who is twelve years younger than me, is alive and we are in contact, even now, every fortnight.'

Paulette found it impossible to talk about Ravensbrück or their release.

'I've already described Auguste. I could not have done anything I ended up doing without him, he was my better half. All my time in France depended upon his wisdom; he knew his country inside out. When I returned to France in February 1944 it was because I didn't want to let *him* down above all others. He later told me that if I hadn't returned he would have chucked it all in.

Auguste's reaction in Ravensbrück was totally in keeping with features of his character which came out in the two years I lived and worked with him – he was enormously warm and affectionate but he was also tremendously in charge of himself; he never let go. I suppose we had that bit in common.

You don't talk about a great friendship – it is.'

'I was asked to go to a camp that had no Allied troops there at all. We flew in, in uniform, and were treated as liberators! . . . I flew in the first plane to land at Copenhagen airport and the pilot told me, with a grin, they didn't know whether it was mined or not. The Danish Resistance who were seeing Allied forces for the first time gave us a tremendous evening and the leader presented me with his mistress for company. Very kind. The next day we drove back to the Harz Mountains to pick up Auguste – he hadn't thought it necessary to go up to Copenhagen!

Soon after that I got in touch with all the units and said it's over now. The French filled their jeeps with French wine and we were away!

I'm not a miserable man but, apart from Belsen and getting Auguste to Ravensbrück, the SAARF period was blank and grey and one of those certain areas in my life when I didn't know what I was doing.'

SAARF was disbanded on 1 July 1945 and an 'official' account of its value managed to ambivalently back up his honest, dismissive tone: 'A short-lived and obscure unit, SAARF was a strange note, most of the hardened veterans of airborne and special operations who served in it would have agreed, on which to end one's wartime career. And yet one must wonder whether some of these men have not looked back and felt increasingly a sense of satisfaction that their last mission was a humanitarian one.'[3]

During this period there had been attempts, backed by SOE, to try and get Francis transferred to the diplomatic world, but privilege can be as ineffective against institutional snobbery as non-privilege – as two letters from his Personal File effortlessly show:

From: AD/E To: V/CD Copy to: A/CD, F. 7 Mar 1945
LT. COL CAMMAERTS (JOCKEY)
– Col BUCKMASTER has tried to obtain employment for Lt. Col. CAMMAERTS (JOCKEY). It was considered that he would do well with the Foreign Office, but he was turned down because his father is BELGIAN.
– He was then offered the appointment as Ministry of Information Press Officer in S.E. France, but the Foreign Office are again standing out against the appointment for the same reason.
– I gather that the FRENCH know of, and have raised no objection to the appointment.
– I feel that, in view of CAMMAERTS' record, this objection ought to be overruled.
If you agree, could you approach the Foreign Office, or, if you think necessary, enlist S.O.'s support.

From: AD/B To: CD ADB/710 Copy to: A/CD. 9 Mar 45
Lt. Colonel F.C.A. CAMMAERTS.
We spoke.
The Foreign Office Personnel Branch confirms that in view of the possible 'inheritance' by the Foreign Office of certain M. of I. personnel, the latter have agreed to enforce F.O. rules of entry.

As this officer's father – Professor Emile CAMMAERTS, an elderly and distinguished Anglophil [sic] – is a Belgian, Lt. Colonel CAMMAERTS cannot be accepted for the suggested employment by M. of I. as Press Officer for S.E. France.

CAMMAERTS, a British subject by birth, has already applied for employment in H. M. Foreign Service and has been turned down. He had a rather regrettable interview when he was told that the proposed work was of a confidential nature and no foreigner could be employed. CAMMAERTS has only spent ten months (holidays) of his civilian life out of the U.K.

The Foreign Office Personnel Branch tell me that it is unlikely that Mr Eden can be persuaded to over-ride this ruling on personnel and I attach in amplification of this attitude a copy of a letter received last November by A/CD from Peter LOXLEY referring to MUNTHE, whose satisfactory Foreign Office employment was terminated when it was realised that his father was not a British subject by birth.[4]

Diplomacy's loss would be education's gain.

The sense of shame that had begun to creep up on Francis in ruined Hamburg would be further nourished by the behaviour of the Allies-as-victors in post-war Germany. After SAARF he was posted to the British Military Government responsible for a sector of the city of Berlin and to head its Economic Section dealing with Food and Agriculture – a strange songline reaching back to Lincolnshire!

The overriding problems facing the Allies were demilitarising and governing Germany and controlling the rebuilding of its economy – at least until the 'Iron Curtain' descended and split it in half. After two world wars Germany regaining her place among the European nations was to be severely monitored. Divided into four zones – British, Russian, American and French – the overall political authority rested with the Allied Control Commission's four senior military commanders – Montgomery, McNarney, Zhukov and Koenig – and under them a Coordinating Committee of lesser generals and civilian expert advisers. Progress was almost nil.

Berlin, in turn, although in the Russian Zone, was also divided into four sectors, though the Russians, in view of their losses in the capture of the city, blindly resented the Western Allies' share of its occupation; it was a tense city.

A friend, driving an open jeep across the frozen width of Germany to join Francis, registered at first hand the dreadful scale of destruction that civilian and military target bombing had wreaked: '. . . the huge capacity of the coal mines and the steel mills of the Ruhr had been sharply reduced; electricity was in short supply and large parts of the rail network had been destroyed. The German people were not just defeated, they were bemused and, not surprisingly, they had lost the will so essential for recovery, retaining only the will to survive.'[5]

The friend, Roy Close, ex-1 SAS, had met Francis in a Brussels night-club – the Kremlin – through their respective 'girlfriends' having been at school together. They had remained in contact, and when Roy's regiment was disbanded he was posted to Berlin and served as a representative on the Trade and Industry Committee; knowing little of either, yet the experience proved a launch pad for a distinguished career in industry and economic development post-war.

They shared a house in the Grünewald, a leafy upmarket suburb, with a happily adjacent mess, but a rather disagreeable colonel as president. On one occasion overhearing them discussing radical policies being proposed by the newly elected Labour government – reform in education and social security and a free National Health Service – he called it 'socialist nonsense' and asked them where they'd met. Without batting an eyelid Francis replied – 'in the Kremlin'. The poor man, puce, could only explode into 'bloody Communists!'

Both gregarious, both good drinkers, both reachers-out, a great deal of fun was had, yet conversely there was ample time to mull over the scene and reflect on significant Allied disagreements just below the surface.

Roy Close again: 'The French were suspicious of getting factories working, repairing the mines, etc, while in France electricity was rationed, French factories could work for only three days a week and French people were unemployed.' True in general yet Britain, France, America and Russia were busy identifying machinery and materials they could remove as reparation. The biggest irony was that, as the Iron Curtain descended, 'the Allied intention of not wanting to restore Germany as a European power turned to the strengthening of Germany as a buffer against the Russian Communist threat. This led to dedicated efforts, mostly by America, to provide German industry with new machinery and materials to replace those taken as reparations. So defeated Germany got the new stuff and the victorious Allies got the old!'[6]

At the day-to-day level, rotating chairmanships led to national differences dictating political rather than economic decisions. Bureaucracy ruled the world of 'us amateur soldiers doing jobs we were never trained for'. The centralised government of Russia meant that every issue or item on a committee agenda had to pass through the crucible of the Moscow mind – often returning in a totally unpredictable manner. As an example, on one occasion, Francis, on his committee, 'in an effort to secure land for agricultural and horticultural production, proposed the setting up of a purchasing cooperative in land round Berlin. The Americans did not like the idea because it was "kinda socialist", the French thought it spoiled the Germans, but the Russians opposed it because it would "interfere with private enterprise"!'

It would feel to Francis and others that, with one war won, the fields of the next conflict were already being prepared: 'From the privilege of pacifism we had always anticipated this – war achieves nothing and at the same time as it kills it corrupts. No one can be sane in war or immediately post-war. The instruments of war destroy something personal, destroy hope for improvement; only occasional friends saved my despair.'

'Francis was so intellectually ahead of us all,' recalled Roy, 'very powerful, culturally knowledgeable, his articulacy marvellous, always probing at the pros and cons of thought. In today's language he was a mover. At that stage I was gauche and in awe of him.'

But Francis counters: 'Yes, but they were never one-sided conversations because I wanted to know! It is probably true I didn't mention my growing sense of shame at our behaviour as victors, but I did with others, journalist friends. There are always things in life you don't want to talk about – it's how I *felt*. Roy was a proud SAS man from an "unprivileged" background in north London; he taught me as much as I taught him.'

Social life was active and a favourite club – Die Mauve – a place where the film director Roberto Rossellini and his actress wife Ingrid Bergman would drop in, together with writers, artists, etc – well frequented. Francis's lifelong love of sailing was also richly satisfied,

But on the dark side was the policy of non-fraternisation, a potent contributor to Francis's sense of shame; it ranged from regret to fury:

> 'I was so ashamed of the way the victors were behaving when they should have been generous, forgiving, not actively exploiting the situation; all four sets of Allied troops behaved in the same way. The living on the black market and officers getting their non-commissioned assistants to sell their cigarette allowances and coffee in order to buy their girls or what have you. You could

see it growing. At that time a high-up in the administration told me that the troops in Berlin had only drawn one-third of their pay because the rest was coming from the black market. This and living in a heap of ruins. We had been told we shouldn't talk to the local people when what the victors really wanted was to prevent their simple young soldiers from having German girlfriends – basically an American idea. Germany was full of the old and women without their menfolk, anxious to earn. The black market and exploitation of the bombed, impoverished citizens of Berlin even made no distinction between those who had been in concentration camps and others.

Of course there were magnificent gestures – Yehudi Menuhin shaking the hand of Wilhelm Furtwängler was one – but that only served to point up the idiocy of non-fraternisation. We, of course, broke it ourselves, especially in the Russian sector.'

What was inescapable was the extent, on both sides, of the damage done especially when, almost overnight, the policy became one of fraternisation. Help with the practical side of reconstruction meant the need for better understanding, closer contact. At a party given by a group of German intellectuals and the like with Military Government representatives, Roy Close recalled joining a small group in a corner:

They spoke very good English and the conversation turned inevitably to the condition of Germany, the difficulties of being occupied and the danger posed by the presence of the Soviets . . . We were convinced we had listened sympathetically . . . But then suddenly, one of the group – she was a writer, if I remember correctly – said, 'It's no use talking to you two, you hate us so much, you just don't understand.'

Shocked, we protested.

'No, it's true,' she went on, 'the hate and the distrust is in you.'

We thought for a moment and then Francis said, 'It's not hate. Certainly we don't trust you. But you have to understand that we and others like us have two very good reasons this century for not trusting Germany, and we have good reasons, many of them very personal because of things you have done to friends and comrades, not to like you very much. You can't ignore that or pretend those things haven't happened.'

And these were the intellectuals. Even with them there was something – after six years of war – there had to be. But we tried.

For the last seven months of his military career Francis was transferred to the Control Commission – i.e. covering the whole British Zone as well as the Berlin sector – as Liaison Officer between General Robertson and General Koenig, and it was from Koenig that, on 14 July, he received the Award of Chevalier of the Légion d'Honneur with Croix de Guerre from a grateful French nation. This posting, however, like most of the others, 'wasn't very fruitful because I saw General Koenig every day and General Robertson once'. In October 1946 he was demobbed, honoured by the British government with a DSO and a Silver Star from the United States. Like his father, never a fan of medals, one nevertheless caught a glimpse of modest pride in his daily wearing of the thin lapel ribbon of the Légion d'Honneur.

But it seems wrong to leave this 'strenuous loner' at this stage without an example of the magic that goes with charisma. Roy Close:

> There was an occasion, in the depth of the German winter, when he smiled and said – 'Beethoven's Ninth!' I said, 'What?' We were told a re-formed German orchestra was to give a concert in the State Opera House in the Soviet sector. We bought tickets. It was a bitterly cold Saturday afternoon and snow was falling. We took rugs with us and we put on big overcoats. He said, 'You're going to enjoy this. It's a setting of Schiller's poem.' The sight that greeted us was unworldly. At least a quarter of the roof was open to the sky and a part of one wall had been sliced open. We'd been told that, as the orchestra's instruments had been destroyed in the fighting, they had borrowed from a variety of people what instruments they could get hold of. We sat in the 'circle' and watched and listened with sympathy and admiration as the orchestra, accompanied by a choir, came in with shawls and blankets over their shoulders, knitted balaclavas on their heads and mittens on their hands. Snowflakes were falling through the open roof on to the audience and players alike as they played and sang Beethoven's Choral Symphony.
>
> At a time of uncertainty and in such bleak, almost hopeless conditions, that song of brotherhood and freedom was performed passionately by this group of poor, cold and probably underfed musicians. It was spellbinding. It may not have been the greatest performance of all time, but to us it was a deeply emotional and memorable one. It suggested that Germany might be able to find again the soul it had for too long rejected. I see and hear clearly that performance even today. And Francis knew the words![8]

19

SOE was to all intents and purposes disbanded in January 1946 and early in the same year a fire ransacked Baker Street, depriving historians of a great deal of documentation. Previous apparently random filleting of the files further complicated any access to the truth – Francis's Personal File was certainly interfered with, is far from complete, debriefings are written up rather than verbatim and errors remain as fact. But he belonged to a secret, overstressed and understaffed organisation and its secrecy was at the same time its strength and its danger. Bent on smoothing immediate post-war relations with de Gaulle, Tito and certain elements in the US, the government decided it didn't want any problems and one way to avoid that was to close down SOE.

'But they had by that time many thousands of "dependants", not only in Europe but in the Far East as well. All these people, myself included, had to resettle after the end of the war. Of course they tried to help and in my case they came up with the offer of a job in Brussels with the Inter-Allied Repararations Agency which they thought I'd like. I did, but for reasons nothing really to do with reparations which, I'd already seen in Berlin, weren't doing much good to the smaller nations in Europe who desperately needed help.

I jumped at the job because it was splendidly paid, £2500 a year tax free – a salary I didn't think I'd ever have in my life! It meant Nan and the girls could be relieved of the harsh life that still existed in England. Nan's joy at being able to eat shellfish for the first time and butter, which in Belgium was plentiful, had to be seen to be believed. We could go out to restaurants and to the races with the girls.

This isn't sentimentality recollected in tranquillity. Our silence still cast a cold shadow. The return to our mutual profound understanding was very slow because, although I was no longer in uniform and I could revert to my former pacifism, the whole of our immediate past still stood between us but at least Brussels was neutral ground. And there was Belgian family.

We were there for eighteen months. The bitter winter of 1946–7, where the girls' tears on their cheeks froze as we walked them to school, finally gave way to summer car trips to France – a specific attempt to open windows. As well as seeing the snow-capped Alps for the first time, or the Mediterranean, Nan meeting and liking many of the friends to whom I would remain permanently and profoundly attached, marked one of the gradual swing points in our relationship. Initially she was baffled by the variety – many of them were middle-aged, badly shaken men who smelt strongly of garlic; far from physically enchanting, halved by war but with their funny sides, too. Such a one was M. Téstanière. Deeply loveable, he had a birthmark on his face and the wife of the man he was working for had a baby with a birthmark in exactly the same place. They didn't talk about it – he just left and came back ten years later.

But when Nan met them she understood perfectly. That was a magic bit in the slow mending and away from a lot of the pain. There with those people we could rejoice in having won.'

On the other hand three- or four-year-old Jay could hardly bear the heat and neither could her once again pregnant mother.

'I've said I never felt confident that reparations were going to do much good to anyone and they didn't. The shame I felt in Berlin persisted in Brussels; war and the consequences of war were still embedded in my daily life. We seemed to have no idea of how to behave as victors; we *manipulated.* As Deputy Director and with a staff of two hundred, I was in contact with most events. I had two nice Yugoslav chaps on my staff who were very excited by the fact that old-fashioned stuff collected from the Ruhr or Austria or wherever they could see being sent to their country or Poland or Hungary – while others could only see the best being reserved for Germany! Military decisions still drove the economy.

My father had hated the Treaty of Versailles because he was perfectly aware that treating a starving Germany as a pariah was a disaster not just in terms of revenge but also of inevitable reaction, that Versailles built in fact towards a Second World War. This had a direct effect on my feelings post-1945. Germany was becoming the fulcrum of the Cold War. *Déjà vu.*

*

'Then, in February 1948, Christine was born.

The biggest single event in all our lives.

She was a very difficult birth with a very large head. A little later the matron informed me Christine had a very serious case of hydrocephalus: "Shall we stop feeding her?" I asked her, "Do you make these decisions?" And she replied, "Yes, about twenty-five times a year." "What about the doctor?" She replied, "The doctor doesn't even admit it happens. But of course most of the cases are more obvious than Christine – children with three heads or total distortions – but in such cases we don't provide the means of continuing life." Finally I said, "As far as I'm concerned no go – the most important decision-maker in this is Nan and as she is no doubt suffering still from the birth we certainly won't do anything without her."'

Never would Nan let her child go and so she guaranteed for her family and all those who came to know Christine closely, an amazingly unifying *gift* of pleasure and love.

'Nan was told that Christine would only live for three months. She attained her fourteenth birthday – a complete celebration of Cliff Richard, about whom Christine was "beautifully crazy" – organised by her sisters, brother and close friends. As she grew and began to lose her sight and use of her legs, the doctors knew nothing about the overwhelming understanding of her intelligence – they were incapable of thinking about it. But she was a totally unusual child and those doctors I've been able to talk to and who knew her said they'd never heard of a similar case. The illness is wholly destructive of the brain and all its functions. Christine remained very bright and very intelligent until her death.'

Silence.

'I'm ninety. In my bedroom I have a collage of photographs of all the people who have been important in my life. At the bottom of the frame, opposite my eyeline when I wake is Christine at three.'

Everyone spoke of Nan's calmness, a virtue, not of blind acceptance of what was going on, but one often laced with the shrewd, tart put-down; like her husband she could not accept fools gladly. Physically she was an active, organised woman who suffered greatly from a succession of illnesses yet was always her own person and unafraid – except for others. So one wondered how she dealt with Francis's insistence that if they did have another daughter she would have to be called Christine, after Christine Granville.

> 'Our tour helped Nan to understand what Christine had been through and what had brought us together and all that happened. My friends in France talked freely to her about Christine – she wasn't taboo or anything – we'd been all over the area together and lived as a couple for a few months and people knew that. Like calling our son Paul after Paul Héraud, I think Nan understood both names were based on unique feelings. There were very few things we'd really have quarrelled about but if she'd resisted those two names it might have caused profound trouble because it was so deeply important.'

To the charge that the naming might also mean that Nan had a permanent reminder of Christine in her child, Francis's reaction was swift: 'It wasn't the way her mind worked!'

However, to her eldest daughter, Nan's response was more elliptical: 'Among the young men, and they were young men, who went off to the war, the ones who allowed themselves to have affairs survived better.'

Then Francis proceeded to sack himself from the Reparations Agency. On request, he conducted a survey of staff employment and concluded that they hadn't got enough cleaners and drivers and the staff were overworked. But they had ten directors, himself included, with nothing to do except read books or write poems in their offices and their combined salaries would pay for another six hundred staff. Therefore his main recommendation was that he should be got rid of together with as many of the directors as possible; it was gratefully adopted.

No longer a 'phoney senior officer', feeling uncut out for sustained administrative activity, his uncertainty as to what to do next matched that of his leaving Cambridge and the solution would be the same – teaching. The yen to return to the classroom had always been there and his desire to trade in luck and privilege for normal contact as undeniable as it had been in France.

But there was a further link with what he had experienced in wartime France. Like many, many former ex-servicemen and women he needed to match the *intensity* of those scintillating years. He knew the 1944

Education Act and the post-war rise of new towns were revolutionary concepts and he wanted to be actively involved in bringing them about. But for the moment there were barriers.

Interviewed by Stewart Mason, a remarkable innovator in Leicestershire education, he was offered the headmastership of a new secondary modern school in Hinkley, but on learning that the salary was £540 a year he had to turn it down: 'I said I can't live on that with growing children, one of whom is seriously handicapped, and no chance of a house for three years.'

What did, however, keep him tightly in touch with education was becoming, in 1948, the first Director of the Central Bureau for Educational Visits and Exchanges, a UNESCO body being set up to feed the post-war need for bridge-building and cultural exchange between nations until recently riven by war. With his own contacts and countless friendships in France, Belgium and Germany, and his organisational skills honed since the war, it was a post made for him and he for the post. Francis's gifts and imagination lay in his ability to make contact with all classes of people, to set things in motion matched by a compulsive need to make things happen. Once more he could move outwards, get away, expand. The unwilling soldier now had peace on his side.

Francis found a house at Sunbury – four up and six down: 'Nan said she'd divorce me if I bought a two up and two down' – totally impractical – but on the Thames riverside with space for Christine. Niki, the eldest child, remembered it as enchanting: 'You could wake up and look out on the water and the fig tree in the garden, the landing stage and going out in boats with Francis and swimming.' Nan, pregnant again – Paul would be born there in August 1949 – set about transforming the top floor into a rentable flat and the boathouse into a kitchen. Niki is clear that her mother, if she had had a chance of a career, would have taken up architecture or design. On the other hand, from the ages of six to eight her clearest awareness of her father is one of absence: 'Nan covered that beautifully but I was aware that there were always glamorous women around but the absence wasn't a problem – there was a continual sense of movement and people in the house.'

The Bureau for Educational Visits was seen as serving all those involved in European education – pupils, university students, teachers, lecturers, teacher trainers, etc, and the twinning of schools and towns. High among its aims was the strengthening of modern foreign language learning and teaching, equally high on Francis's personal agenda since his first efforts at Penge:

> 'All these elements were important – including trying to solve the problem of the very large numbers passing between London and Paris every year. We had a plan for a huge youth hostel beneath Hyde Park – now the car park – but it was held up over provision of water and drainage. This was all part of our work and we had an open brief and it was something the nation wanted us to do. Yep, my job was similar to my role and work in France – advising, helping, finding finance and using my contacts.
>
> Germany belonging gave us the chance to overcome the iniquity of non-fraternisation; there was possible contact with the Communist world through Yugoslavia and to a certain extent East Germany – the Cold War hadn't got properly started yet. All this meant a lot of travelling and the office itself was left in the sure hands of Vera Atkins who I'd appointed as my deputy.'

Vera Atkins, a Romanian Jewess, both of which facts she hid from everybody, had been SOE's Intelligence Officer and to many people 'she had been SOE!' Alarmingly clever, her formidable organisational skills and brilliant memory masked a secretive, 'cagey', haughty woman who could never admit she might ever have been guilty of having made a single mistake in her life. Nevertheless, in the many months between the closing down of SOE and her appointment at the Bureau, she had single-mindedly, almost single-handedly and against all odds and official indifference, combed Europe to uncover the fate of all of SOE's missing agents, especially the women. After all, she reasoned, she had sent them to their deaths. She succeeded completely, her evidence vital in many a trial of Nazi criminal activity, even if the stark detail is often unbearable. For example, her persistent questioning of, among others, Franz Berg, the crematorium stoker at Natzweiler, the only extermination camp on French soil, ends with a note: 'It has now been definitely established that the above mentioned women (Vera Leigh, Diana Rowden, Andrée Borrel and Noor Inayat Khan) were killed in the camp of Natzweiler on 6th July 1944. It appears that at least one of them was still alive when she was pushed in the furnace.'[1]

But for the dark, secret side of this extraordinary woman, and indeed of SOE's own mistakes and shortcomings, see Sarah Helm's vivid biography of Vera, *A Life in Secrets*. All the rumours of her covert political sympathies received short shrift from Francis: 'MI5 and MI6 were the stupidest people I've ever come across. Of course Vera was not Communist. She had the politics of a right-wing Kensington lady, which was what she wanted to be.'

At this stage in his life, as with the proximity of Vera Atkins, legacies of the war made their appearance almost daily and in unexpected, different ways:

'For example, I loved the travelling involved, travel has always mattered to me. Through my friendship with Dick Taylor, the Cultural Attaché to the American Embassy, a trip to America was arranged for me – then things got funny over the visa. I rang Dick and said the visa issuers must be put off by my friends in France – there were files on me, I had no doubt. I was then told to submit a list of French Communists and near Communists I knew. Dick rang back within twenty-four hours and said, thank God you've mentioned every name – if you'd left one out we'd've been dead; you're pukka and your visa'll come through. As I was a member of the Committee for World Peace, which Paul Robeson, Charlie Chaplin and Frédérick Joliot-Curie, the leading French atomic physicist, who was a Communist, also served on – in every sense I was sweetly insulting McCarthyan America. Then I had to go and collect my visa . . .

I walked into a room three times as big as this and a chap was sitting at a huge desk and not looking up. I walked the 100 yards or so and stood in front of him and told him who I was. He said, what did you do during the war? I said I was a conscientious objector and then I joined the Résistance in France, working for SOE. He looked up and snarled – and you mean to say you were never a member of the Communist Party!? I said I've signed your document which says I was never a member of the Communist Party. Oh, he said, and he looked down, signed the visa and chucked it across the table.'

If the trip to America helped to bury the memory of General Butler, did work with the Bureau lead to Francis personally accepting Germans or had the experience been so *tactile* he could never give them the benefit of the doubt in any sense?

'I don't want to be glib here. This is one of the things that disturbs me profoundly because I have resisted as far as I could the association of all

Germans together because I was convinced there must be some good ones. Yet I've known all my life that if, say, I'm watching a tennis match involving a German I'd hope the other chap would win. I know it's there, I'm so ashamed of it yet I can't do anything to remove it totally. On the other hand, I would never express it. It's one of my major worries.

I've tested it with friendships with individual Germans. For example, Minna Specht – an education reformer – I went to her school. There was an organisation called German Educational Reconstruction which I was very friendly with and helped a great deal. One of her pupils came and stayed with Nan and me when Paul was born. I have always been able to be friendly with individual Germans – it's the fact that I associate National Socialism with a tennis player that I am ashamed of.

I'll give you a specific example. When Boris Becker criticised Germans for being racist and went and lived in Nice I stopped wanting him to lose his matches; it is as silly as that. He became a favoured German. It's awful.

I admire so profoundly some responsible French people and the attitude they took towards Germans. I remember particularly a young French officer in charge of some German prisoners after the Vercors tragedy. He came to me and said could I tell him the details of the Geneva Convention for exercise and diet for prisoners. And I thought that was absolutely marvellous, incredible. A man who'd seen seven hundred of his countrymen slaughtered on the Vercors and these were the people who'd done the killing!'

War would obey no time limit.

'I've just read a newspaper article about delayed trauma, the woman whose rape trauma had returned after fifteen years . . . A dozen or so of my friends have committed suicide since the war and two of them over seventy years old . . . Trauma doesn't suddenly stop. A lot of people have claimed some medical after-effect from the Gulf War – that may well be the same thing. In the First World War they called it shell shock and it was commonplace. But it was never really studied and I don't think that the effect of various kinds of trauma resulting from war have been adequately studied either . . . there's also psychological trauma . . . The horror of the Langlois family – Suzanne's suicide, two brothers – one committed suicide, too, and the other died of TB. There was a lot of TB about, incidentally . . . Louis Malarte went for a year to a sanitorium in Briançon and one of my closest friends in Crest spent a year in one – lack of nutrition and very little vaccine available

– so people were exposed more readily to infection. Everyone wanted milk and very little cows' milk was protected at that time . . . it went side by side with penicillin which was the miracle drug – so that you had a need for drugs that were not immediately available and you also had new drugs which were curing things that before were regarded as incurable! It wasn't an hysterical situation but we talked about it, especially with people like Louis Malarte who knew his medicine.

As I said, the Langlois sister collapsed completely and then there were occasions in each decade afterwards of one or two suicides over the age of seventy. So that the continuity or rebirth of traumas was something that until very recently, when I read that article, puzzled me completely. I always said when I was talking to people who were concerned with the care of those who suffered through the war, and through being in the Résistance, not to forget the effect on the mental development after . . .

Whether it is a question of personality – some able to deal with the experiences, others not, or the severity of the experience, or the weight, for some, of survival through duplicity catching up – I really don't know.

We've talked about Christopher Burney[2] and evidence of his traumas is in his books where it is perfectly clear. I really don't know. There were those who romanticised the experience of the agent – like Peter Churchill; there were those in it for the kicks, like Déricourt, and those who were as professional as they could be, like George Starr and Maurice Southgate, yet Maurice abandoned his family and wandered around trying to get money from old Résistance friends and then he came back and was all right again. There was no pattern to those who were badly affected in terms, for instance, of age or sex – it seemed to have affected men and women of all ages, although I can't think of any who were middle-aged during the Résistance period. But the shock came from the late suicides. Henri Bouchet had a lovely wife, they were totally devoted to each other – I'd known them from 1943 and he committed suicide in 1992 and no one knew why. He displayed no symptoms and she was left a widow and had been born in the valley where we retired at Combemaure and they'd been the first to visit us. All I could imagine, before I read the article, was, "It's incurable cancer and they see this way out". I had no reason to believe that but it was simply how, on earth could it happen to such a man?

As now, with the Iraq War, the psychologically damaged were not treated medically. They were left with their hallucinations, nightmares, flashbacks, depression, bewildered families and sometimes suicide attempts. Until only very recently, I'm told, they were ignored by the Services that sent them into conflict zones. Their value was over.

It didn't have to be fatal. Pearl Witherington, that most balanced of human beings, well after the war was taking her grandchildren to look at the Eiffel Tower when one of them ran forward too quickly and, without looking up, Pearl darted after the child who then came to a stop before three people. When she looked up they were soldiers in modern German military uniform. She froze utterly. She was caught. And that meant she would die.

No, I'm not amazed, I'm not traumatised to some degree, I didn't look too deeply into why I was doing what I was doing. Doubt never became a problem; I'd volunteered because I'd wanted to be of some specific use.'

*

On Monday 16 June 1952, the *Evening News* blazed the black headline 'EX SECRET SERVICE HEROINE FOUND DEAD IN LONDON HOTEL' with the *Star* simultaneously announcing, 'HEROINE MURDERED IN LONDON'. Using almost identical text, emphasis was put on the murder weapon, 'a foot-long dagger-shaped knife with wooden handle', on the immediate and unresisted arrest of Dennis George Muldowney, a porter at the Reform Club in Pall Mall and his reply, 'I killed her. Let's get away from here and get it over quickly.' He had stabbed Christine Granville at around eleven o'clock the previous evening .

Most of the daily papers picked up the story on the Tuesday in a generally non-hysterical fashion and Christine, her record and problems received sympathetic and sober treatment. 'ACE WOMAN SPY FOUND PEACE TOO DULL'; 'WHAT DOES A HEROINE DO WHEN WAR IS OVER?' On the Wednesday, the *Daily Mail*'s – 'BRITAIN FAILED MURDERED HEROINE SAY FRIENDS' began to spell out the detail. 'Britain gave her the George Medal and OBE but very little practical help', they said, 'so she became a ship's stewardess and a hotel employee – not from love of adventure but necessity.' Aidan Crawley, former Parliamentary Secretary, who knew her well, said 'I blame the country to some extent for the way she had to earn her living after the war. Her great ability should have been recognised. There were few women in the world like her. She was brilliant but unfortunately had no paper qualifications.'

The same article predicted that her funeral, the following Friday, would be attended by Polish princes, counts, generals and colonels, secret agents, FANYs and representatives from the Vercors, by Anton [sic] Kennedy and his cousin Captain Ludwig Popiel, twice awarded the Virtuti Militari, the Polish equivalent of the VC. He had dined with Christine on the evening of her murder and one of their past exploits together is recounted: 'Popiel had helped her smuggle from Poland a new type of anti-tank gun which the French military authorities wanted. Captain Popiel and Mrs Granville brought the heavy gun by skis across the Polish frontier. It was then hidden in two parts under the body of a car when the Hungarian police swooped on Captain Popiel's hotel in Bucharest and was finally taken to France in a diplomatic bag.'

A small group of her dedicated friends made it their business to try and ensure that the facts that got into the news regarding Christine were correct; above all, that there should be no misrepresentation, and in this they largely succeeded. In the case of Francis, such 'stand-by' activity led to unfortunate domestic consequences – Nan and the children were besieged in Sunbury, curtaining themselves off from the press outside, the girls terrified, but with Francis in central London. The *Daily Graphic*, *Daily Sketch* beneath its headline 'CHRISTINE, GM, DEFIED GESTAPO', had on the Tuesday reported: 'Last night her former Secret Service Chief Lt-Col. F. Cammaerts said, "She was the bravest woman I ever knew and certainly one of the finest members of the Service."

In the London Offices of the Central Bureau for Educational Visits and Exchanges, Lt-Col. Cammaerts told me, "I knew her when she was working in Special Services in France. She saved my life by walking alone into a Gestapo office after two other officers and I had been arrested. She bluffed the Gestapo into releasing us. I know much more about her work but I am bound by the Official Secrets Act not to tell all I know."'

Unlike many mourners at her funeral on the Friday 'who will not tell their names', Francis was one of those willing to stand up for Christine, even to allow his photograph to be used. 'Only Andrew and her close and dear friends such as Francis Cammaerts, John Roper and Patrick Howarth, who knew how little honour had been paid to Christine in her lifetime, were saddened by the ironic sight of the representatives of so many august and military bodies, who, having ignored her needs when she was alive, were now gathered solemnly to pay homage round her dead body.'[3]

So what had happened?

> 'When she came back to London with me, Warsaw was blowing up. She wanted to find Andy and see if they could do anything to help. He was at Bari on the heel of Italy, then the centre of SOE activities directed towards Poland, and she flew to meet him, eager to be parachuted in. But it was

just too late and there was nothing that could be done. We met every time she was in London, not as lovers but as very close friends. Just as I had a beloved wife and children, she had Andy and we'd always understood it would be so. Consequently I, like others, was trying to help her find something that would suit her. Knowing the terrible pain she'd suffered from the events in Warsaw, especially the Uprising on 1 August 1944, and now the hard knowledge that she couldn't go back to Poland, she was a deeply unhappy and unsettled woman. I suggested one or two things like working for an honest travel agent but other friends of hers in high places were trying to find desk jobs, which was never her. Neither did she want a long course of retraining. And, of course, because of her enormous independence she wouldn't wait for others to help – she'd go looking for something for herself. And she did for years.'

She made it perfectly clear to John Roper that she was not prepared to accept any job which was offered to her on the basis of what she had done in the war.[4]

*

Francis:

'One of the fiercest factors in Christine's make-up was her inborn dislike of authority and it was terribly important and best illustrated by her refusal to accept any officer class decoration. The only one she wanted was a Military Medal, which is only awarded to non-commissioned officers. That was very typical and I'm quite sure based on the experience of her arrogant aristocratic father and the suffering that her mother, a beautiful Jewess, had had to submit to.'

After a spell in Kenya, an accident to Andrew and a wild idea of going into partnership in Australia to buy up car agencies, including Porsche, which fell through, she was back in London, broke. She then hit on the idea of becoming a sea stewardess – it would get her to Australia where perhaps the scheme could be reworked out with the other partners and saved. She would travel and meet ordinary people and, in May 1951, she joined the Shaw Savill liner *Rauhine* on her maiden voyage to Australia and New Zealand. There she was kind to a bathroom steward, Dennis Muldowney, who helped her in her jealous persecution by some members of the crew (stewardesses, like all crew, were obliged to wear any wartime ribbons!). Muldowney appointed himself her protector. Unaware that he was a violent schizophrenic, her grateful pity for the lonely little man would fuel his obsession with her into tragedy. The Australian scheme died a death.

Back in London, after every voyage Muldowney would tag along behind Andy and Christine, dazzled by her circle of friends. For Andy, 'He was unbelievably thick-skinned. He was small, dark, insecure and he was a mass of obsessions and neuroses. We thought him a dangerous simpleton. But none of us had any idea of just how dangerous he was going to become. He was like a dingo dog trotting at Christine's heels.'[5]

For Francis: 'Muldowney was completely out of his depth in Christine's orbit. I thought him a pathetic bore, but Christine explained his background and his futile, miserable life. She told me he would not leave her alone. She said the only thing she could do to escape from him would be to pretend to sign on for another trip, and then to get as far away as she could until he came to his senses. I rather agreed with her, as I could see that he was becoming intolerably clinging.'

In her sympathetic biography of Christine, Madeleine Masson fully traces the terrible tension between Muldowney's possessiveness and jealous rages and Christine's feeling of responsibility for having introduced him to a way of life wherein he was lost. She said that his lack of intelligence made him vulnerable and she hesitated to hurt him. But she was pathologically hounded and stalked every minute she was in London and he himself not working. Finally, she made plans to leave England and join Andy at Liège to try and work out her complete escape. Tragically, her flight was cancelled, Muldowney burst into her room at the Shelbourne Hotel, 1 Lexham Gardens, accused her of driving him out of his mind and threatened to kill her. He could only be calmed when she asked him to accompany her to her appointment.

Back from her meal with Ludwig Popiel, she was in the process of taking a pile of her uniforms for storage down into the basement when Muldowney reappeared. After demented demands for the return of his letters if she was in fact leaving England, he struck. 'By the time medical help had arrived, she was dead.'

On Tuesday 30 September 1952, on his way to execution, Muldowney made only one remark. 'To kill is the final possession.'[6]

'Christine Granville's death,' recalls his eldest daughter, Niki, then ten years old; 'all that I remember is seeing Francis's emotional crying, nothing else.'

Christine had never talked of the degree of her love for Francis.

20

Although on the one hand Francis admitted the four years at Sunbury 'had not been a success' domestically – travel, squash or meetings in the evenings, and beery cricket at the weekends feeding the continual need to 'be away', – on the other hand,

> 'the corresponding period I'd spent with the Bureau had given me a wonderful opportunity to travel the length and breadth of the country and meet everyone who was creating change and seeking to turn the 1944 Education Act into reality. Among them was John Newsom, the Chief Education Officer for Hertfordshire and an outstanding educationalist.
>
> One day he came into my office and said, I've heard about the unwillingness of the government to expand the Central Bureau properly – would you like to come back into schooling? I said yes, but the problem was the old one – money and family. He said, I've got a school with a house in Stevenage – Alleyne's Grammar School – which will need steering towards ultimately becoming a comprehensive. I want you to apply I did, was interviewed, appointed and began my nine year tenure.'

The Bureau offices were in Hamilton House, the headquarters of the National Union of Teachers, at that stage being run by Ronald Gould, who was also Chairman of the Governors of the Central Bureau, a man who would continue to be influential in Francis's career. Twin souls where educational thinking was concerned, Ronnie Gould was perhaps the more tolerant of the apparent slow rate of change – 'It will happen, Francis, it will happen, it is happening.'

If luck is very often related to the accident of geography, personality is the factor which can make luck work. Just as privilege had helped before the war, so luck had played its part during it and would continue post-war, but the influential people in the new world Francis was about to inhabit were not offering a sinecure: they were responding to a man they felt had the will and ability to achieve what was necessary and important. Educationally what drove this man, they recognised, was not ambition but a quiet, fierce morality. It would be France all over again.

> 'It was a period of genuine excitement: not only were we turning a four-hundred-year-old Tudor grammar school of some 170 boys into the first stages of a mixed comprehensive, we were waging war on the eleven-plus, moulding a new form of education, in fact a new form of society. What was happening in Scandinavia was happening here. Stevenage was profoundly attractive because it had a *future,* it was a "New Town"; people were willing to make it work and there was a vibrancy in the staff who came in precisely because it was a New Town and in one of the areas of England that required huge expansion in housing and secondary schooling for all; the school was literally on the geographical cusp between old and new. Of course, this gave birth to real difficulties, too – the social problems of those who came from east London were to do with them not knowing anyone, or the buses; they were all young parents with no one to give them advice. They were desperate at first to get back to an uncle or auntie. It was very big and serious.
>
> Nevertheless, the improvements in the fifties were clearly quite dramatic in spite of much feebleness of the secondary modern nationwide. That was due to the fact that when the 1944 Act said "education for all", to the normal voter that meant grammar school education for all, which, within the post-war need for restart and equality, was patently undesirable. And stupid.'

'Francis was *exotic* when he hit Stevenage,' recalled David Harding, a former head boy who has remained a long family friend.

> He and Nan brought glamour, great flair and style and how, on his salary, one can only guess. When Nan had redesigned and repainted the old school house it was as if Heals and Habitat had suddenly opened a branch in Stevenage! Suddenly we saw paintings and sculpture as part of a house – like an art gallery!
>
> Francis always seemed to want to introduce everybody to the good life. His impact was palpable, never the same tailor-made suit daily, soft white shirts, ties from Liberty's, tall, military-looking, moustache, with a whiff of de Gaulle about him yet with his big head and sloping shoulders he

could have been a French railway driver with cosmopolitan tendencies. All this thrilled many of us – this was London, New York, the Continent – and, of course, there were the Gitanes. Yet despite his total air of command there was gentleness, humour and intelligence creating an aura in which you knew you were respected and your point of view would be heard. Discipline wasn't something he wanted to talk about and most of the quasi-public school rituals were eased out. Having to administer corporal punishment left him white with shame and his family would quietly leave him alone before and after the event to recover in his way.

In the provincial backwater which was Stevenage, post-war grey like the staff, Francis was *dangerous*, especially to the old-fashioned and the entrenched. But, backed by Newsom, having the money, and because there were new members of staff constantly coming in, Francis was not too often faced with his genuine dislike of sacking the teachers who should have been removed. He had too much respect for the skills they actually had. Education was for life, life-long.

Francis:

'There's a big word here – the *independence* – of schools under John Newsom. When I was appointed he told me, you'll have nothing to do with salaries – they are fixed by trade union agreements – but all the rest of the expenditure of the school is at your disposal and that of your staff. If you'd like to buy a wonderful painting and have no books, exercise books or pens – that's all right by me. If your colleagues don't like it you'll have to convince them. We also had the freedom to get round the absurdity of the eleven-plus which was still operational and the fundamental fault line in secondary education.

This I did by not automatically admitting the top ten names from the eleven-plus exam results. I'd talked to every primary school head and said, will you make a list of pupils you think will benefit most from coming to our school, or will get more from going to the secondary modern because we know that the marks mean absolutely nothing. So that way we were admitting candidates who had 20–30 per cent less marks than someone who previously would have had 20 per cent more.

In the first three years I helped to twin Stevenage with Autun and very deliberately carried over international exchanges from the Bureau into the school, e.g. apart from France and Germany, a communication with a school in Johannesburg. We welcomed the pupils and the two teachers who came with them who said, we don't think they'll want to go back! The pupils didn't talk about apartheid but the teachers did and they discouraged any talk of any return visit! There were no black boys in the school, nor in the primary schools.'

His young son, Paul, can only remember this period, as far as Francis was concerned, as one of having an active, present father because of sailing and, incidentally, creating in him a life-time passion for it, and camping. 'The memories are rich – I can still smell the latrines of pubs, taste the fried bread, jam sandwiches – exciting things we never had at home!'

Francis:

'We took groups of parents, teachers, pupils on the Broads. That was possible because John Newsom realised very quickly after the 1944 Act that there was a lot of money that had formerly been left by elderly widows to help their children and grandchildren financially through university but was now no longer needed through government provision under the Act. The sum of money was enormous and unusable; millions of pounds, stagnant, just sitting there.

John knew the only way of touching it was to get an Act through Parliament specifically for Herts Education Committee to be able to use the moneys – which were specified – in the interests of Herts children instead of the original designation. It succeeded.

Everyone else then tried to get theirs through Parliament and it was stopped. No other authority was able to do it. But that is where Barton Sailing Centre came from – six boats were acquired and, incidentally, a lot of international travel was also financed by the money.

Sailing is like teaching – you sniff it! It's a lovely sport, very enjoyable and I went on enjoying it until we went to Nairobi!'

David Harding:

In the nine years I was at Stevenage, the expansion was 800 per cent – a continual raft of new buildings, complete new assembly hall, huge expansion of the gym, masses of new classrooms, new science block, etc. Though most of it was planned before he arrived, he would hire extra huts just to keep pace with the arrival of new pupils, let alone trying to influence the whole curriculum and the culture of the school. All a fantastic success.

Hertfordshire led on new buildings and Alleyne's was a prototype. And Francis was the key man.

His was a creative invasion of French classes, though only rarely – out went the grammar, in came *Le Petit Prince* and we all learnt 'Chevaliers de la Table Ronde' as future party pieces in one lesson. Many of us went on French exchanges at the age of twelve – my exchange is now a judge well into his sixties and we're still in touch. In 1959 it was arranged for me to go on Voluntary Service Overseas to Guyana through Roy Close, who was working for Booker Brothers there, and I was sent up country and lived in a tin hut with a dozen black workers and infiltrated their society by playing in their calypso band – they taught me the bongos! And we had to be smuggled through the kitchens to play in white clubs; Francis utterly loathed racism.

Francis had real connections, lived at a different level – Richard Hoggart or the US Cultural Attaché would present the annual prizes, not the Chairman of the Governors.

'France, Germany and Belgium gave me the confidence to do things I'd never done before. I came to believe that to run a school you've got to be a good teacher and I taught seventeen hours a week – English, French – even maths – whatever was necessary.

The downside of this was that most evenings I was out. I was learning my trade. Yes, nightly committees and sport took me away from Nan, the girls and Christine and can be construed as selfishness. But when I was actually doing it I don't think I felt guilty; *post facto* it was very different. It sounds a bit like the old paradox, a good educationalist makes a lousy dad. They nearly all do, because you're giving other people's children the attention you ought to give to your own and in my experience that's not unusual.

But the sport selfishness – that was me not recognising the value of my presence. That's being reasonably honest. Looking back on it, I know it was wrong and part of the poison Mill Hill had injected into my system. The importance of sport and its selfish enjoyment was something I wasn't aware of at the time. I certainly had no fanciful notions of keeping physically fit or anything like that, but my failure was my failure as a husband and a father; it's something I think about a lot and in some ways it's due to Nan.

She was a perfectionist and, if you like, I didn't feel I could make much of a contribution to those things she could perfect. A local infants school needed an admission class teacher – she took over; as our school rose to a strength of six hundred we lacked a caterer for a year – she took over and in that way she was able to exercise her major interests – children, cooking, art and decoration. As we were building the school she was talking to the architect and telling him what to do. She got a lot out of it and she loved being involved. She did for the school what she'd done for Sunbury – she made everything work and that meant and included the whole of the non-teaching part of the school.

If I was "away" Nan was certainly "home". I wouldn't go as far as to say it was a lack of balance, because I don't think our partnership did lack balance.

On the other hand, there were things I ought to have done which I neglected to do.

What I did do was a lot of reading to Christine and I spent a great deal of time on that, a legacy from my father's Sunday. After all, I come from a family of actors and it was all Paul ever wanted to be!'

Paul remembered him reading 'Norse fairy tales, all of Ransome, C. S. Lewis, Dickens – absolutely fantastic, he was a wonderful reader. Then the Shakespeare play readings on a Sunday – boys would come and take part – a stunning concept and success. Francis even testified at the Lady Chatterley obscenity trial in 1960 – "This book I'd let my ten-year-old boy read!" – but I can't remember that he did but he would have.' D. H. Lawrence – a gift from his friend John Lloyd.

'Our two daughters were sitting eleven-plus at this time which they both failed but made up for so incredibly later on. They were becoming young women, yet, like us all, were enormously influenced by the experience of Christine.

Christine had a wonderful intelligence; she could follow a complex story and listen to the whole of a Dickens novel without uttering a word then ask about characters and create them in her mind. I felt that was a contribution I made and it took a reasonable amount of time. But that certainly didn't excuse my neglect of other things.

She was a very exceptional child. The experts said of her they'd never come across any dual-handicapped child with such a brilliant intelligence and who could, at her age, sustain a conversation with literally anyone and everyone.

After she'd got to the end of the possibilities of the Sunshine Home in East Grinstead, which we'd all trusted, we took her up to another wonderful school near Shrewsbury – the only one for the dual handicapped; she'd lost her sight and the use of her legs. We wanted to find somewhere where she could make friends; and we all spent a weekend there and the Head, called Myers, a most gifted man, said, she can't come here – we've no child (and they had them up to sixteen and seventeen years old) who could talk to her for five minutes. She's much too bright – you would be defeating what you are trying to do by sending her here. So we had to transfer her to a Dickensian school in Malmesbury, which was dark and terrible, but she did have friends there and they were mostly physically handicapped. And she'd be home for holidays.

I didn't feel I could do anything except reading and talking to her. Because everything else Nan did so well.

My guilt where Nan was concerned dated way back to the time when I was no longer earning a living. From that moment I was sharing a partnership with her and making really no special contribution, I began to consider how I could have made the partnership a better one for her than I had and what got in the way. There were a number of things, some of which we've covered, but there was another, important one – the absurdity of the stiff upper lip which I'd been forced into. It was profoundly destructive and when Christine died, for example, I didn't help Nan at all and I should have been able to. The stiff upper lip has been the source of much pain at certain periods in my life when I have made mistakes because of it – not because you set out to be like that but that is the way you have grown up, and it takes a lot to actually perceive it in yourself and be able to act differently. All this is being conscious of the inadequacies of your social upbringing.

This hinted at the certain formal tone in his relationships; it was not a coldness, but a mannerism.

David Harding:

There was something about Francis – and many I have talked to spoke of it in the same way – where one felt there was a final emotional barrier to being allowed to be either close to him or to feel he was close to you; a wall. He was even shy of saying anything emotional directly. He was very 'in the head' but with an incredible gift for friendship. His was a very cool approach to living. Only rarely did he allude to some special relationship from the age of twelve or thirteen. I felt he had aspirations for me which made me feel special and singled out, yet he only barely nodded in the direction of a 'special relationship' on a couple of occasions. Once, when we were buying wine at Gassac, the assistant said, 'Are you enjoying buying wine with your son?' Francis just smiled and Nan said to me softly, 'He was rather pleased with that idea' . . . or he may not have heard the question!

During the beginning of the second year in Stevenage news came from Radlett that his father was gravely ill. Suffering from angina, he had become very frail and was now unconscious. 'I went and stayed with him for twenty-four to forty-eight hours. Just holding his hand without any real conversation. I don't know that it had any significance at all. For me it was the only family death I attended.'

Two of his sisters have abiding memories of Francis, for long periods, standing at his father's shoulder gently wiping away the nasal phlegm with cotton-wool.

'It's impossible to recall passing thoughts but if I am right I was thinking what he had done for me, contributed to me, over thirty-seven years. It added up to a very great deal.'

Silence.

'I'm not avoiding the issue. I'm very little aware of what people call pain, tragic suffering and so on. Those concepts don't mean very much to me. I didn't sit there holding my father's hand and weeping internally.'

Silence.

'He loved crude Flemish humour. When I was young he told me about a man who was preparing a great feast for his wife and a chicken got up and crapped on the table – which he covered quickly with a silver top because it was nearly time to eat. Then the wife came in, very authoritarian, double-checking everything. "Have you done this" – yes – "have you done that" – yes. And she was furious and said, "Merde!", and he said, "Yes, I've done that" and lifted the top. From my earliest memories there was a closeness – we had giggles together.'

Silence.

'He was reaching the end of a life that I thought had been a great life. I hadn't been happy about his religious preoccupations at the end because I didn't share them. But that didn't mean I was against what he was doing any more than he had been against what I did as a conscientious objector; that was life – he believed one thing, I believed another.

The "cells", the conversion to High Anglicanism, largely took place when my brother died. They had become very close before his death and he sought relief. People's attitude to death and the deprivation of people they loved dearly has often puzzled me. In my father's case it was complete bewilderment; how was it that the only possible answer as far as he was concerned for his pain was God? The anarchist turned arch-conservative? He wasn't bullied into it, it was his own path. And then he had to follow the Anglican line – Catholicism was impossible after what it had done in Belgium to Protestantism – so he went with that and he returned in a sense to socialist thinking by helping to create Christian cells![1]

That religious development in him happened while I was in France. My brother died in 1941 and I went into France in 1943 after training. So apart from the conscientious objection tribunal I didn't have an opportunity to talk to him about my brother's death, although he would write very movingly about it. I knew about the cells and I could only think of Communist cells and I was always sorry I didn't have a giggle with him about it all. But there it was – he was doing this thing which I was told was an enormous help to a number of people.

Until my father died I met him regularly when he was in London – at the Atheneum. Right up until she died, I hardly ever saw my mother although she survived my father by eleven years. After we moved to Stevenage, and since the family had repudiated Nan to a very large extent, I had little chance to talk to him alone between 1952 and his death.

I don't think I'd ever stopped thinking about him. He was like Nan and Paul Héraud – whenever I was in a quandary I'd think how would they have solved this, what would they have done; not necessarily for the solution but the method. I'm simply talking about people whose actions and thinking you respect so much that you know they are better than your own. And we'd talk in French together about the rest of his life, the family as a whole, his involvement in art and, yes, I'm quite sure that when he found solace in religion he was very much affected by his love for Rubens and Italian art which was largely the art of religion.

We talked very little about the war. We talked about the politics behind it, the impossibility of neutrality for small countries after what had happened. I wouldn't say he'd washed his hands of politics; he just didn't think he had any part to play any more. No, the big thing we talked about was facing up to Pieter's death. In other words we talked about what a crushing blow to him it had been. He didn't want to talk about the RAF. For him the big breach was the war and the death of my brother.

We didn't talk about what I'd done. I think he knew that wasn't something to ask about. He regarded medals as being as idiotic as I do. It turned out he knew I'd taken part in the Résistance almost from the beginning. I think his non-asking, his silence, was linked closely to the loss of Pieter, a closing of his mind in certain areas. He also recognised that there were certain things I wouldn't want to talk to him about – Christine and my arrest, for example. It was in a sense too highly emotional to relate to our relationship at that time. I think both of us had to be careful not to find any confrontation.

The sympathy was fine. The love hadn't changed.'

A few of Emile's gifts to his son are hinted at – both highly sociable creatures with a talent for friendship, essential modesty, an intolerance of 'woolly thinking' or waste, the energy, a capacity to organise, a love of the intellect and fundamental seriousness and above all the art of the teacher.

Emile died on 2 November 1953.

David Harding:

To his great credit Francis never played the war card. I never really knew about it until the *This Is Your Life* programme in 1958. I was fifteen or sixteen before my parents said, 'Do you know what he did?' Little by little it crept out. He could have had an instantaneous following in 1952 from a whole school of boys but he'd made an absolutely conscious decision to draw a line. There were too many war 'heroes' who were not, the truths of many events were still darkly hidden. Christine Granville's life and murder and the outcome for a host of French Communist Party members he was still close to as yet unclear. I'm not surprised he wouldn't talk of it – those reasons alone would have made me go quiet for some time. No, for him all that mattered was – let's get back to education – that's what we fought for!

David Harding again:

I want to pick up on the point about 'fine educator and lousy dad'. No, Francis kept an eye on his children and Nan. He made it clear he would back their decisions, facilitate what they wanted to do whenever he could. No doubt in part a legacy from his father but it was forward thinking at the time.

They were three kids who developed in the most extraordinarily different ways and were encouraged to be themselves and expand into what they wanted to be. None are particularly conformist – Niki, after nursing had let her down, all over the place – Club Med to sailing boats across the Atlantic and settling into a life in an ashram in Mexico; Paul, from misadventures in Kenya to Special Branch, to entrepreneurship in France, to riding schools and the RNIB. They were all given an extraordinary freedom to think outside the norm. Jay is the most conformist but she rediscovered herself with a first-class degree in mid-life after a devastating three-year marriage in Iran. 'Reflected glory' was not on the agenda – they were more important than that. The disparate ways they have developed is testimony to the Cammaerts letting them fly – 'Fly and we'll support you if you need our support!' When Jay returned from Iran with baby Kia and discovered her ticket was one-way – she needed to fly and Nan brought up the baby to teen age to let her. This Jay, with her husband, Wole Bo Wey, has a thousand times repaid by caring, intimately, for her parents in their final years.

Francis:

'As a child Jay was a perfectionist, like her mother, and she remembers things which most children wouldn't and she suffered the feelings of failing the eleven-plus for thirty years. And that was the kind of child she was. You couldn't change that. When she took her degree, aged forty, and got a first, she wrote to me and said if she had got an upper second she would have regarded it as a failure. That was the residual emotion thirty years later of what society had called her failure.'

David Harding:

Francis was *fearless*, he loved the encounter with those brighter than himself, he delegated effortlessly – and that wasn't laziness – it was trust in the

> capacities of others; he never picked unnecessary battles when they didn't mean very much to him. He was imaginative. I can't see how you could operate in France, in a war situation without imagination, without scanning people around you, without anticipating their reactions, etc, to any given moment; without imagination he wouldn't have survived ten minutes. Transferred to teaching, and apart from the same ability to assess people, he was a man who imagined possibilities and made them happen – the placing of the Henry Moore statue between the two schools so that they both benefited is a case in point, and there are a hundred others. His whole attitude to education was imaginative – it was a period of grey and he was colourful and made things colourful.

The desire to move on was logical. The school, like the New Town, had by now begun to settle into its future path and its academic record was good.

Negatively there was the probability, after nine years, of new ideas and ways of expressing them becoming habit, of succumbing to the rust of repetition. John Newsom's deteriorating health meant him leaving education for publishing. An important support was gone and it probably helped make the move inevitable.

His active contact with primary and secondary teachers across the board, and his ceaseless union work, had convinced him that if comprehensive education was going to mean anything, the teachers had to control it. 'Teacher unity was absolutely central to what I was trying to do.'

Lastly, training mattered.

> 'The entire system was moving towards getting graduate-equivalent status in order to raise the whole self-confidence of the teaching profession, to ensuring that there was equal pay with graduates, mixed sex residential colleges and a Bachelor of Education degree. It would prove a formidable revolution. And I wanted to be there.
>
> At that time we heard that Beryl Paston Brown, a gifted Principal, was leaving Leicester and so her job was coming up. I'd met her and went to see her. She knew I was applying, I think she liked me and thought I had a contribution to make. I said to her, why are you leaving, because you're obviously the person to continue this college, which is expanding and growing, and she said, "Men aren't yet ready to accept orders from women and it's better I go to Homerton and you come here."'

21

The elevation from an old wattle and daub school house on the A1 – 'a leftover from the time when there were more pigs than pupils in the school – which meant that you couldn't install central heating; the place was kept up by damp' – to Scraptoft Hall, east of Leicester, a three-storey Queen Anne building, delighted the whole family. The Hall and its adjoining parkland had been bought and developed in 1954 as the site for the City's new Teacher Training College and the Hall became the Principal's Residence. It took a year to gut and rebuild, thus rewarding Francis's seemingly insatiable predilection for working in the middle of a building site.

'I loved the Hall – I thought it was a very beautiful place and that was it.'

> 'As usual, there were problems over finding lecturers for maths and physics. Here at least I had the help of a brilliant man, Frank Lovis, who had been working at the New Maths in schools for some time and, also, very early, did a lot of work with companies producing the new technology and got a lot of stuff into the schools, and so we were able to pull the maths, which was very important, out of the deplorable situation it was in at the start. He was an international rugby referee and guaranteeing him absence for his games was my way of saying "Thank You".
>
> Beryl Paston Brown had appointed a lot of good people – like George Kitson, a future Principal of the Central School of Speech and Drama in London – from whom I learnt a great deal. He'd started on teaching differently and conducting the relationships that students needed day to day, and before I left I asked him to take a year off and create an Annexe to serve a hundred mature students. By the time I left Scraptoft 30 per cent of the students were over thirty years old and it is now part of Northampton University.'

At that time there was a fierce dichotomy in Leicestershire. The City of Leicester retained the eleven-plus, the County did not. In fact, under Stewart Mason, its highly innovative Director of Education, it sought to introduce a modified comprehensive system all of its own – the famous 'Leicestershire Plan'. As early as 1957 it involved the abolition of the eleven-plus and instead of the rigidly divided structure of the past – primary, secondary and grammar schools – it substituted a two-tier system of non-selective comprehensive schools with a break at fourteen. Within it, too, went the abolition of streaming, the move to group and individualise study and, significantly, the matching of new buildings to these new procedures. Together with Oxfordshire and the West Riding, these 'rural schools' of Leicestershire were the pioneers of the breakout of primary education.

Like Francis himself, Mason believed passionately in the value of art and his school corridors were alive with constantly changing original paintings. If Scraptoft was going to choose schools for the students' teaching practice, it was seldom likely to favour the City. In any case, the City of Leicester Education Department had been, from day one, in Francis's eyes, rejectable: 'When I was appointed to Scraptoft I was asked by the Chief Education Officer if I would be interested in joining the Masons. And I joked, I wouldn't join any secret society that couldn't keep its secrets better than the Masons. Unknown to myself, I'd planted the seeds of busy enmity.'

What occupied him was his union work and support from the strong Education Department of the university under Professor Billy Tibble and contact with Brian Simon, the eminent historian of British education and a Marxist, who, among a host of other responsibilities, ran the bible of comprehensive education, the magazine *Forum*. There were people like Robin Pedley and Caroline Benn around – everybody was mobile, interactive. When Leicester University became independent of the University of Birmingham, contact was even easier and the sanity of such contact a world to be rejoiced in.

As at Stevenage this was genuinely a period of *change*. It was the golden age of post-war expansion in education and Francis was where he always wanted to be – in the middle of a revolution.

Tom Adams, an ardent socialist and Headmaster of Taylor Street School in Leicester, a converted factory, clearly remembered Francis's arrival on the Leicester scene:

It was at an ordinary NUT meeting. Nobody knew who he was. We vaguely knew he was from the College – but the Principal – no! Then he turned up again and took a large part in all the discussions. After such meetings we'd make for the pub and he said, 'I'll come with you!' He and I seemed to think alike on so many things and we'd both been conscientious objectors. Within a few weeks he was proposed for a seat on the Executive which had been left free by the College and within three years he was our President.

I invited him to dinner. He and Nan were very quiet as a couple. We had a boy playing upstairs and they were both keen he shouldn't be left out of things. Then it emerged that this was the first time they'd been out, socially, together, since the death of their daughter. From then on it was friendship.

As a person Francis had a need for people. I don't think he liked his own company very much. It was always the *way* in which he related to people that impressed. For instance, in our pub the repartee with the darts-players was unbelievable – yet they soon got into the habit of abandoning the board quicker than usual and getting down into conversations they wouldn't possibly ever have had – discussing real philosophy though they had little idea it was philosophy. They saw him as a big man but he didn't act like one.

Years later I would see him quietly walk into his staff room and everyone knew he was there. When his successor did the same, no one looked up.

He invested highly in trust. He trusted his students and they knew they'd not be betrayed; he never let anyone down yet at the same time if anything was wrong he'd say so. We were both intuitives – get something tried out then, once that had been done, move on. He was an anarchist without being anarchistic.

Above all, his pacifism ruled his politics.

A great deal of his energy went into smoothing the relationship between the College and the schools; he was always working to make us understand the problems of the students in the schools. He was always endeavouring to raise the profile of students to what they ought to have and to be.

In teaching terms he was original in believing that, if you trust people, especially students, with freedom, by lessening constraints, you get the best from them because they are free. 'These eighteen- to twenty-year-olds have got to be in contact with the larger issues – whether it be Art or Revolution. 1968 didn't rock the College – they were already there!'

He was passionate about teacher equality and status – equality with universities and within schools. He wanted a complete union of teachers, all teachers, a huge union. He was tremendously ambitious for the NUT. He wanted aspirations to be bigger. The idea behind it all was that teachers themselves should take hold of education.

Most of the people he was involved with actively were working class and I remember someone asking him why was it, with his upper middle-class upbringing, he was so able to work with everyone? And very simply he began talking a bit about France and he said the teachers in his life have been the people he'd met and they'd been from all over; he'd been lucky.

The presence of men in a college that had previously been all-female was a powerful determinant in Scraptoft and they quickly dominated student affairs. Mixed colleges meant that studenthood should become an adult affair and the responsibilities that go with freedom would be tested on a personal as well as a professional or academic level. Yes, the younger students could grow up together – the whole experience was equivalent to the modern gap year; yes, if you offered freedom you at the same time offered the freedom to make mistakes and there were mistakes; but, much to Francis's delight, the older intake provided a balance and were an enormous help in realising what it was the system was trying to achieve.

On the occasion of one 'mistake' two students came to Francis for advice – she was pregnant but didn't feel that she should be deprived of the chance to finish her studies, an argument that Francis, having offered his congratulations, fully supported. He invited them to discuss it with himself and Nan and it was Nan who came to the rescue. The student would take a year off and have the baby then, the following autumn term, return and finish her training. While she was involved with her daily studies Nan would look after the baby, a big, almost predictable, commitment. This was not a singular occasion.

Freedom wasn't all about sex, or destructive:

'There were things of which I felt enormously proud. For instance, the students perceived the problem of immigrant children which, in Leicester at that stage, was quite small. Nevertheless, problems existed. They ran classes for Asian mothers because they had particular language and religious difficulties and also for the Afro-Caribbean families. Without talking to anyone about it they ran classes in the evenings for these mothers to help their children through school and it went on, as far as I know, for a decade. They took place at schools and centres which were close to where the mums lived. They were marvellously wise about it and I only discovered it by one mother coming up and saying how grateful she was for what the students had done! So I had a look to see what was happening and it was tremendously impressive. The students had gone on teaching practice, seen the problem, felt free to do something about it and did something about it. When the schools saw this kind of commitment they were only too pleased to become involved; exactly what was wanted.'

Francis's central role in this panorama of emotion and intention, parochial and national participation, in freedom versus prejudice, can best be illustrated by the early career of someone he regarded as his and Nan's 'great success' – the College's first female Union President. 'Her importance was that she got herself elected.'

From a literate working-class evangelical family in Leicestershire, one of seven children born in ten years and not allowed to run on Sundays, Priscilla Strutt could claim that the world of *Oranges Are Not the Only Fruit* shadows her own story and the vocabulary and idiom of both are identical – 'You don't need an airing cupboard when you've got Jesus'. Very bright, school could be and often was, alien, it being pointed out at assembly 'there are girls who can't play for the school on Saturday because they have to earn money'. Later, when she lost her faith, she could reassure her mother, 'You didn't waste my upbringing; I learnt music, love of words and the ability to preach from you', and regard her father, who early on lost his belief, as a working-class aristocrat – 'he had ideals'. Teaching, rather than university, she was encouraged to regard as 'the best you can hope for' and she ended up at Scraptoft, her choice because her headmistress had dismissed it as having 'a rather progressive Principal, I hear'.

I was taking everything in at once, trying to make sense of the world. I couldn't take history – I was a creationist. I was a socialist yet I didn't believe in nationalisation. I would be thirty before I could abandon my belief and become a 'happy heathen'. I was still looking for a structure, I still thought I needed a religion – luckily I didn't find one.

The centre was the bar. If you wanted time with Francis you headed for the bar. Word got round – he's in town! Francis loved it, he loved us, we were the future. If you weren't too shy you could park your bum on a barstool beside him and he'd chat to you, find out who you were and buy you one drink, but usually we bought our own, no rounds. By the second year Francis had made it clear to me that he saw my value as a human being. For him I was a classic – working-class, ignorant but bright with a feel for politics. He did for me what he did for many, many others – he changed the course of my life, not by telling me what to do but by facilitating the chance to change.

The image of the sixties was a promiscuous one – actually, we were mostly very confused. But as tyro teachers we got the good, necessary stuff – how important it was to see the whole child and to see the child as part of the whole. I won the Union Presidency in my third year, then, having held off and held off, finally succumbed to sexual congress just before Christmas after a breakfast with toast.

I was Student Union President, it was my final teaching practice and I was violently sick every morning. I was still twenty so an adult signature was necessary in order to have an abortion – or, if that was impossible, I'd have to arrange one myself. Dr Philip Bloom in Harley Street agreed to sanction the abortion if I could get an adult signature. I remember being totally beaten by the intercom at his door. I went to Francis who came down from a dinner, full of bonhomie, to see me supported by two friends. He promised to consider the situation. When we met he said, 'I can't do this. You're a grown-up and I feel very strongly that I am not *in loco parentis*', and he wouldn't compromise. So he wrote a long letter to both psychiatrists (you had to be sanctioned by two) saying that, as far as he was concerned, I was an adult capable of making up my own mind and if they wanted him to endorse my decision he would happily do that – but he would not sign *in loco parentis*. It had all come down to Francis or a backstreet abortionist. I really admired his stand.

I had the abortion, cash down first, on 10 March, and the 14th was my mother's birthday and my friends sent flowers from Leicester in case she'd discover they came from London. My philosophy has always been 'Here I stand, I can do no other', which later grew into 'If you don't protest you collude'. Francis never said 'I helped you over an abortion'; no, what he did say was 'I supported you over one of the most life-changing decisions you will ever make and I've never regretted it.'

No, I didn't fancy him – I felt his power – women love authority because we're denied so much. I probably fancied Nan more. My respect for her grew into love. She had a bright mind, with a narrative thread always there. Christine's birth had been so difficult. Jay, who loved her mother completely, said once that Christine's disablement disabled the whole family – the others feeling they didn't get the attention they deserved.

After staying with Nan and Francis, once, the children and I were aiming to cycle across the Massif Central and at one point we were talking about the approach to Le Puy. Francis dug out maps, insisted on certain routes and pointed out the best places to stop. One was aware this was the man from the Résistance talking, total recall and knowledge and, of course, when we did the trip it was full of roadside memories of the war; he'd directed us there deliberately, the effortless educator, facilitator and enabler. 'Maps are my fingers,' he'd murmured.

Francis firmly believed that nine years was the maximum period anyone should stay in one place. It was enough for introducing new ideas, then for making them work (or dropping them) and, finally, for consolidation and making sure the right people were in charge to continue the work. Longer than that was repetition. Stevenage had been fine in this regard but Scraptoft fell short.

'Educationally, it was a matter of regret. What had been talked about in the 1950s was now being put into practice – we had three- and four-year courses set up and we were finishing with the Certificate. *Pace* Ronnie Gould, it all took time.

By 1966 I had been head-hunted by the Kenyan government for the post of Professor of Education in Nairobi. After the call I'd gone down for lunch with Nan and told her I'd said no, there was too much to do here. She said, "Don't be a bloody fool. Now we've lost Christine we can go to Africa which you've always wanted to do; you go back and ring up and say you'll apply." I did. In an interview in London, Jomo Kenyatta told me I'd got the post because of my war record! I was fifty and for some obscure reason even then fifties were a barrier in employers' minds, so maybe I was lucky. But the Masons wanted to mar my going.

The nice caretaker at Scraptoft came to me and said his daughter, aged thirteen, had read a story published in the College magazine which was a bit sexually outspoken and she didn't know what it was about. Today it would be regarded as rather prim but I told the editor I'd look into it. I held a meeting of all my colleagues, asked them if they'd read the story, told them I'd read it and thought it well written but that it posed a problem. Because a students' magazine was not subject to national or public control, and we didn't want it to be, there was nevertheless a danger if a row arose and I said I'd like their support in talking to the students, explaining the problems of censorship and the problem of a student magazine in relation to young children. If any of them wanted further action to be taken, please to let me know. As they were going off on holiday I wrote to all of them and told them I'd seen the students, we'd agreed we didn't want to impose censorship but I'd asked the President and the editor, if they had any doubts about any contributions, to come and talk to me about it before they actually printed anything. I asked my colleagues, if you don't agree with this please let me know straight away. Everyone said that was fine and we were all happy. Masons on the staff made no objection at that stage.

Before going to Kenya I was summoned to the Education Office by a small sub-committee of the education committee who were all Freemasons and were determined I should leave under a cloud. I told them what I'd done and that the staff were on my side. They said, "You're running a brothel." They'd read the story and that was their attitude. It was part of a build-up to making sure that I wasn't replaced by someone who'd be likely to continue the obscene things I'd been up to. They succeeded in stopping an excellent candidate who later became Secretary of the Commonwealth Institute – Jimmy Porter – but they didn't manage to taint me long term. On returning from Kenya I was interviewed for two of the top jobs in the country – Director of the British Council and Chief Education Officer of the Inner London Education Authority. Silly folk. But what they did manage to achieve was to place their candidate in my stead at Scraptoft. Full stop.'

Francis would be leaving not only an educational revolution in full flood but also, for the moment, the added responsibilities he'd assumed in his union work. If he committed himself to a course of action it was for long term, and union work was no exception.

He was professionally very unapologetic about the 'time away' such activity called for, believing fiercely that it helped the school or college because of its *national* nature. But it was on the personal level that the consequences of such regular absence, nurtured by his war and immediate post-war 'freedom', gradually impinged and in later years became, especially where Nan was concerned, a further twist to their 'silence', the source of his already admitted guilt – the whole process triggered, silently at first, by the death of Christine in the second year at Scraptoft.

Tales of this unique child with her sunny sensitivity, high intelligence and acute awareness of others, are manifold and everyone who knew her has their own to tell – a sister with teenage torments crying in her sleep to wake and find that 'Christine, already blind and six years younger, had left her bed, crossed the room on her behind and was stroking my hair and murmuring, like an adult, "It'll be all right". She had no negativity in her. She would prop up her head but the moment she knew people were within her orbit she'd drop her arm; she never talked about pain and that was what was so surprising and even shocking when she'd go into her crises because she'd never discuss them. Like her parents she couldn't stand fools and she couldn't stand pity; pity has to have compassion not curiosity or duty. She could "see" the pious coming and she'd say, "I've plenty of love in my life, you don't have to worry about me" and I'd say, after they'd gone, "how could you tell?" and she'd say, "pity has a smell" – then grin.'

Friends and her impish brother Paul speak of spending willing hours with her immobility in silence or riot – she could be effortlessly scatological in her vocabulary – while others testify to her blazing need to know – 'explain navy blue'. Part of the problems lay with this intelligence: in her 'schools' it had always been difficult for her to find friends of her own age and the value of Scraptoft was that there were different kinds of people available, students, male and female, to surround her. Paul, when working for the Royal Institute of Blind People, was daily reminded of the world of his sister – dominoes with raised dots, teddy bears with bells on their heels so that you could know where they were, teddy-bears your own size that could be hugged, the utter necessity for the tactile in the world of the blind. But he remembered her, too, in the school at East Grinstead: 'She'd have all the children there around her – it was like the laying on of hands – children so difficult to deal with. There was a boy who could just giggle so she'd giggle with him and hold his toe. She knew that touching any other part of his body was impossible – she knew where to touch him and that he needed to be touched.'

But as she grew towards puberty anger at her condition and its frustrations found a typically comic outlet – she'd call for 'cracked-pot time'. All cracked or chipped crockery was kept to be smashed and, whenever the occasion demanded it, any member of the family, from Nan to her youngest child, could and did go outside and hurl the plates or whatever at a concrete wall, screaming away individual frustration. On one occasion Christine was presented with an old fashioned yellow mixing bowl and she ran her hand around the inside of it, then, 'No, no, no, I don't want one that isn't cracked.'

In the final crowded party organised by the students – from which Francis and Nan quietly absented themselves – she was upright on a sofa; a late arrival hesitated at the door to the corridor at the noise and bustle within and she called out, 'Come in, come in! Don't stay out there!' 'How does she do that!' marvelled her brother.

Niki concluded, 'She had this out-and-out desire to be fourteen. She said she didn't want to go past it because she wouldn't have a normal life and up to fourteen she felt she could live till then. At the time of the party I felt she was in the finest form she'd been in for years. Then, ten days later, she slipped away.'

As the family, plus dog, made its way towards their new base in Nairobi, excitement and anticipation served to mask momentarily the fact that internally relationships had floundered since the death of Christine.

Christine's body had been donated to science; there was no burial and no public chance given for the students or anyone to mourn. Francis and Nan offered no explanation for this decision even to their other children, who were not consulted, and as Jay, the second-born, dryly confirmed, 'It was as if she had been swept under the carpet.'

But both parents were sensitive, good, deeply caring people; Nan especially, a carer *par excellence*, had given her all for her child even, to some extent, at the expense of the others. It was reckoned that with her skills she could have done everything necessary for her daughter on her own, but she had chosen to share her with everybody and perhaps, to a large degree, denied herself; Francis's contributions we have already touched on. One can only surmise, therefore, that their grief and pain as parents was so strong that they just stuck together over her death or Nan's complete control might've gone. Or were they both being consistent? Do not dwell on the past, it is the future that counts. It certainly echoed Francis's declared feelings on the death of his brother and father. He had no tolerance of mourning. That was associated with religion he had rejected long ago and, as for 'celebration' in a church or the paying of people to 'perform', that was 'totally unacceptable'. 'So,' he concluded, 'I had to avoid being like that and I shut things down which was absolutely wrong in terms of my children. Christine's departure was far too administrative, efficient. Some kind of vehicle came and took her away and I was totally incompetent.'

This still seems more like an aversion to method than a reason. Nobody offered any other explanation for their action, though their grandson made a tentative guess: Francis never liked things to go wrong, his life had been and continued to be incredibly successful. Only the fate of Christine, tragically disabled, was beyond their control.

The fallout was nevertheless long lasting. To the young Paul and to Niki it felt like abandonment. They had been excluded, not confided in, not consulted, so they 'didn't matter'; their love never given a chance to weep. Consequently both, in their differing ways, 'moved away', increasingly, from the family: Paul into adolescent wildness and Niki, with equal determination, ultimately to Mexico. There was a great deal of their father in those actions. Jay had reached Iran and returned alone with a son, Kia, who in Francis's words, 'gradually replaced Christine at the heart of the family with his achievements'.

But the one person, much to his later shame, whose behaviour seemed not publicly to be affected was that of Francis. Although for ten years he could not mention Christine's name, he could have, but didn't, help Nan in their loss. It was a perfect chance to change direction, change behaviour but *his* 'awayness' did not alter; he was as much involved elsewhere and absent from the home, and this he would duplicate with gusto in Kenya and Botswana. Nan had long since had to accept the fact that, for Francis, home did not come first; it was where he returned to eat, change and go out from.

But Christine's death and the decision to go to Kenya would ultimately liberate Nan and in so doing provide a solution to the shadow of the long silence between them. She was a person who had never given up on her own life.

22

'As Head of the Department of Education in the University, I wanted to employ a local secretary and I appointed Essey Senvumo, a Ugandan aristocrat who belonged to one of the families close to the Kabaka, or King; Uganda was still very feudal in its hierarchical structure. Essey stayed for ten years after I'd left – she was very good, very efficient and very thorough. Again my luck – I've always been blessed with omnicompetent secretaries.'

The part of the University of East Africa in Nairobi was formerly the Gandhi Memorial Academy, financed almost exclusively by and for Indians, descendants of the 31,983 labourers who, from 1902, had crossed from India to work on the construction of the great railway. When it was completed seven thousand decided to stay on, and, denied the right to take up farming, turned to trading and gradually spread the use of money rather than barter into the economy.

'But to newly independent Kenya it was a minority institution of people they didn't like very much because they ran commercial life. One of the disasters was education – the government of Jomo Kenyatta had decreed "we're not going to have teachers educated in an Asian institution" and wouldn't allow any resources to go into teacher education. They were only three years past a savage, bitter civil war, remember, fought to secure the rights of the Kikuyu and the Kamba nations – I never use the word "tribe" – and the government insisted on the need for Kikuyu priority. The situation was saved by the Carnegie Corporation in New York who were very interested in assisting the transfer from colonial rule to independence. They persuaded the government that there was bound to be a loss of teachers from the only post-secondary institution in Kenya and they had to have some teacher education there otherwise graduates were going to stagger into schools with no guidance. Hence the reason for my appointment.

Arthur Porter from Sierra Leone, my Principal, an excellent, wise, diplomatic academic, who saw me through my early days, said what I really had to do was to make the department an up-to-date *Kenyan* affair; that was the most important part of the work on hand.

In fact, good work had already started – for instance, history had still been taught as if no African civilisation had existed before the arrival of the whites. So a programme of studies, where the evidence came a great deal from the work of Richard Leakey and the discoveries of ninth-century ironworks, etc, was used finally to put the colonial presence into its proper perspective.

The first thing was to find Kikuyu scholars. Kikuyus were the majority in government and it was they, very largely, who had fought the civil war because they'd felt immorally restricted in their need for land and bitterly resented the presence of European settlers and reservations in Kenya.

And we've come to "Tom Mboya's Airlift". Graduates were needed for key jobs in Kenya and Mboya had made an agreement with Walter Reuther in America to fly several hundred school pupils, men and women, to universities there backed by the American Trades Unions.

So, in turn, Nan and I flew to America in 1968, again financed by the Carnegie Foundation, the aim being for me to go round the universities and try and get good Kenyans to come back and teach in the country. It wasn't very successful, overall; we found about six Kikuyu and a number of lost souls who couldn't really cope with American university education but we also found some very good gifted and personality gifted people, one of whom I had even identified to be my successor. Unfortunately they all "came from the west".

Originally the west of the country – Kisumu and the area around Lake Victoria – were part of Uganda and the boundary between the two countries was down the Rift Valley and all the Luhyan part was west of it, while the Kikuyu and Kamba were to the east. Later this was changed and the ill-informed and unthought-out policy of the colonial government thus had a profound influence on the way East Africa developed. Tanzania was nationally reasonably sensible; Uganda exploited its medieval aristocracy and royal family but Kenya, with its western border now on Lake Victoria, was left with the deep divide of the Rift Valley between west and east, leaving the powerful Kikuyu and Kamba nations running the government in the east and the huge numbers from northern Luhya territory occupying the "west".

Added to our problems, too, was the fact that among all the different groups of missionaries, only the British Quakers had had the wisdom to say, we won't spread ourselves all over the country, we'll find one locality, which they did and that was part of the Luhya and it became totally Quaker. Quakers were keen on education and among the number of women graduates from that part of the Luhya territory about four out of five came from one small village alone.

'Probably the most gifted educationalist in Kenya at that time was Salome Nolega. She had been head girl of the girls' grammar school, which had been evacuated outside the zone of hostilities during the civil war. To all intents and purposes she'd run the school, then become a teacher, and when I got there she was Principal of a college in Nairobi. A stunning woman in every sense.

One of the first things I was asked to do by the government was to produce a survey of teacher education throughout the country and make recommendations for its future development. For this I linked up with Salome and Joseph Lijembe, replacing the brother of a junior minister in the government, who, coming from the Falls of Lake Victoria, was regarded as "a bit too western". We visited every college and talked with every staff member and student over a period of several months. I think there were fourteen colleges in all but most were tiny places of less than a hundred students, single-sex and with very modest standards of study. All except two were set up and heavily influenced by one or other of the Christian Missionary organisations and, apart from the Quakers' own college, still very old-fashioned in educational method. The two colleges with three to four thousand students were both in western Kenya and there lay our problem – there was so much of the west in qualified education and it was difficult to get a balanced staff; the difference between the nations was also vast because of language. When we got to Kenya there were 120 identified, different languages, divisible into about fifteen language groups. But even within those fifteen a lot of people who were said to be Luhya speakers couldn't understand someone from a village 20 kilometres away. Among all this was Kiswahili which everyone spoke very badly and which was entirely local and non-literary. One of the fourteen to fifteen languages was used in the first two years of primary school; after that they went into English, thenceforth the language of teaching throughout late primary, secondary and post-secondary study. One terrible problem to emerge from this was that there were already some very gifted Kenyan writers and they were forced for financial reasons to write in the colonial-oppressive language and not in their mother tongue. These problems were political as well as literary because they were forced into a line of semi-rebellion; being obliged to write in English dictated the nature of their writing. No books were sold except in English; it was culturally destructive. Even a writer as powerful and important as Ngugi Wa Thiong'o, a friend, had to wait until the 1980s before his work, written in his own language, Gikuyu, would be published

In school terms the cultural problem in Kenya was relatively minor because all Kenyan children had at least three languages! Worldwide, multilingualism separates the haves from the have-nots yet it is vital because, outside the English, probably 90 per cent of the children of the world have to have more than one language if they are to survive.

After the survey, we lined up our recommendations. These were that the colleges be joined together, reducing the fifteen to eight, that they should all be under the Ministry of Education, not the Church, and that a salary scale for the teachers in colleges should be about or above that of the teachers in schools. Talk about continuing where I'd left off at Scraptoft.

We made recommendations on the quality of the colleges as they were and identified the real need as being the removal from education of the missionaries who very often even quarrelled among themselves. The bottom line was that the teacher education institutions had to be Kenyan, run by Kenyans and taught by Kenyans and my job was to try and set that up as quickly as possible. Every recommendation was implemented and the Report welcomed because it was deliberately the end of the missionary.

Giving degrees in education meant first of all that you had to teach what their country was all about – which they didn't know. For instance, Salome, travelling with me, had never seen an elephant, never seen a lion or a crocodile and never seen snow. All these things could be shown because we had them on the doorstep. So in that way the basis of the course became the study of their own country, including the problem of the differences in language. Like everywhere else we had to develop their most urgent needs – mathematics and science – and we were backed well by senior government figures.

Finding people with teaching abilities wasn't so difficult. I have a feeling that a lot of Africans are good at teaching. This stems, I think, from early childhood – the baby in every African nation I encountered was treated in the same way. As soon as it could toddle it was an adult and given an adult job to do which nearly always involved looking after an animal; it was an adult, part of the community, contributing to its community and the child was never useless. That gave adult Africans a much better start than we have, to my mind, because they were not children who were patronised and talked down to – they were talked up to. So teachers were talking to young adults. Teachers in turn were older so they deserved respect – age deserved respect – and the whole thing was structurally based on age and communication ability related to age. What you didn't have was the awkwardness of the relationship between different people of different ages we often find in Europe. Witness the respect my former pupil showed to Tom Henn at Nairobi airport.[1]

Progress was slow. I had to consider myself as a visitor, there to help. I felt I was very much in the same position as I was in France during the war – I wasn't there to tell them what to do and how to do it. I was there to indicate certain problems which struck me and to discuss them.'

Jay, who saw her father working at close quarters, elaborated:

Francis was sent *to manage change and that was what he was good at*. He knew what he wanted to do and he found the right people to help him; often they did the work. But, again, it's worth saying, he had a way of deciding if you were a goodie or a baddie. Great as he was at delegating, if you were not reckoned, nothing interesting came your way and you soon got the idea. It wasn't very diplomatic but on the other hand with all his committee work he couldn't always act like that – you'd never get anything through – and he had it within him to be much more subtle to get what he wanted going. He had different styles for different occasions but when he was the boss he was not going to faff around with people who were not going to help the cause.

As in the Report he wrote at the end of his work in 1972, his educational writing was very intelligent, lucid, but informed by real dreams. He was so clear. It was that which impressed others – 'Here's someone who knows what he's talking about, good!'

The Report was full of practical ideas for the future. He anticipated 'Distance Learning', i.e. using television, etc, to overcome shortage of resources devoted towards education. He could manoeuvre between educational need and political reality, he could join countries together to pool resources; no one was to be excluded – 'education is a continuing process which should not seem to have terminal periods'. He recognised the relationship and its problems between an agricultural economy at the mercy of international ruthlessness and the need to finance the ambition of a nation's increasing awareness of itself. Adult education ('Informal Education') could use the buildings of their childrens' schools, school examiners should become school consultants, exams should include consideration of personality, motivation and late development instead of seeking immediate results; above all teachers mattered – from pre-school to university.

'Back to Salome. The Kenyan politicians were terrified of her because she was probably the most able human being in Kenya at the time. As Principal of her college in Nairobi she was therefore of enormous political importance. So they shifted her out to a huge secondary school right on the Ugandan border – as far away from Nairobi as they could manage. I used to go and see her and sent a lot of students to her for their teaching practice. She stayed there till I left and she remained there when I was in Botswana, and I came up and had an evening meal with her in 1982–3. She died of cancer about two years after that. It was very sad.

Yes, she carried out the policies we'd set out and more that she would have invented herself. Her school of, I think, eight hundred girls was one of the happiest places in Kenya, all down to her. I asked her once why she'd never married and she said, "There isn't a man in Kenya who could afford my bride price. My bride price is twice my salary and no one's got that kind of money." A male friend overheard this conversation and he said to me, she may not have been able to accept the amount of the bride price but there was a man who touched her heart. You know she's got two children? To call it "touching her heart" – that was the kind of effect she had.

Salome represented another salient fact. One of the most dramatic things we witnessed was the emergence of women. In less than a decade they came from slavery on the land, with no reading, no writing, to become some of the brightest graduate students in the country. They weren't slaves but they were in fact slaves. More than 50 per cent of my students were female and by the time they achieved their degree – it had taken ten years – it meant they'd made their start during the civil war.

No, I don't know of any succeeding in business. Business was so dominated by Asians and they on the whole didn't tend to encourage women. They might have entered business, but I can't say.'

If Francis, at the height of his powers, was willingly travelling 2400 miles a month – 'it's a large country!' – the family adjusted as rapidly, individually in their private way. Nan loved Kenya. Now with her own car and released, however unwillingly, from her responsibility for Christine, she felt she could have 'a proper life at last'. Modestly, she taught in the shanty town in Nairobi and, while Jay found work in an art gallery and later in London with Roy Close at the National Economic Development Council, before returning to Kenya, Nan reared Kia, allowing his mother 'to fly'. In later life he could say, 'Nan was my mother but Francis was always my grandfather. She did everything *not* to replace Jay yet she was the only constant in the first twenty years of my life – until I'd gone through everything at university.' In addition to all this, within the context of traditional Kenyan hospitality, she still found time to run their usual open house.

The survey and report over, Francis brought a wide range of people to the house and, said Jay, 'we did a lot of family things'. Despite serious recurrent illnesses, Nan felt freer and the curse of the silence began to fade in the face of their parallel maturities and, despite periodic difficulties, they existed, strongly, side by side, not apart. To one child she could admit, 'I've been angry with your father most of my life; I've been angry with *men* most of my life and, given other circumstances, I'd probably have been better off with women!' Yet to Kia she'd confess that, difficult, hard as things were, Francis was the man for her and she wasn't sorry she'd married him.

Paradox persisted in Francis's personality and behaviour – the man of clear, articulated moral values who rarely wished to be at home; perhaps home meant his mother. Sylviane Rey, remembered by the family as a 'gorgeous person', while recounting his qualities of gentleness, calm courage and sense of humour, could still be hurt: 'After having lived for some time in the Drôme (in retirement) Francis disappeared without explanation, disappointing those who still valued him but, *no doubt, no longer having anything to bring him. He is not a sentimental man.*' The cause might have been the proximity of Nan, who had known of their previous friendship, and as Katharine Whitehorn, a friend of both women, wryly pointed out, 'where a beautiful friendship is concerned a sensible English wife resents the French even more!'[2]

But the observation still stands and is consistent with Francis's attitude to death – even of those closest to him. A modest man who never mentioned the honours bestowed on him for his educational work, let alone his very real scorn for his wartime medals, was at the same time the man who clearly wished to be acknowledged and acclaimed.

But the strangest paradox still lay in his relationship to Nan.

This 'strenuous loner' with 'a Casanova edge' whose affairs were many, this charismatic, tolerant enabler, facilitator, who would understand and forgive a student a multitude of sins or defend with intelligence and compassion the waywardness of a friend, became extremely intolerant of any slighting or questioning of Nan. In Jay's words, 'she was in this *bubble* Francis put her in'. Francis 'was in a fury if someone was not good to her and would then think nothing good of them; they would be dead'. Life with her was difficult; without her it was unthinkable, rudderless. Those who had really known the couple would even feel that Francis was Nan's creation; he was the achiever, immensely nuanced, but she was the lodestar.

One story will illustrate this 'fury'. It is Paul's account.

Once in Kenya, everything could happen. Carole, a lovely girl who Nan helped, suggested we take Nan to the Game Park to have breakfast and watch the sun come up. Nan was thrilled – she had recently had a serious hip operation in Nairobi. Everything we did at this time was outrageous and this was no exception. Carole had made some cookies, very powerful, and after Nan had eaten her first she declared, 'They're very interesting, I'll have another' and she did and – disaster. She began hallucinating, seeing tigers stalking in the trees, she couldn't feel her lips or her hand and on the way back getting quite paranoid which happens sometimes when you have too much – you get jumpy about other people and everything else – and in her case, because she'd given up smoking in Scraptoft, it was the tobacco.

Nan took to her bed and when Francis came home and saw the state she was in he insisted on calling a doctor, which she wouldn't allow. Then he turned to me – I was to blame, *I had put Nan at risk*, and he hit me once, in the chest. I was much lighter than I am now, but I was pretty fit, having played a lot of rugby, and I hit the wall, which was six to seven feet across the room, about two feet off the floor and, like in a classic *Tom and Jerry* cartoon, I slid slowly down. He was so ashamed at what he'd done he left, wordless and white.

I was completely gobsmacked; after so long at being untamed and my misdemeanours always tolerated, I'd got a response. I could do things to him, myself, my friends, *but not to Nan*!

In terms of shame Francis equated the blow with the death of the Milicien.

Francis:

'I was ready to leave Kenya in 1970, after four years, but the postal strike in England stopped me from applying for a job. Generally speaking the movement had been forward but the Department of Education at the University of East Africa ceased to be and it became the University of Kenya – so I stayed on for another two years. But in that period the University changed profoundly and the conflict between the students and the governing authority became difficult. I think that in all the newly independent countries there was at the political power centre a fear of two groups of people – the students and the teachers – and they didn't want either of them coming along with their bright new ideas.

Many French, Portuguese and British nationals, like myself, were perfectly ashamed of what harm our countries had done as imperial powers. So our reasons for going and working with the new independent nations was to try and make up a tiny bit for the appalling idiocy and violence of colonial thinking. If we could help things to emerge which would lead towards more self-confidence in the countries themselves, so much the better. We had to recognise that Nan and I went there at a very favourable time but then things began to go very badly, especially after the death of Jomo Kenyatta in 1978.

On the whole I was pleased to be going back. What I thought I ought to do had come to an end. I didn't think it was wise for a white helper to take too prominent a part in the change towards local control. Kenya increased my love of Africa a great deal and I left with few regrets. In Exmouth, I'd find a totally different situation – they were reducing teacher training instead of increasing it – it was cut back, threatening to abolish us. But one way I was able to continue my interest in Africa was by inviting Africans to fill the places the British government didn't want us to fill with British students! In they marched – students from Kenya and Botswana!

'Both domestically and professionally, Rolle was in many respects a repetition of Scraptoft – a house to restructure and powerful changes in teacher training which, as I've said, I hadn't expected but which immediately fired my unionism once again.

The College had some obvious attractions: it was beautiful, in a lovely position, we had the sea, and a very good school for Kia. Jay and Paul we'd left in Nairobi – they'd find their own ways. The Principal's house needed great help from the County Education Property committee, rattling as it was with the hidden whisky bottles of the previous Principal, Doris Spicer. She had been a sad and depressed figure; it wasn't that the students disliked her, they just didn't *know* her. As usual there was a wonderful secretary who helped the Registrar keep things going.

So while Nan got together with everybody in the place, passed a course in horticulture at a Poly and took over the family finances because I'd made a mess of them, I focused on the College.

In my customary search for balance it was obvious that the education of the very young was not being catered for anywhere else, including the two other colleges in the region. Then we had to find the suitable education staff which wasn't easy because few were unaware of the movement afoot to change teacher training. All the touching up of disciplines was difficult because of the atmosphere of reduction and everything became a bit rushed, because I arrived at the beginning of September and was immediately ordered to cut down on our admissions by 3 per cent during the next month! Rolle was a college of seven to eight hundred students and each year we were told to admit fewer and fewer – and that was when the African students were slotted in, to everybody's benefit. The English teachers said afterwards that they had learnt a great deal from them, especially over child rearing.

In fact, this coincided with the Ministry of Education in 1973–4 increasing per-overseas-student-cost and the Kenyan High Commissioner in London, who we'd known in Kenya, rang me up and said the President wanted to see me. He's staying at the Dorchester; can you manage tomorrow? I said yes. I was shown up to Moi's suite and he dropped down on his knees in front of me and virtually kissed my shoes crying, "You must save us! We want to send our students to England. We don't want them going to America or Russia, but with the cost your government has imposed we can't afford to send them here." I said I entirely agreed with him but that the government would hardly be likely to listen to me. He said, "They must!" We shook hands, I left and had a drink with the High Commissioner. It was extraordinary, pathetic and evidence of Arap Moi's inadequacy as Kenyatta's successor.

Of course they came but he wouldn't have known about it. It was done through the Permanent Secretary of the Ministry. They sent a dozen at a time and we had national days for them and so forth. As far as I know the policy continued for four years after I left.

Soon after my arrival, I was asked if I would accept the chairmanship of ATCDE, which was finishing that year. I was elected as the union's last national chairman, which also meant that, in parallel, I became the joint president of the less genteel, more robust National Association of Teachers in Further and Higher Education (NATFHE). This was the period of the polytechnics. Although I would appear to be spending more time in London than Exmouth these positions helped, as they had before, in the sense that when we got coverage in the national press and I was mentioned, so too was Rolle College.

This paid dividends when, in about 1977–8, we were one of thirteen colleges proposed for closure in 1979. We were saved by Shirley Williams who, as Secretary of State for Education, was able to slow down the government process, which had been imposed simply to save money, and she did what she could to stop the flood with, no doubt, the Treasury pushing her hard.

I had known her immediately after the end of the war and while Roy Close and I were still in uniform we made a number of friends who included Shirley and Peter Parker, among others. The subject of our discussions was always education: it was friends talking, mostly in Oxford.

The campaign to save the College was all-encompassing. First of all we had a staff meeting and decided on a series of activities to include the Students Union and we were all unanimous. I wrote to every school of any former student of the College where it had been their first teaching job asking that if they had been pleased with the nature and quality of them would they write to the Secretary of State and say so; Shirley told me they were getting seventy letters a day! The letters, the visits, the demonstrations – all was worked out and the students, the staff and the trade unions behaved beautifully. On one protest on the pavements outside the Ministry of Education, Shirley crossed to me and a great friend of ours – Doris – came up and said, could she have a word with the Secretary of State? Shirley said, "Sure – what are you studying?" Doris said, "I work in the kitchens." And Shirley said, "That just seals it!" The whole campaign lasted about six months.

Towards the very end, I remember being at the NUT conference as an ordinary member and I was joined in the gallery by Shirley and her whispering, "I think you've won" and she told me why – our common sense and *the map*. Correspondence with the Ministry had intimated that the college at Bath would look after the education of the very young and it was at that point that we produced a map which showed that *Bath was nearer Bradford than it was Penzance*! Bath was in any case not suitable educationally. We had sent that map to everyone concerned. Distance won. At Rolle it took me a whole day to visit students in the South West.

You can't stand still in education.'

But neither was Nan motionless. Having transformed the residence in Rolle for two years, despite further operations, in 1976 she began planning for their retirement. Neither wanted to live in a suburb or a village where it would take too long to get to know people, so a city it would be, and the only city they both knew and loved was London. In 1975 she found a house in Coldharbour on the Isle of Dogs, near to The Gun (conveniently opposite Lady Hamilton's house), where Nelson used to muse over his wars. Nan knocked £5000 off the asking price and, commuting between the two places, set about busily converting it fit for the whole family at one time or another to use. Francis immediately approved: 'By the time we sold it after Botswana she made more money on it than I made in all my professional life, including my pension. I always loved the riverside – you don't need a garden when you have the river to look at.'

23

One of the first appointments Francis had made at Scraptoft in 1961 was that of a rather remarkable, diminutive young woman, Alice Crutchfield, 'a typical heroine of the infants school'. In Northern Rhodesia, a non-believer in formal teaching at that age, she'd taken head-on the language problems of children of Polish miners, the conflict of black and white and the creative value of play – why not use abandoned anthills as clay! 'As the children become confident in one skill they can, and do, transfer that to language.'

'When she first came to Leicester, because she'd spent ten years with infants, talking to them *in their language*, careful never to use words they couldn't understand – a revolutionary adventuress – at first the students used to laugh at the way she spoke. She came to me and said, "I have to go – I can't teach students; I've been teaching infants too long. What can I do?" I just said, you don't have to ask me, I trust you, you do it. She did, the students grew up and she blossomed into the lifelong friend of hundreds. When I wanted to know about Africa I talked to Alice.'

In 1980, Francis, still at Rolle College and one year from retirement, was approached by Keetle Masogo, Permanent Secretary in the Ministry of Education in Botswana, with an intriguing offer. A combination of reports from several students who'd been sent to Rolle, and the uncompromising recommendation from one Alice Crutchfield, then working in Botswana – 'the only person you want is Francis Cammaerts!' – had led to the approach.

> 'Keetle Masogo, came to Exmouth and said to me, "I understand you're retiring and taking your pension next year. Will you come and help us. Our government's policy is to give every child in Botswana nine years' schooling. We're a huge country with a very low population. We can't afford to give boarding education, which means we have a lot of very small

schools which include a few pupils going to university and others who can't read or write or understand English. We want teachers who can handle a situation where you've got those two levels of ability in the same classroom. We understand you've been working with the government on mixed-ability classes. You are just the kind of person who can help us launch a college to produce teachers of that kind." It was deeply flattering and impossible to resist. I rang Nan who was in London and said, would you mind continuing our teaching career for another five years? And she said, not if that is what you want. So I said yes. I didn't think I was upsetting her plans but she would suffer medically in the coming years and couldn't make her usual 100 per cent contributions.

Leaving Rolle brought its usual regrets, students and staff having been so confident and aggressive, relationships had been happy and mutually respectful. Kia and Jay had Coldharbour and were "high-tension", both taking their degree courses, and so we had Africa once again!

When I arrived, the College wasn't there! On my own because Nan couldn't come out at first, I stayed in a hotel in the capital, Gaborone, and started work at the Ministry of Education on all the issues involved in setting up the College.

If the big problem in Kenya had been too many languages, in Botswana it was that there weren't enough. There was only one really local language, Setswana, which pupils and teachers alike spoke outside school; English was never used as a social language by anyone, yet it was the single teaching language from the first years. When you take six-year-olds and teach them in a foreign language from the start you're creating a huge problem and the result was that the pupils were two years behind those in Kenya.

"Now, what'll you do about it?" I was asked and I said, "I'll tell you but you can't do it. If you conduct the whole of primary education in Setswana your children will learn far, far more. But being 20 kilometres from the apartheid border – 20 kilometres of completely open land without even a tree to stop the rifle fire – you're not going to be able politically to do it. You know the idea would be rejected because many, many Botswana citizens work in South Africa and are crying out to be taught Afrikaans!" They needed to sup with the devil. Yet while we were there a South African helicopter could land within five miles of where we were living, gunmen get out and shoot dead one of our top students, get back in and fly off, a situation no one in Botswana could do anything about.

As to minimising the effect of all this educationally, teaching teacher awareness of the problem was all one could do. Obviously the children were slow at learning because they found it very difficult to understand and the slow and backward children found it almost impossible.

They had a young university with few lecturers – usually refugees from South Africa or expatriates. The locally trained teachers were mostly two-years certificate graduates, which was all right for an urban primary school, but not much good for anything else, let alone handling the mixed ability and age differences – our overriding problem.

Yet this remarkable nation already had schools in the middle of the Kalahari Desert, where you needed a four-wheel-drive vehicle to get up the main street and to travel in convoy to reach schools in the most remote parts. So, although there were still children who didn't get to school or who didn't go, the parents were not punished and consequently the State was moving rapidly towards almost 100 per cent schooling. It was an indication of a people lifting themselves up by their bootstraps to turn themselves into a reasonably prosperous country – selling stock to Europe where their lean beef was appreciated and negotiating cannily over their diamonds and so ending up in the top league in terms of expanding economies. This was being achieved without profound corruption – it was Seretse Khama's lead from the start bearing fruit and the reason the country had enjoyed unbroken peace from 1966 to the present day; its Gross Domestic Product in 2004 was almost as high as that of Mexico.

Even in the reaction to the plague of AIDS, which threatened the nation with extinction – I've just read that an estimated 120,000 children have lost at least one parent, where life expectancy since 1990 has fallen from sixty-five years to less than forty years – I still feel the presence of Seretse Khama in the fact that Botswana was the first African country to aim to provide antiretroviral therapy to all its needy citizens. The name Seretse means the clay that binds together.

It is a small nation. At the time we were there, out of a population of five and a half million, only 1.2 million lived in Botswana. Two million were in Bophutswana, inside the South African border and many, many more in South Africa in the mines.

There were no Quakers or Catholics as in Kenya, but there was the London Missionary Society and the number of church attenders was something like 80 per cent. It was enormous and there was a lot of contact with traditional thinking but the introduction of education was so general and non-competitive that it was all very different. The Churches in Europe were less interested in the few million in Botswana than in the ten to fifteen million souls in Kenya.

'But my overall dream was the setting-up of the College which was only a third constructed. An important factor was that Molepolole, the site of the College, lay on the edge of the Kalahari Desert and covered a country slightly larger than France. Some higher ground existed to the east and in the north, and the Okavango Delta provided almost the only perennial surface water. Water is the blood of Botswana. Eighty per cent of the population lived in the east where rainfall, falling on only 5 per cent of the surface of the land, produced good pasturage and allowed arable agriculture; four inches of rain was a good year.

So, imagine my astonishment when I looked at the plans and saw provision for a huge swimming pool! I asked the architect, was there sufficient water not only to supply a swimming pool but also service about one thousand people who were going to need flush toilets and showers – where was it coming from? He said from the Okavango Delta. It's five hundred miles away. And I said, what's the loss between the Okavango and here? Apart from evaporation, the cracks in the rock surely meant that water would disappear and fall to a depth which made it uneconomic to recover? At the University there was no map anyone knew of indicating the places where the water travelled underground. The next time I went back the pool had vanished.

After water came the need for me to get to know and understand everybody. Molepolole had a population of 80,000 so I had enough to start with. But one utter pleasure was experiencing the democratic system of the Setswana people which was to place every quarrel in public before maybe four thousand people at a time. There were no rules of debate and everyone, of whatever age, had the right to attend and to speak for as long as they liked – it was called a *kgotla*.'

The most famous series of *kgotlas* took place at Serowe when Seretse Khama and his English wife, Ruth, returned from exile in England, after the British Labour government had colluded with racist South Africa (through British need for gold and uranium) in regarding his mixed marriage as politically capable of destabilising the whole sub-continent and had therefore declared Seretse unfit to govern his country, despite his intelligence and being of royal stock. Only after national and international uproar was he allowed to return in 1956. His uncle, Tshekedi, who had acted as Regent since Seretse's fourth birthday, demanded they divorce.

'Initially the *kgotlas* were absolutely against the white wife because they could not accept the possibility of a cross-bred future ruler. The cross-breed was a rejected person. When Seretse came to speak he said he wouldn't talk about his wife but only about his return and his dream for Botswana. They listened to him and they believed him and most of those who were against him at the beginning of the meetings voted for him by the end. It was his return which was discussed by everyone and, maybe, the suspicion that converted the *kgotla* towards his cause was that Tshekedi was suspected of wanting to hold on to power. As far as I know Seretse didn't actually use that argument but the people who supported him did and it was the suspicion of Tshekedi that swung the people and he gave way and went into self-imposed exile.'

In 1966 Seretse was declared the First President of the Republic and remained so until his death in July 1980.

'He was a great man. On the day the College officially opened Ruth was a guest of honour, an equally impressive woman.'

'Because the building progressed very slowly there was no teaching until it was ready – it took about a year and a half. This gave me time to set about recruiting staff from everywhere and that had to move as fast as possible to satisfy local needs and expectation and we had to build up towards a nine-year programme. We needed twelve lecturers. Interestingly, as in Kenya, one didn't have to cater for heads of schools – there the women especially jumped into the job as if they'd been doing it all their lives.

To deal with the problems posed by the range of mixed ability meant you had to change basic thinking. Whether you took a class of thirty or forty even fifty individuals, *you had to try and find an activity, an action, a direction to fit each individual.* As teachers they understood the problem reasonably well because it was a situation they'd have come through themselves. The high-flyers you taught apart but not at another school. It was treating them in the same way you treated children needing special help, where it was vital you knew what the common practice was among their people and work and develop from that. It was the same with the albino – a frequent African problem.

'After the first eighteen months, with the College built and teaching in full swing, the next stage for me was looking to how things would go on working well. I'd already recruited my successor and, as in Leicester and Exmouth, I became heavily involved in the question of staff salaries because it was only on salary separation from the secondary that the government wouldn't play.

I talked to them about the Pelham Scale. You don't have to use it for ever, but if you can for a decade or so it would give you the chance of establishing the fact that *the teachers who are in teacher education must be good teachers and they must have proved themselves in the past; every child deserves the best teachers.* They listened and nodded and said they understood – but they didn't adopt it. I said the salary dispute was not necessarily to do with money but with status. But the possible introduction of the Pelham Scale meant you were treating some form of teachers differently and that might have been too sensitive an issue at that stage.'

The fact that these were truly early days is testified to by Solade Adams, a geography teacher from Sierra Leone who had gone to Scraptoft for special tuition and practice in organisation by Francis and others as he was being groomed to become Principal of his own College. Over the years they had met 'internationally' at conferences where a great deal of the success the meetings achieved was down to the 'live-wire' Englishman. Solade joined the staff at Molepolole where:

Time was of the essence and almost without books and adequate equipment. Francis pioneered the College with he himself teaching as well as organising. He taught English with British newspapers until the required stocks of books were delivered. He encouraged his colleagues to use all the resources they had, private books, books from friends and lending libraries to get the Institution started. Staff taught subjects not their forte. I taught Nutrition to the Home Economics Students although I belonged to the Department of Education! From its opening by President Masire the College took shape. Francis worked assiduously, sometimes to the detriment of his health. He was very determined in his convictions and sometimes would appear stubborn; he envisaged more than some professionals and administrators saw yet he got on well with everyone he came in contact with. He believed in and trusted adolescents. He had a great sense of humour and enjoyed his Castle Beer.

In his last Christmas card he wrote cryptically, 'It was lovely to hear

Solade's voice even for a second or two. Friendships never end.' THAT WAS FRANCIS. Our friendship spanned a period of forty-two years.'

'Of the six years I spent in Botswana Nan was there only half the time. Although the children were OK by now she herself had had a bad time. Nevertheless, she got out to Botswana when she could and made her habitual impression on people. Normally you went down to Johannesburg and took a BA flight home from there. Then they opened the international airport in Harare and she was on one of the first planes to use it. There was a terrible African storm, when the sky goes completely black, and her plane was flying into it – and that is a vision that will stay with me until I die: I thought she wasn't going to come out of the other side of the cloud, it was so black.

'I finished because I wanted to go home and now we had a home. I'd gone originally for five years and it had slipped into the sixth, and I'd had my seventieth birthday out there and managed to get all the employees of the college to have a drink with me at different bars. That was incredible and very important – it wasn't just an excuse for a good time but respected the African's respect for age. As I'd been getting older I thought, I've got to drop this, there aren't many teachers around at seventy-two years old . . .

And there was family – all the family developments – I felt I ought to have been there to help, whether it was Jay's studies or Paul's second marriage, Kia's career – whatever – all those things had happened without me and guilt came into my life.

Days before I left I can remember one student asking, when are we going to get a local Principal – he didn't know I'd overheard him – but it confirmed what I already knew. It was time to go. I left during the vacation, that is to go before the results of the first degrees were out; I didn't want to make a big thing of it.

What I am proudest of is having done what I was asked to do – create a College! It was growing and growing and the maximum number of staff, non-teaching staff and students would be achieved within a couple of years. It was lovely because it was a totally new and totally different experience, but with the rich bases of the enormously civilised, traditional way of living and, initially anyway, concentration on the practical everyday rather than theory.'

Don Thompson, his successor as Principal, is in the best position to talk of Francis's legacy:

> At my first meeting with him he said, what would you like to drink? I said, a beer. Pint or half? Pint'll do fine. Good, he said, I tend not to reckon people who only drink halves. And we were away.
>
> Botswana was one of the first – if not *the* first – African countries to offer nine years' free education to children. Francis, working with the relevant people (and friends!) in the Ministry of Education, formulated the curriculum of the new junior secondary schools *and it has remained substantially the same in ideas and practices to the present day*. He wanted rounded citizens, so home economics and agriculture had to have their part – had to be well taught and teaching practice meaningful – and that was the responsibility of the Molepolole College of Education.
>
> On one occasion he suggested we go and watch a film together – *Children of a Lesser God*. It was the story of a speech teacher at a school for the deaf in America who falls in love with a sign language-using deaf woman. Francis emerged very quiet and obviously moved by what we had seen. When he did speak he said the film had 'illuminated his own experience' and he began to talk a little about his dead daughter, something I'm convinced he'd never have spoken about to me if we hadn't seen the film.
>
> Just one last personal memory of him. To watch him playing snooker at the Golf Club with his close friend Len Adams was like entering a cathedral. Absolute silence had to be observed during play, which was interrupted only when beers were brought over from the bar, a not infrequent occurrence. He was also a regular at the Bull and Bush, to my knowledge the only English-style pub in Botswana. He enjoyed his beer and the social context and connections which went with it.
>
> In Botswana he was The Man.

Botswana, like Kenya, had masked a dark side. Illnesses had begun to take their toll and heavy drinking and occasional fierce affairs were his way of overcoming them. Nan, suffering herself, felt he was becoming an alcoholic and that in Botswana there was no one to rein him in. At least in Coldharbour, back in the heart of the family, he would have a chance. Once stabilised, life could resume, only with care.

Two further factors conspired to add to the pain. In Botswana, in Kia's words, Francis had been paid 'two tenths of nothing', something in a poor country he could both professionally and socially accept, but which meant that very little money at all went back to Coldharbour. Nan was forced to rent out the house but on Francis's return Coldharbour was reoccupied.

The second factor was that Francis was far from happy.

> 'For the first time in my life I was contributing nothing to the relationship, I had no function and, having plenty of time to think about it, this was the point at which I began to reassess my past behaviour and the guilt to settle in. We've gone through the reasons, or excuses, for me acting the way I did, but those who "move away" tend usually to "come back". This I found myself doing but I had nothing to offer – I'm cack-handed, anything technical, mechanical and I'm lost. In a word, I felt superfluous.'

The logical solution to both problems was to sell Coldharbour – 'we're sitting on a goldmine' – and Nan offered Francis the chance of going to live in France, which he jumped at. After most of the fine profit from the sale had been divided among the children, a house was found at Combemaure, south of Crest in the valley of the Drôme, and from there Francis could see in the distance the massive, sheer-sided plateau of the Vercors . . . Given her schoolgirl French and the charged memories for Francis in even the most hidden of byways in the *département*, it was an incredibly generous gesture by Nan.

But, she was now free from the shadow of their former silence, as was Francis. In 1989 they were almost fifty years on from 1942. Each had, in the meantime, created positively in their respective worlds and together their humanism, humanity and adventure had given their children huge and diverse experiences and, above all, the freedom to make their individual journeys. Nan still had her tart exasperation and Francis his dawning, rooted guilt, but both were played out, like their former games of 'black Scrabble', in a new silence, the silence of habit and sharing, of acceptance. Kia recalled:

> Their games were lessons in trench warfare. They played Scrabble to the death. Nobody said anything; there were no whoops when one or the other won. The Scrabble board was a battlefield, a war game. They had their own variations on the rules which were absolute. It was played in two languages and you could play either – which gave Francis a slight edge –

but it was an arena where Nan could pit her own intellect directly against Francis's because, while she couldn't compete with his day job, she could demonstrate that she could win.

When I was a child, Sundays at Rolle College meant Sunday roast, clear up and I vaguely remember Nan and Francis washing up – like a weigh-in – then the 'game'. At fourteen or fifteen I was bright enough to play but they didn't really like it. It was virtually the only occasion when they weren't reasonable – either of them. No, it was their game. They kept cumulative scores – I've never seen numbers that big – they kept scores from dozens, hundreds of games.

That was the two of them.

Francis had been ill again, this time necessitating the removal of 'a chunk' from his spine which the surgeon kindly placed in a jam jar and left at his bedside. Nan, herself unwell, was terrified he would never see the house completed, but recover he did.

The rapprochement with Paul was a positive in the six years at Combemaure, as was his delight in his two grandaughters, both born there, and his 'stakeholding' in the region. He was a proudly remembered figure, revered by many, and nothing had given him greater pleasure than when, on his journey back from Botswana and visiting Beaurepaire he, as a foreigner, had been given the singular honour by the mayor of presenting a medal to the wife of the farmer on to whose ploughed field he had landed after bailing out on his return from England in 1944; the award, by the French government, had been for services to the Résistance.

Part of his time was still devoted to helping with claims by the families of those who had worked with him, as he had done immediately after the surrender of Germany, principally by identifying the participants and the validity of their service. Despite the length of time that had passed and the cold agony of having to admit that he had only known most of their grandfathers or grandmothers by their field names, his was a valuable voice when it came to distinguishing between a false application, say from a collaborator, and the true *résistant*. In addition there were problems stemming from the variety of organisations involved – escape routes, information services, foreigners, people at home and those who were engaged in top dangerous resistance work. Nevertheless, he persisted and some battles were won.

For someone who personally detested awards, failure to recognise properly the contribution or sacrifice made by many of his former companions angered him greatly:

> 'Both the British and the French were terribly slow and dragged their feet on the awards issue. As I've said before, all this was a reflection of the political situation of the New France officially trying to avoid any idea of others being important in the liberation of France; absurd and just about understandable.
>
> Immediately after the Liberation there were agents set up to be responsible for the proper tying up for the future of those who had been recruited into the Résistance. I for one was not consulted – I would have obviously nominated Auguste, he knew all our people – but they appointed a rich contractor in Nice, who didn't even know Nice, let alone the rest of the area. I'd talked to Yves Farge about it, pointing out that what we were concerned with were those left behind, the children, we weren't the least bit worried about rewards except possible financial rewards in the case of real necessity. But I couldn't interfere; it was a French government decision.
>
> On the British side I'd asked early on how the government would handle the question of those who had helped me and those who had helped the Résistance as a whole. At that time I was still in the army, still under orders, working without any secretarial back-up. I talked to the wonderful Brooks Richards, because he was in the Embassy in Paris, about what we could do and naturally he was completely aware of the diplomatic situation. Brooks said, "After a lot of heavy breathing, the government has decided on the formation of the King's Medal for Courage in the Cause for Freedom", a British military award which didn't compare with anything and, I think, was used to recognise acts of courage by foreign civilians or military personnel during the Second World War. I then gave Brooks a list of about 175 people who needed recognition and he pushed the whole lot through, but it then transpired that it was an award that couldn't be made posthumously, which took all its value away because the only people who wanted them were the widows and orphans of those who had died. I can't begin to envisage the mind of people who sat down one morning and thought that up; unspeakably crass.'

Years later, at Le Pouget, he suddenly fell silent and stared at the portrait of his father, as he often did when about to touch on something personal.

'I've got to write soon to the Buckmaster people again – they keep on making mistakes. They've built this monument at Valencay on the Loire to the agents of SOE F Section who lost their lives for the liberation of France and they can't decide whose names should be on it. They'll only put people who were actually killed before the Armistice. So anyone who survived and died early, as so many of them did, or committed suicide, has no chance of being remembered.

When the project came up I was invited to react and I wrote and said, if Christine Granville had died saving my life would her name have been on the Valencay? And they said no. Because she came from North Africa and not from London. Ah.'

Then the negatives gradually began to overtake Combemaure – illnesses all round, too many people living in the same space, the building work taking too long, tension distorting relationships and money had drained away once more. Nan and Francis felt they had to move out and the saving grace appeared in the form of Jay's new husband, Wole, an immensely gifted Nigerian IT consultant. He was very generous but disliked having no say in the situation and resolved it by taking off with Jay and Nan in search of a new house and the sun. They finally settled on Le Pouget – Francis took one look at it and said, 'I can die here' – both knowing they would be protected in their last years: for Nan a matter of seven, for Francis eleven. All differences in differing ways were in time resolved.

In a corner of the calm, cool lounge of the house in Le Pouget, sculpted on many levels into the ancient rocky citadel of the village, boasting fine panoramic views of the lower Cevennes to the north and the arc of the Golfe du Lion and the western Mediterranean to the south, Francis sat every day, his beloved local wines within easy reach. Upright but frail in casual jacket and tie, almost military in bearing – the very description would displease him – slim, still very tall, brown eyes alert, watchful, assessing, reflecting a paternal structure to his mind, yet possessed of a spirit, untrapped by age, capable of exploding into chesty laughter. Framed by a niche in the wall, enclosing a Kenyan bird sculpture in wood, he was the epitome of Englishness, happy in a French house.

The scimitar mind still sharp and issue-conscious found little difficulty in dealing with the continual trail of journalists, historians, friends, family, TV crews and radio producers in both languages who sought him out only to reel away impressed. Almost deaf, he couldn't answer the telephone but his cards – 'what can't be expressed on a postcard isn't worth considering' – became items treasured by their possessors. What amazed his son was that 'he hasn't moved from his chair for well over a year and he knows everything that's going on! Everything!'

I told Francis that Jay had just introduced me to their neighbour, 'Little Francis', and he had not moved his hand before I'd offered mine.

> Yes, he's still living his discomfort sixty years on. Early after the occupation, the Germans made an offer to the French population saying that they would send a prisoner back for every three workers who volunteered to go and work in Germany. Francis volunteered but this first scheme didn't work – there were practically no volunteers; three-for-one wasn't a fair deal and even the one didn't come back. So they had to drop it and promulgate the STO law that everyone between eighteen and forty had to go and work in Germany unless they had a written reason why they shouldn't. That was when the numbers in the Résistance soared.
>
> He was criticised for having accepted the German 'bargain' but he's still got lots of friends in the village, he still talks and people shake hands, but when we had our occasion for Nan his wife Annice came but Francis didn't.

And soon we were treading warily across the murky terrain of *épuration*, a word that means 'purging' but in practice included the settling of old scores, identification by gossip, revenge and often unlawful killing. It is a word that even today can trouble the French, sister as it is to 'collaborator'.

> 'The identification of what was collaboration has never been possible. A little cornershop keeper in a small town the size of us here where there was a German presence – did he serve the Germans who came to buy things in his shop with a frown or a smile? It was as close as that.
>
> Then, at the other extreme, you had those who volunteered to help Germany and many there were who betrayed their friends. There were all these levels and it took a long time to sort them out. I'm sure bad feelings were important and sometimes lasted for a very long time but my experience of the whole of south-east France is that it died quickly and that probably half a dozen people were killed. But half a dozen people.
>
> It was a strength of feeling that started in the shame of 1940 and the whole argy-bargying about what resistance was and who was running it and who was wise, who was stupid, accusations about what happened to

the money and if there hadn't been resistance there wouldn't have been reprisals, etc. All that surely went on. But basically life resumed in a dignified and honourable fashion and the residual dislikes probably existed long before as they do in all villages. Negative *épuration* has been hugely exaggerated – there were far more civilised legal handlings of very difficult situations generally throughout France than were given credit for; better that bastards like Roger Bardet and Déricourt escaped without serious punishment than that innocent people should have suffered.

Yes, when one thinks of the Vercors and Oradour you'd imagine it would leave a bitterness which could never be resolved. But as my miner friends in the north-east said, it'll take about four years and we'll be embracing our fellow workers down the mines. And that was a reasonable time to put on it.'

Francis knew of times when people did things that were wrong, bad and dangerous but he would not talk about them

'Others have told me afterwards that indeed so and so killed so and so who wasn't guilty of any really . . . but I had no means of testing, judging. But I never encountered anything that I disapproved of.

'When we first came to Le Pouget and I was chair-bound, Nan was still very active, physically working hard, especially on the garden three flights down. Both she and Jay were very protective – Jay still is – but I hated Nan having to come up from the garden just to look after me, keeping her away from her creative work. Both had to do it, I know.

Nan always had this need to be perfect as a woman. During the whole of our sixty years together I never saw a broken fingernail or slightly misplaced make-up or any kind of physical neglect of herself.

And not just appearance but *deeds*.

Everyone she had reason to associate with became her friend – the catering and cleaning staff, the gardeners, builders, architects: they were always the ones who drew her major interest and she'd be called "the Head Woman Without a Hat"! She complimented the workers here by calling them "artists" and the manager of the enterprise said it had transformed their lives. Her original political leanings were towards people like them, ordinary people. Contact was achieved through a friendly intimacy which was tantamount to a gift.

I know you suspect me of gilding the lily but that is because her virtues far outweighed her weaknesses. It is very difficult to talk about Nan's faults because of those black four years during the war. They were terrible and make criticism look thin yet, for good or for bad, they hardened her into a positive, independent being, someone who never looked back. Of course I could and do look back on the same period with considerable pleasure and have come to realise that it was what largely made me however good a teacher I am. Hence the initial imbalance. Yes, she had faults, we all do, but her contributions and virtues swamp them. There have been other very important people in my life – John Lloyd, Harry Rée, Paul Héraud – and I can't think of *their* faults!

It is the nature of the kind of love I'm trying to express that you are entranced by the virtues and skills and you shrug off the defects. That shrugging off is part of my loving.

She said on a couple of occasions that she had been sorely tempted to leave me, not because of affairs, we both had those and we had an understanding – monogamy was impossible, but any departure from it should never be allowed to threaten our relationship. Nor because of my drinking – that worried her medically more than as a reason to leave me. No: as we have dealt with, the most dangerous occasion for me was after the death of Christine when she needed help and I did not see her call. The second occasion was in Botswana where I still hadn't learnt how corrosive self-indulgence was. But this time I was terrified she meant it. Without her I would be lost. There was this smell of darkness about it. It couldn't happen. Mercifully she stayed.'

At the end of March 2002, and Jay in the UK with flu, Nan became ill with undiagnosed thrombosis and the threat of gangrene and blood poisoning real. Jay returned and Francis was able to visit Nan, sedated with morphine, twice during her last five days.

An illustration of her need to be perfect as a woman are the last words she spoke to me in the hospital room: 'Please leave, I'm not in a state to receive.'

Three final images.

Paul:

Watching Francis with my daughter Juliet and suddenly he was talking about Christine. Since Nan's death he has occasionally begun to talk about his feelings and here he was saying that 'she'd died forty years ago, a young girl much the same age as you are, your father must have talked about her'. And he was describing her 'valuable' life – but never, ever, even now, mentioning his behaviour at the time. He read Juliet's essays on Locke or ethics and wrote back to her about them and he was marvellous.

Then I realised the overwhelmingly important thing was that they did that amazingly right thing – giving Christine the life they did. As badly as some people may think Nan and Francis handled her death, it is as well to remember how they handled her life. They gave her as good a life as she could possibly have had and she benefited from that. I can't be critical of them because now, as a parent, I have no idea how I could have done what they did and to have guaranteed the wonderful life she had and the impact she had as a person. I have no idea. And I don't think you can until it happens to you.

Kia:

A very impressive statue. I'm still very impressed with him as he is. I love him dearly but there is quite a stiff reserve in our relationship even now. He is my grandfather not my father. The way I relate to him daily is I will go downstairs after he's had his nap and tea, sit with him and read my book. Every now and then he'd put his book down and make a comment on whatever – sports, current affairs or something interesting he's just read. This would last for five to ten minutes, then we'd carry on. There is something very stiff upper lip about it all. It's relaxed but it is a formal relationship. When I didn't do the chats one week, I learnt later from Jay he was quite upset!

I had relatively few presents as a child. The few I did were good ones on birthdays and Christmas – but none in the middle. It was an ascetic household with very few possessions; functional. Francis finds it hard to buy presents for people because he doesn't lack anything.

Yes, he has charisma but also a pretty unshakeable self-belief based on a relatively compartmentalised view of life; and within it one thing doesn't spill over into another. If you ask a direct question there is never any evasion no matter what the subject; but no information will be volunteered. It is a civilised relationship. Nan was the same.

On the other hand, I can't recall a single conversation about Christine.

The former Children's Laureate, Michael Morpurgo, his nephew, wrote movingly in the *Guardian* of *his* relationship with Francis:

I thought of him very much as my grandfather, a grandfather's grandfather, and after I had named him as my adoptive grandfather he wrote me one of his cards. It began, 'Dear Grandson' and when I went to see him two months ago in France he greeted me warmly, as he always did, but this time with the words 'Hello, Grandson'. I felt honoured, and more moved than I can say. It was a moment I shall never forget . . .

. . . the truth is that for most of my life he was not someone I knew well until late in both our lives, and I held him in great awe, so conversation was not easy, for Uncle Francis was a legend in the family and with good reason.

For a start he looked the part. At 6 foot 4 inches he was a hugely imposing presence. He towered over everyone and age never diminished that. And his voice had a deep resonance that was as compelling as the unflinching look in his eye. But it was what he had been, what he had done in his life that made him legendary to everyone in the extended family . . .

. . . we talked a lot, wrote each other letters. He came here to Devon with Nan and his family. We went to see them in France. Already a grandfather myself, this is where I really got to know him. With each visit the legend fell away and I began to know the man. My uncle became my grandfather. We learnt how to be silent together, to be comfortable with each other. I knew with each visit we were on borrowed time, and I treasured every hour. He had a good end, the end he deserved. Just a couple of weeks before he died he celebrated his ninetieth birthday. His family, his real grandchildren and his friends were all there. The mayor of the village made a wonderful speech. He was a much honoured man, a much loved man.

The great oak tree in our family has fallen. This grandfather has lost his last grandfather.[1]

Francis died peacefully on his way to hospital on 3 July 2006.

Abbreviations

ABWEHR Police under Admiral Canaris responsible to the State. Expired 1 June 1944.
ANVIL Allied invasion from the South of France.
AS Armée Secrète. The Secret Army. Set up by de Gaulle linking all opposition to German occupation. The Army of the Future.
BCRA Bureau Central de Renseingnements et d'Action. The body for unifying resistance, the military included.
CAD Committee of Action against Deportation.
CFLN Comité Francais de Liberation National. Original committee set up by Jean Moulin.
CGE Comité Général d'Etudes. Committee for general Studies set up to examine the existing and future French civil administration.
CNR Conseil National de la Résistance. Set up by de Gaulle and originally organised by Jean Moulin.
DMR Délégué Militaire Régional. Gaullist leaders of Résistance, later under direct orders from BCRA.
DZ dropping zone.
EMFFI Etat-Major des Forces Françaises de l'Intérieur. The State organisation for FFI run by General Koenig.
F (SOE) Special Operations Executive – French Section. This independent section was British as opposed to RF which was French.
FANY First Aid Nursing Yeomanry – British nurses who helped SOE. Several served abroad.
FFI Forces Françaises de l'Intérieur. The French forces of the Secret Army.
FTP Francs-Tireurs et Partisans. Communist and fellow-traveller branch of French armed resistance.
GESTAPO Secret Service under Himmler, responsible to the Nazi Party at home and in occupied territories.

LLL Liberté, Libération et Libération Nationale were early Résistance groups, the first two fusing into Combat.

MASSINGHAM SOE HQ in Algeria.

MEW Ministry of Economic Warfare. The non-military body 'in charge' of SOE.

MUR Mouvements Unifiés de la Résistance. Left-wing.

OG Operational Groups. American.

ORA Organisation de Résistance de l'Armée. Formed by Vichy on the dissolved 'armistice army' of Vichy.

OSS Office of Strategic Services. The American equivalent of SOE.

OVERLORD Allied invasion of Normandy.

P et C Ponts et Chaussées – the Highways Department.

PTT Postes, Télégraphes, Téléphones.

SAARF Special Allied Airborne Reconnaissance Force. Set up briefly to check concentration camps, etc.

SAP Service d'Atterrisages et Parachutages – the French Landing and Parachute service – basic to SOE.

SAS British Special Air Force.

SD Sicherheitsdienst. The powerful Nazi Party Security Service – the SS.

SHAEF Supreme Headquarters Allied Expeditionary Force. The Headquarters of the Allied Invasion Forces run by General Eisenhower.

SIS British Intelligence Service.

SNCF Société Nationale des Chemins-de-Fers Français, the National Railway Service.

SPOC Special Projects Operation Centre – body set up which linked SOE and OSS in Algeria.

STO Service du Travail Obligatoire – the German law, the Forced Labour Service which obliged French males to serve German needs in Germany.

STS Special Training Schools – SOE's secret training schools

TORCH Allied invasion of North Africa.

VICHY The name given to Pétain's government under German rule; the government sat at Vichy.

WAAF Women's Auxiliary Air Force.

WEHRMACHT German Army.

W/T Wireless telegraphy.

Notes

My conversations with Francis Cammaerts over a four-year period are as they appear in the text. Where his memory of events does not differ from well-known accounts in books, I do not quote the books. That does not mean that my huge indebtedness to many authors and sources and the kindness and understanding they offered must be forgotten. I am very beholden to them all and gratefully thank every one. Quoted texts are acknowledged in these Notes. Every effort has been made to clear copyright and the author and publishers will be pleased to hear from any source they have not been able to contact.

Preface

(1) Hugh Verity – *We Landed by Moonlight* – p. 71, Crécy Publishing Ltd, (www.crecy.co.uk) 1978
(2) E.H. Cookridge – *They Came From the Sky* – p. 83, Heinemann, London, 1965
(3) (SOE) Personal File. Report 6

Chapter 1

(1) Jeanne Lindley – *Seeking and Finding*: *The Life of Emile Cammaerts* – pp. 29–34, S.P.C.K., 1962
(2) Op. cit., p. 40
(3) Op. cit., p. 59
(4) Op. cit., p. 73
(5) Op. cit., p. 93

Chapter 2

(1) (SOE) Personal File
(2) By Willheim Rauber
(3) Jeanne Lindley – *Seeking and Finding* – p. 137

Chapter 3

(1) N.G. Brett-James – *Mill Hill School Magazines* Blackie, 1938
(2) Conversation with author.
(3) Ronald Blythe – *The Age of Illusion 1919–1940* – p. 129, Penguin, 1963
(4) Patricia Cockburn – *The Years of the Week* – pp. 7–8, Macdonald, 1968
(5) Op. cit.
(6) Emile Cammaerts – *The Poetry of Nonsense* – p. 31, Percy Lund, Humphries & Co Ltd, Bradford, 1925

Chapter 4

(1) Harry Rée – Russell Miller – *Behind the Lines* – p. 11, Secker and Warburg, 2002 (reprinted by permission of The Random House Group Ltd)
(2) E.H. Cookridge – *They Came From the Sky* – pp. 71–77

Chapter 5

(1) Conversation with author.
(2) Emile Cammaerts – *Upon This Rock* – p. 50, Cresset Press, 1942
(3) Op. cit., p. 62
(4) Hugh Dalton – *The Fateful Years* – p. 368, Muller, 1957
(5) Madeleine Masson – *Christine* – p. 146, Hamish Hamilton, 1975
(6) Marcus Binney – *The Women Who Lived for Danger* – p. 190, Perennial, Harper Collins, 2002
(7) Madeleine Masson – *Christine* – p. 164

Chapter 6

(1) M.R.D. Foot – *The SOE 1940–46*, p.63, Pimlico, 1999

(2) Personal File – of Lt Macalister – 9 Oct 1942
(3) M.R.D. Foot – *The SOE 1940–46* – p. 64, BBC, 1984
(4) Personal File – Group B Finishing Report, December 1942
(5) Leo Marks – *Between Silk and Cyanide*, Harper Collins, 1988
(6) G. Rheam – Report in Personal File

Chapter 7

(1) Peter Churchill – *Duel of Wits* – Hodder and Stoughton, 1957
(2) M.R.D. Foot – *SOE in France* – p. 205 (reprinted by permission of The Random House Group Ltd)
(3) Op. cit., p 205
(4) E.H. Cookridge – *They Came From the Sky* – pp. 89–91
(5) Op. cit., p. 91
(6) Madeleine Masson – *Christine* – p. 165n

Chapter 8

(1) M.R.D. Foot – *SOE in France*, p. 253, HMSO, 1966
(2) M.R.D. Foot – *Six Faces of Courage* – p. 30 Eyre Methuen 1978
(3) Op. cit., p. 32
(4) Op. cit., p. 43
(5) Op. cit., p. 44

Chapter 9

(1) Frederick Douzet – '*Cammaerts et le Reseau Buckmaster Jockey*' – Thesis University of Grenoble, 1988–9
(2) E.H. Cookridge – *They Came From the Sky* – p. 96
(3) Xan Fielding – *Hide and Seek* – Secker and Warburg, 1954
(4) E.H. Cookridge –*They Came From the Sky* – p. 100
(5) Hugh Verity – *We Landed by Moonlight* – p. 133
(6) M.R.D. Foot – *SOE in France* – p. 419
(7) Denise Domenach-Lallich – *Demain Il Fera Beau* – Editions BGA Permezel, 2001

Chapter 10

(1) Personal File. Report 16 Oct 1943
(2) Arthur Layton Funk – *Hidden Ally* – p. 9 Greenwood Press, 1992 reproduced by permission of ABC-CLIO LLC, Santa Barbara
(3) Henri Rosencher – *Le Sel, La Cendre et La Flamme* – p. 151, Private Publication, 1985

Chapter 11

(1) E.H. Cookridge – *They Came From the Sky* – p. 104
(2) Personal file, Mentioned in recognition for DSO
(3) E.H. Cookridge – *They Came From the Sky* – p. 105
(4) Note – the explanatory notes of name – Drôme, Vaucluse etc would not have been used in the Message, only the letters
(5) Personal File. Report 26 March 1944
(6) Personal File. Cipher Tel 19 April 1944
(7) M.R.D. Foot – *SOE in France* – p. 376
(8) M.R.D. Foot – p. 377
(9) Francis:

'Several of those arrested had been executed by the Germans including Marc Taperell, son of the present Consul in Paris. All the relatives of course were anxious to see justice done. Pierre Agapov was commissioned by us and held the rank of Captain. He returned from Germany in June and was arrested by the French in Marseille. His "trial" was to take place in August 1945 and I travelled down to Marseille to assist.

Janyk came back from Germany alive and we were able to say to him – you were betrayed by Agapov what do you think we ought to do? And Janyk said, oh, he's been through enough. So we all agreed the non-lieu (no ground for prosecution) should be recommended.'

(10) Max Hastings – *Das Reich* - p. 30. Henry Holt & Co, New York, 1981
(11) de Gaulle - *Memoires*
(12) Francis's BBC Foreign Service broadcast – August 1945
(13) G Millar - *Maquis* – p.40, Heinemann, 1945
(14) M.R.D. Foot – *SOE in France* – p. 120

Chapter 12

(1) M.R.D. Foot – *SOE in France* – pp. 395–6
(2) Henri Rosencher – *Le Sel, La Cendre et La Flamme* p. 275
(3) Personal File. Report 7 July 1944

Chapter 13

(1) Personal File. Report 16 Apr 1944
(2) Pierre Dalloz
(3) Pierre Tanant – *Vercors* pp. 148–181
(4) See E.H. Cookridge, p. 129n
(5) Messages from E.H. Cookridge pp 127–135
(6) The Peugeot car factory at Sochaux near Montbeliard, in the Doubs Valley, had been converted by the Germans in order to make tank turrets for the army and Focke-Wulf engine parts for the air force. The RAF chose it as a target on 14 July 1943. No bomb landed within a kilometre of the site but hundreds of French civilians were killed. Seated under a peach tree some kilometres from the action, Harry decided that there had to be a better way of putting the factory out of action. Already in contact with one member of the family – Rudolphe Peugeot – for financial loans in running his circuit 'STOCKBROKER', Harry suggested a plan whereby effective internal sabotage could be carried out against the assurance that the factory would never subsequently be destroyed from the air. Naturally Peugeot demanded proof of Harry's good faith and of his ability to guarantee immunity from bombing. Harry told him to compose his own code phrase which, on agreement by the RAF, the BBC would then transmit at a pre-arranged hour, '*La Vallée du Doubs est bien belle en été*' – 'The Valley of the Doubs is very beautiful in summer' came through clearly.

Peugeot then sent for the foreman of the tank turret machine shop and introduced him to Harry who made one tour of inspection and never there-after set foot in the place. A team of saboteurs was assembled and their escape route via Switzerland arranged. While waiting outside the factory gate for someone to produce a key, the saboteurs played a game of football with several uniformed German guards. When a home-made bakelite bomb fell out of a saboteur's pocket a German guard politely handed it back. The power station and the main transformer of the plant were blown up, the assembly hall collapsed in flames and large stocks of finished tank parts were destroyed. Effectively the factory remained out of production for much of the rest of the war to stand as one of the great sabotage coups of the conflict.

Although Bomber Command honoured the embargo on Sochaux, it did not extend such grace to other targets. It had its own agenda of industrial blanket bombing, an agenda in which the idea of dislocation through bribery, with no civilian loss and less need for huge future post-war reconstruction costs as an arm of policy, had no place and 'one of the most interesting innovations of the war', was shelved.

See also M.R.D Foot – SOE in France – pp. 287–8

(7) M.R.D. Foot – *SOE in France* – p. 391

(8) Op. cit., pp. 393–4

Chapter 14

(1) Xan Fielding – *Hide and Seek* – Secker and Warburg, 1954

(2) E.H. Cookridge – p. 108

(3) Madeleine Masson – *Christine* – p. xxii

(4) Op. cit., p. xxiv

(5) Op. cit., p. xxvii

(6) Op. cit., p. 61

(7) Marcus Binney – *The Women Who Lived for Danger* – p. 87, Perennial, Harper Collins, 2002

(8) Alberto Turini di Priero – *Le Temps du Refus* – p. 35 Groupe Calade, 2004

(9) Henri Rosencher – *Le Sel, La Cendre et La Flamme* – p. 306

(10) Op. cit., p. 306

(11) Op. cit., p. 306

(12) E.H. Cookridge – pp. 132–134

(13) Pierre Tanant – *Vercors* – pp. 148–181

(14) Op. cit.

Chapter 15

(1) Capt Léquyer

(2) Arthur Layton Funk – *Hidden Ally* – p. 69, Greenwood Press, 1992

(3) Souvenirs – *Homage à Paul Héraud* – p. 5M Ribaud Frères, GAP, 1946

(4) Op. cit., pp. 6–7

(5) Arthur Layton Funk – *Hidden Ally* – p. 66

(6) Madeleine Masson – *Christine* – p. 189 and letter in note
(7) Op. cit., p. 200
(8) Op. cit., p. 201
(9) E.H. Cookridge – p. 145

Chapter 16

(1) Xan Fielding – *Hide and Seek*
(2) Op. cit.
(3) Op. cit.
(4) Op. cit.
(5) Arthur Layton Funk – *Hidden Ally* – p. 111
(6) Op. cit., p. 121

Chapter 17

(1) Arthur Layton Funk – *Hidden Ally* – p. 153 note
(2) Op. cit., p. 155
(3) The infamous reduction of the whole town to nothing. One of the horrors of the war.
(4) Madeleine Masson – *Christine* – p. 213
(5) M.R.D. Foot – SOE in France – p. 413
(6) Op. cit.
(7) Op. cit., p. 248
(8) Op. cit., p. 441

Chapter 18

(1) E.H. Cookridge – p. 95
(2) Martha Gellhorn – *The Face of War* – pp. 195–202, Granta Books, 1998
(3) IT
(4) Personal File
(5) Roy Close – *In Action with SAS* – pp. 181–193, Pen and Sword Books Ltd, 2005
(6) Op. cit., p. 183
(7) Op. cit., p. 192
(8) Op. cit., p. 193

Chapter 19

(1) Sarah Helm – *A Life in Secrets* – pp. 258–261, Virago, Little, Brown, 2005
(2) Christopher Burney – *Solitary Confinement* – Macmillan, 1952
(3) Madeleine Masson – *Christine* – p. 247
(4) Op. cit., p. 226
(5) Op. cit., p. 238
(6) Op. cit., p. 247

Chapter 20

(1) Cells – small intellectual working groups

Chapter 22

(1) 'In the early 1970s Tom Henn flew once through Nairobi and asked if I would come to the airport – which I did – as he couldn't get off the aircraft, suffering terribly as he did from arthritis. Seeing a lad on the security staff whom I'd taught, I said to him, 'My teacher is on that aeroplane and I want to go and say hello to him – can you help me?' His eyes widened in disbelief and he said, 'You a teacher of teachers and your teacher is still living? He must be the most venerable man in the world! Of course I'll come and talk to him and will ask him one thing – will he allow me to touch his hand!' So he drove me out in a jeep, I took him aboard, told Tom the story and he was tickled pink and kissed the terrified boy on both cheeks.

It was the last time I saw him alive. It was like a certainty, a sure confirmation of all Kenyans' respect for age. The older you are the more venerable you are. At family ceremonies it is the oldest who speaks, very often a woman, and she does so on behalf of the family and you can't interrupt – they have the right.'

(2) Sylviane Rey – letter to the author.

Chapter 23

(1) *Guardian*, – 11 March 2006

Select Bibliography

M.R.D. FOOT — *SOE in France*, H.M.S.O. – 1968
SOE 1940–46, B.B.C. 1984

HENRI MICHEL — *Bibliographie Critique de la Résistance*, Sevpen 1964
Jean Moulin l'Unificateur, Hachette 1964

H.R. KEDWARD — *Resistance in Vichy France*, New York 1978

W.J.M. MACKENZIE — *The Secret History of SOE*, St Ermin's Press 2000

*

MARCUS BINNEY — *The Women Who Lived for Danger*, Harper Perennial 2002

HUGO BLEICHER — *Colonel Henri's Story*, Kimber 1954

RONALD BLYTHE — *The Age of Illusion* 1919–1940, Penguin 1963

CHRISTOPHER BURNEY — *Solitary Confinement*, Macmillan 1952 and 1961

EMILE CAMMAERTS — *The Poetry of Nonsense*, Percy Lund Humphries & Co 1925
Upon This Rock, Cresset Press 1942

ALBERT CAMUS — *The Rebel*, Hamish Hamilton 1953

PETER CHURCHILL — *Duel of Wits*, Hodder & Stoughton 1957

ROY CLOSE — *In Action with the SAS*, Pen and Sword Books 2005

PATRICIA COCKBURN — *The Years of the Week*, Macdonald 1968

E.H. COOKRIDGE — *They Came from the Sky*, Heinemann 1965

HUGH DALTON — *The Fateful Years*, Muller 1957

DENISE DOMENACH-LALLICH — *Demain Il Fera Beau*, Editons BGH Permezel 2001

XAN FIELDING — *Hide and Seek*, Secker and Warburg 1954

M.R.D. FOOT — *Six Faces of Courage*, Eyre Methuen 1978

ARTHUR L. FUNK — *Hidden Ally*, Greenwood Press, Westport Connecticut 1992

MARTHA GELLHORN — *The Face of War*, Granta Books 1998

SIR C. McV. GUBBINS — *Resistance Movements in the War*, J.R.U.S.I. 1948

MAX HASTINGS — *Das Reich*, Henry Holt & Co., New York 1981

SARAH HELM — *A Life in Secrets*, Little, Brown 2005

PAUL HERAUD — *Souvenirs à Paul Heraud*, Rubard Freres Gap 1946

RENE HOSTACHE — *Conseil National de la Résistance*, Presses Universitaires de France 1958

PATRICK HOWARTH — *Undercover – The Men and Woman of the SOE*, Phoenix Press 1980

PAUL LEVERKUEHN — *German Military Intelligence*, Weidenfeld & Nicolson 1954

JEANNE LINDLEY — *Seeking & Finding*, S.P.C.K. 1962

LEO MARKS — *Between Silk and Cyanide*, Harper Collins 1988

BRUCE MARSHALL — *The White Rabbit*, Evans 1952

MADELEINE MASSON — *Christine*, Hamish Hamilton 1975

GEORGE MILLAR — *Maquis*, Heinemann 1945
Horned Pigeon, Heinemann 1946

RUSSELL MILLER — *Behind the Lines*, Secker & Warburg 2002

ELIZABETH NICHOLAS — *Carve Her Name With Pride*, Heinemann 1946

J. OVERTON FULLER — *Madeleine*, Gollancz 1952
Double Webs, Putnam 1958

PASSY (COL. A. DEWAVRIN) — *10 Duke St*, Solar, Monte Carlo 1947
Missions Sécrètes, Plon 1951

ALBERTO TURINI DI PRIERO — *Le Temps du Refus*, Groupe Calade 2004

HENRI ROSENCHER — *Le Sel la Cendre et la Flamme*, (Private) 1985

JACQUES SOUSTELLE — *Envers et Contre Tous*, Laffont 1947–50

DAVID STAFFORD — *Churchill and the Secret Service*, John Murray 1997

PIERRE TANANT — *Vercors, Haut-Lieu de France*, Arthaud, Grenoble 1948

JERRARD TICKELL — *Odette*, Chapman and Hall 1949

HUGH VERITY — *We Landed by Moonlight*, Crécy Publishing 1978

PAUL WEBSTER — *Petain's Crime*, Pan 1990

Index